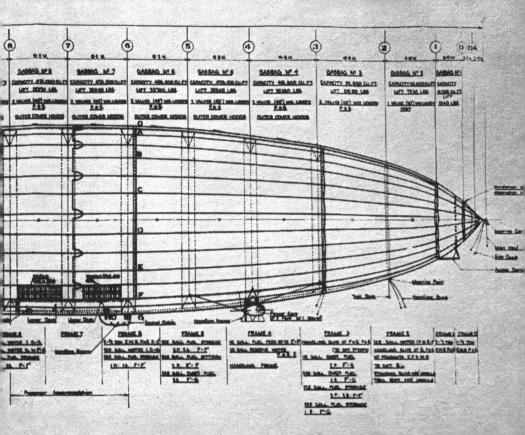

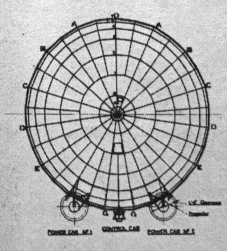

IXXW VIEW. (LOOKING AFT)

D1223681

WITH ADDITIONAL BAY

DRAWING Nº RKX/Al.

ALSO BY S. C. GWYNNE

Empire of the Summer Moon:
Quanah Parker and the Rise and Fall of the Comanches,
the Most Powerful Indian Tribe in American History

Rebel Yell:
The Violence, Passion, and Redemption
of Stonewall Jackson

The Perfect Pass:
American Genius and the Reinvention of Football

Hymns of the Republic:
The Story of the Final Year of the American Civil War

British postcard showing R101 over St Paul's Cathedral in London.
The giant airship was wildly popular.

HIS MAJESTY'S AIRSHIP

The Life and Tragic Death
of the World's Largest Flying Machine

S. C. GWYNNE

SCRIBNER

New York London Toronto Sydney New Delhi

Scribner
An Imprint of Simon & Schuster, Inc.
1230 Avenue of the Americas
New York, NY 10020

First Scribner hardcover edition May 2023

SCRIBNER and design are registered trademarks of The Gale Group, Inc.,
used under license by Simon & Schuster, Inc., the publisher of this work.

For information about special discounts for bulk purchases,
please contact Simon & Schuster Special Sales at 1-866-506-1949
or business@simonandschuster.com.

The Simon & Schuster Speakers Bureau can bring authors to your live event.
For more information or to book an event, contact the Simon & Schuster Speakers Bureau
at 1-866-248-3049 or visit our website at www.simonspeakers.com.

Maps by Jeffrey L. Ward

Manufactured in the United States of America

1   3   5   7   9   10   8   6   4   2

Library of Congress Cataloging-in-Publication Data

Names: Gwynne, S. C. (Samuel C.), 1953– author.
Title: His Majesty's airship : the life and tragic death of
the world's largest flying machine / S. C. Gwynne.
Description: New York : Scribner, 2023. | Includes bibliographical references and index.
Identifiers: LCCN 2022058230 (print) | LCCN 2022058231 (ebook) |
ISBN 9781982168278 (hardcover) | ISBN 9781982168285 (ebook)
Subjects: LCSH: R101 (Airship) | Airships—England—History—20th century. |
Aircraft accidents—England—History—20th century. | Air travel—England—
History—20th century. | Thomson, Christopher Birdwood, Baron, 1875-1930.
Classification: LCC TL659.R101 G99 2023 (print) | LCC TL659.R101 (ebook) |
DDC 363.12/409420904—dc23/eng/20230123
LC record available at https://lccn.loc.gov/2022058230
LC ebook record available at https://lccn.loc.gov/2022058231

ISBN 978-1-9821-6827-8
ISBN 978-1-9821-6828-5 (ebook)

To my daughter, Maisie

CONTENTS

HIS MAJESTY'S AIRSHIP

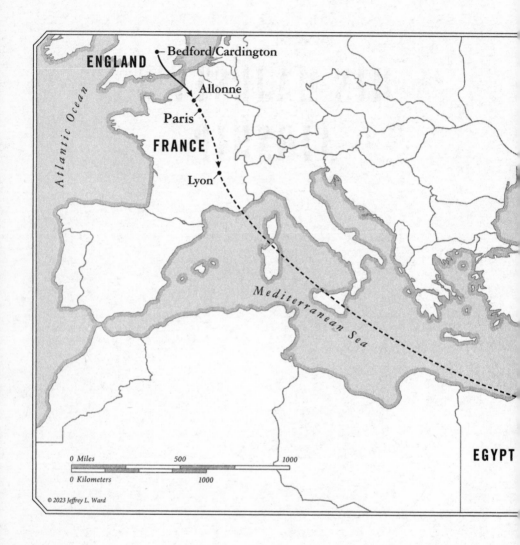

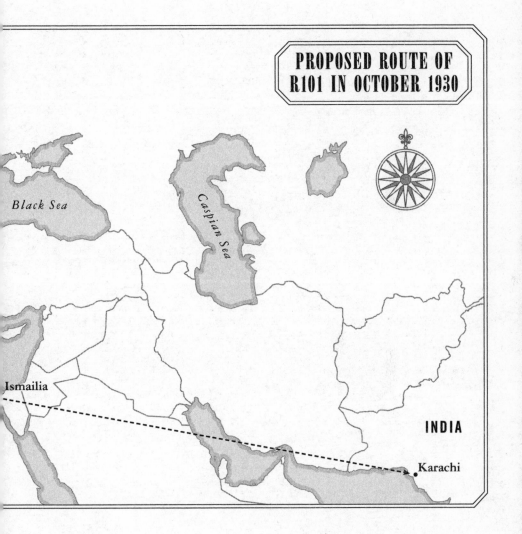

CHAPTER ONE

DREAMS, PIPE DREAMS, AND IMPERIAL VISIONS

Our story begins in the company of the Right Honorable Christopher Birdwood Thomson, First Baron Thomson of Cardington, Privy Councillor, Commander of the British Empire, peer of the House of Lords, ex-brigadier, ex–General Staff, ex-Cheltenham, ex-Woolwich, ex–Royal Engineers, ex–a lot of other things. His official title is Secretary of State for Air, which has a nice Shakespearean ring and is an apt description of what he does for a living. He is also, according to his lengthy dossier, a talented multilinguist, a devoted Francophile, and a writer of some note. He is exceptionally tall. He has an elevated forehead, a strong Roman nose set between frank, wide-set eyes, and an understated, late-imperial mustache.

The date is October 4, 1930.

Lord Thomson is traveling this day from London to Karachi, India, by airship, a five-thousand-mile, single-stop journey over some of the earth's most hostile terrain that no one, lord or otherwise, has ever made.[1] The idea is a bit crazy, in the way that experimental projects often are. But relatively few people, in this time and place, appear to think so.

Thomson must first drive from his London residence to Cardington, sixty miles north of London, a place that sounds—based on his titles and honorifics—as though it might be a Renaissance country estate in rolling pastureland. Cardington is instead a gritty little industrial

1

suburb of the small city of Bedford. Lord Thomson of Cardington has chosen it deliberately as part of his title, just as the imperial heroes Lord Kitchener of Khartoum, Lord Roberts of Kandahar, and Lord Wolseley of Tel-el-Kebir chose theirs. But instead of a battleground of empire, Thomson is lord of a sprawling manufacturing complex—the center of the exotic world of British rigid airships.

He leaves his flat in Westminster in midafternoon and travels north in his chauffeured blue Daimler with his private secretary and valet, crossing through Trafalgar Square, Piccadilly, and Regent's Park, thence into the gray rolling countryside of Hertfordshire and Bedfordshire.[2]

They stop for a cup of tea in Shefford.

Near Bedford, the Daimler climbs to the top of a hill, from which the city and its Cardington suburb are visible on the level plain below. Thomson, who has been deep in his ministerial papers during the drive, asks the driver to stop. Thomson unfolds himself from the car, all six foot five of him, in Savile Row overcoat, homburg, and neatly folded pocket handkerchief. He crosses the road and gazes over the farmland toward Cardington, where, two miles off, his eyes come to rest on an astounding sight. He has seen it before, but never from this distance, and the experience of wonder is the same every time he sees it. Secured to a 180-foot mooring mast, nose-to in a rising southerly breeze, floats the silvery form of an object larger by volume than the *Titanic*: His Majesty's Airship R101—in the vernacular "R hundred an' one." Even from here, there is something implausible and physical-law-defying about it, a giant silver fish floating weightless in the slate-gray seas of the sky. One of the largest man-made objects on earth is lighter than the air through which it glides. The ship is flanked by two equally gigantic airship sheds, so huge they loom like medieval cathedrals over the spreading farmland.

Thomson gets back in the car, and they descend through the gathering dusk and rising wind to the Royal Airship Works in Cardington. The time is just before 6:00 p.m. The 777-foot-long, steel-framed, linen-draped, hydrogen-filled airship, with fifty-four aboard, is set to leave for India within the hour.

Despite his Cheltenham manners and ministerial calm, Christopher Birdwood Thomson is a man obsessed. He has been the driving force behind a scheme to connect the far-flung outposts of the British Empire through the new medium of the air. He has taken firm hold of the national building program whose purpose is to show the world that it can be done. Flying R101 to India will be the proof. R101 is his baby. Or perhaps more accurately, the spawn of his gauzy, rainbow-inflected vision of a future in which fleets of lighter-than-air ships float serenely through blue imperial skies, linking everything British in a new space-time continuum.

"Travelers will journey tranquilly in air liners to the earth's remotest parts," Thomson has written, "visit the archipelagos in southern seas, cruise round the coasts of continents, strike inland, surmount lofty mountain ranges, and follow rivers as yet half unexplored from mouth to source. . . . They will obtain a bird's-eye view of regions made inaccessible hitherto by deserts, jungles, swamps, and frozen wastes . . . high above the mosquitos and miasmas, and mud and dust and noise. By means of the airship man will crown his conquest of the air."[3]

These were extravagant promises. But in the fall of 1930, when airplanes are still uncomfortable, dangerous, and in constant need of refueling, Lord Thomson's vision seems entirely plausible. Planes are short-hoppers, the Lindbergh miracle notwithstanding. Oceangoing ships are irremediably slow. Airships, on the other hand, can span empires, specifically the one belonging to the British, which has grown by a million square miles and 13 million souls since the end of the Great War. "I always fancied the dirigible against the aeroplane for the overhead haulage in the years to come," wrote Rudyard Kipling, reflecting the fashionable thinking of the day.[4] If Lord Thomson can't bring the imperial dominions, mandates, protectorates, colonies, and territories closer in space, he can bring them closer in time, which is really the same thing. The interval required for global travel—with regular passenger and mail service—can be reduced from oceangoing weeks to airborne days.

In 1927 a British air minister named Samuel Hoare flew by airplane from England to India to show how easy and practical it was. He instead proved the reverse, at least to airship promoters such as Thomson. Hoare's 6,124-mile journey in a de Havilland Hercules trimotor required twelve bone-rattling days and twenty stops.[5] By comparison, an ocean liner can make the passage in two weeks. R101 can do it in four days, with one stop. The king-emperor of England could be in Canada one week, Australia the next, South Africa the next. Why not?

Thomson, moreover, as secretary of state for air, is the perfect man for the job. He is a fully formed creature of empire: born of it, raised into it, a disciple of the not-quite-yet-out-of-date idea that it is the white man's destiny to rule. He has spent large chunks of his career fighting for it in South Africa, West Africa, and the Middle East. In the coming days he will fly over parts of the empire he helped create. R101's single stop will be in British-controlled Egypt, by the Suez Canal, lifeline of the empire. The symbolism is impossible to miss. As Thomson himself wrote in 1927, linking the empire by air "will not only confer air power, it will also consolidate the Empire, give unity to widely scattered peoples unattainable hitherto, create a new spirit or, maybe, revive an old spirit . . . and inculcate a conception of common destiny to the mission of our race."[6]

But even deeper purposes are working here. Thomson's destination this day—India—is not only the shimmering jewel of the British Empire, where 150,000 Britons still rule outright over more than 300 million Indians, but also a die-hard imperialist's idea of what twentieth-century imperialism ought to look like. India is also the place where Thomson was born. Though he left India for England as a child, he still feels India's deep pull.

His voyage has been carefully arranged to coincide with the Imperial

Conference in London—a meeting of the eight dominion premiers—where the future of the empire, and specifically the future of airships, will be discussed.* Thomson's trip is thus a piece of stage management on a global scale, a public relations stunt unseen before, even in the gaudiest days of empire. If all goes well, he will make his ten-thousand-mile round trip along the most imperial of all routes, returning to England trailing clouds of glory, having proven his theory just in time to deliver a paper on the future of airships to the conference. If he succeeds, he will be rewarded with more money and more airships and the opportunity to play out his grand vision. The newspapers have already reported rumors that the new viceroy of India will be named at the end of the conference. Thomson is the betting favorite.

Thus R101, en route to India on October 4, 1930, carries more than just her crew and cargo. She is by design a ship of empire. She has been built that way and promoted that way, and succeed or fail she bears with her the dreams not only of Christopher Birdwood Thomson but of millions of other people, too.

AT THE MAST, RAIN FALLS, the wind is rising, the air is electric.

The last light is dying in the leaden sky. Cars and bicycles jam the main road. Headlamps and flashlights glow in the gathering dark. Some blink out messages to passengers and crew in Morse code.[7] "Farewell." "We love you." A million people including the prince of Wales have thronged to visit the silver monster in the past month, but there has been nothing like the crowd today. Many have been drinking, and a sort of imperial delirium has settled upon the crowd. They sing the hymn of empire: "Land of Hope and Glory." *God, who made thee mighty / Make thee mightier yet*. Flashbulbs pop. With great hurry and bustle the

---

* The Imperial Conference was held periodically and attended by the premiers of Great Britain and of its dominions: Canada, Newfoundland, South Africa, India, Australia, New Zealand, Irish Free State, and the United Kingdom.

last loading is done, while men in uniform exchange greetings and goodbyes. They are all waiting on Thomson. Above them the massive ship bobs and shifts restlessly in the wind, her six acres of surface area causing her to pivot about the mast like a weather vane. More than one observer finds it strange and even unsettling to see such a gigantic piece of industrial machinery move so easily.

Around six fifteen the air minister's big, boxy Daimler pushes through the traffic and up to the wooden buildings at the foot of the tower, where Thomson greets officers, crew, and fellow passengers. They represent the elite of the British airship corps, and all are going to India with Thomson. Many are legends in the service. Among them is George Herbert Scott, one of the greatest airship legends of all, the man whose 1919 voyage to New York and back in a modified Zeppelin design was the first east-west crossing of the Atlantic of any aircraft, and the first round trip. Scott, though not in formal command, will set routes and make the final decisions whether to go, based on the weather.

In small groups those assembled ride the elevator to the top of the mast and board through a hatch in R101's nose, tiny figures vanishing into a cavernous space. The ship is unlike any other machine that has ever existed. She is bigger, for one thing, in both length and breadth, than anything that has flown before. Her great high-tensile-steel framework holds 5.5 million cubic feet of hydrogen gas in enormous billowing gasbags, which can lift more than 160 tons, the greatest load ever carried by any aircraft. Measured by displacement alone, R101 is nearly twice the volume of United States Lines' SS *Leviathan*, the largest ocean liner in the world.[8]

The most striking thing about the airship's interior is its luxury. The effect is of a prewar steam yacht married to a warship's admiral's quarters. From her sixty-seat art deco dining room, trimmed in white, gold, and Cambridge blue, to her commodious lounge with its windowed promenades, she is meant to suggest the grand ocean liners of the day.

She even features, in the midst of so much explosive hydrogen, a *smoking room*. But the opulence is all surface: in an airship where weight saving is everything, there is none of the heavy-oak-and-marble solidity of a Pullman car or a steamship. The gold-trimmed pillars are not pillars; they are illusions created by ultralight aluminum alloy, balsa, linen, and paint. Walls and ceilings are paper-thin. Like the ship's outer skin, which is nothing but a fragile layer of linen treated with "dope"— celluloid varnish meant to maintain tautness and keep water out—and stretched over light steel girders, the entire structure has the feel of a giant Chinese lantern.* The less the weight in the frame, the more cargo that can be lifted.

Which does not mean, R101's hyperkinetic press office is keen to remind the world, that the ship is not safe. R101 is all about safety, the office insists. Safety first, safety last, safety deliberately overengineered, safety based on hard-won lessons of the past, safety rooted in technical wizardry. The safest aircraft of any kind ever built. She runs on heavy-oil diesel engines, which have never before been deployed on an airplane or airship, and whose fuel is extremely difficult to ignite. Fires are bad in any aircraft, but measurably worse in hydrogen-filled airships and still worse in hot, tropical climates, where R101 is headed. The Beardmore Tornado diesels are much heavier than gas engines, but Great Britain is taking no chances. R101 is said to be virtually flameproof. Her metal structure is so much stronger than it needs to be—R101's engineers used a 1921 British airship crash as a model of what not to do, then doubled down—that it is said to be unbreakable. Her unique gas valves allow precise altitude control even in stormy weather. Her final, seventeen-hour trial flight was flawless. "'Safety first' may not be a very paying proposition in regard to politics," Thomson told the House of Lords, "but I am sure it is the right thing in regard to airships."[9] A prominent

* Blimps have no or minimal superstructure or frame. They are essentially steerable balloons. Rigid airships such as R101 consist of gasbags inside a hard frame.

German airship engineer has called R101 "the safest conveyance on land or sea or in the air that human ingenuity has yet devised. . . . She is a great, strong thing."[10]

Part of this is pressroom hyperbole, of course. But Thomson and the men who designed and built his airship believe it. They are thus proposing a revolutionary change in the nature of air travel. The early twentieth century has seen more gruesome crashes, of both airplanes and airships, than anyone cares to remember. Forgetting just how dangerous flying is is critical to the industry's progress. Pilots and passengers who think they are likely to die are unlikely to fly. But those who do fly still die in large numbers. In 1929, the most lethal year on record, there were *fifty-one* commercial-airliner crashes with fatalities. The 1920s saw several infamous examples of rigid airships plunging to earth. R101 will show that the dignified flight of an ultrasafe airship—serene, low-speed cruising above the land, with passengers waving to people on the ground and watching deer run through forests—is the future of long-distance travel.

The loading continues.

There are a few odd moments. As George Herbert Scott waits for Thomson to arrive, two stewards walk by carrying tins of biscuits. Scott, who has been frantically trying for the last few days to lighten the ship, which has for the first time been simultaneously inflated to its maximum limit and loaded to its full design capacity of 160 tons, orders the men to throw away the tins and save the biscuits in paper bags.[11]

Which might seem like prudent, if slightly overfastidious, weight management.

Then, to everyone's astonishment and dismay, the great Lord Thomson's baggage arrives. He has already insisted on dressing up the lounge and entranceway with an expensive, heavy 2,630-square-foot Axminster carpet, weighing over a thousand pounds.[12] Now come his effects: two large cabin trunks, as though he were leaving for several months instead of two weeks; four suitcases, with his ministerial papers included; two cases of champagne for his state dinner in Egypt; and, finally, a rolled-up ten-foot-long Sulaimaniya carpet from Kurdistan, which requires two men to carry it and does not fit in the lift. The total weight of just his personal luggage is 254 pounds, compared to 350 pounds for the entire crew of thirty-five.[13] It seems impossible that Thomson doesn't understand about weight in airships.

AT 6:36 P.M. R101 slips her mooring and swings free. A cheer rises from the crowd.[14] Normally the ship moves upward and away from the mast. But now, suddenly, she lurches earthward. Such a movement by something 777 feet long and 130 feet wide is something to see. It arrests the attention. To stop the fall, Captain Carmichael "Bird" Irwin releases a massive amount of water ballast—four-plus tons of it, almost half the ship's total—which pours from the bow in a great waterfall, drawing an even louder cheer from the onlookers, who are not quite sure what they are seeing.[15] The ship responds, the nose buoys up. R101 slides away from the mast, her control car glowing white and her running lights, port and starboard, winking red and green. Her five Beardmore Tornado diesels throb and thrum into the nearly complete darkness.

As she moves off, watchers on the ground can see Lord Thomson himself, flanked by Sir Sefton Brancker, Great Britain's director of civil aviation, leaning on the promenade rail, illuminated from behind by the bright windows of the saloon. One eyewitness will recall that the two men, and other passengers, too, appeared "starkly clear."[16]

Six weeks before, Thomson wrote to his girlfriend, a Romanian princess named Marthe Bibesco—who looms large in the narrative of his life—to tell her how thrilled he was about his upcoming trip to India. In the letter he expressed his keen desire to experience bad weather while flying in an airship, something he had never done: "To ride the storm has always been my ambition, and who knows but we may realize it on the way to India." Then he added, "But not, I hope, with undue risk to human lives."[17] That was a bit like saying, "Damn the torpedoes, as long as no one gets hurt." It seemed an odd and almost naïve thing to say, as though he were not about to make the most perilous journey in the short history of aviation.

BRIEF HISTORY OF A BAD IDEA

R101 may have been built in a British factory by British workmen and British scientists and engineers with massive funding from Parliament and the entirely British purpose of stitching the old empire together, but at her core she was something else. Though her builders and designers would have objected to such a characterization—they would have insisted on the Britishness and originality of her many innovations—the truth was that her lineage was rooted in the town of Friedrichshafen, Germany, in the last years of the nineteenth century and early years of the twentieth century. R101 was, in form and function, a *zeppelin*—a word that came to describe large rigid airships and did not enter European languages until the early twentieth century. Like all zeppelins, R101 was built of circular, transverse metal frames that were connected by longitudinal girders and a hard keel. Like all zeppelins, she was covered with doped cloth, and her engine cars—or nacelles, as they were called—were suspended, port and starboard, below the hull, as was her control car. Like all zeppelins, her lifting mechanism consisted of a series of gigantic hydrogen-filled gasbags suspended within and attached to the transverse frames. Control technology—rudder to steer right and left and elevators (flaps) to move up and down—was fundamentally the same, as were the basic flying principles and techniques, which included the use of hydrogen-gas valves and water ballast. R101 was just the largest, most expensive, most streamlined, and most technologically sophisticated zeppelin-style airship ever built.

But what, exactly, was a zeppelin?

*   *   *

AT DAWN ON AUGUST 4, 1908—twenty-two years before R101 set out for India—a stout, bald, seventy-year-old German nobleman with a magnificent walrus mustache named Ferdinand von Zeppelin stood in the gondola of his 446-foot-long airship and gave an order peculiar to lighter-than-air vessels: *"Luftschiff hoch!"*—"Up ship!" And up the giant, pencil-shaped vessel went, from the dead-calm waters of Lake Constance, up into clear German skies. The old count beamed. Up, too, came cheers from the small crowd below. The ship turned, accelerated to its full speed of 30 mph, and glided out over the lake toward the town of Konstanz, the count's birthplace.

The vessel was called LZ-4. The letters stood for *Luftschiff Zeppelin* (Zeppelin airship). Her objective that day was to do something that no aircraft of any kind had ever done or even come close to doing: fly continuously for twenty-four hours to a destination hundreds of miles away, turn around, and return home. No heavier-than-air machine had been able to stay aloft for more than thirty-eight minutes, as the count's competitor Wilbur Wright had done in 1905.* The Wright brothers had made solo flights. Count von Zeppelin was taking eight people with him.

As his airship cruised at low altitude up the Rhine Valley, a remarkable thing happened: tens of thousands of people filled city streets and town squares to watch. They were crazy with enthusiasm. They behaved as though they had just won a war. Some laughed wildly, others sang or cheered, still others wept openly.[1] Cannons were fired from castle battlements. Beer steins were drained. Up in the control car, slung beneath 530,000 cubic feet of hydrogen gas, the count, who could see all this happening quite clearly, gazed benignly down.

He was, at this moment, the most famous aviator in the world.

---

* A month after this flight by the count, Orville Wright would stay aloft for sixty-two minutes.

He had not always been so popular. Until recently he had been considered by most people, and most Germans especially, a failure. Many would have added modifiers: a clownish, bumbling failure, a caricature of a mad and hopelessly inept inventor. He seemed, too, to be from another world, a place more like a feudal kingdom than Europe of La Belle Époque. His immaculate clothing, morning coats, yellow silk gloves, yachting caps, polished manners, lordly bearing, and fondness for challenging people to duels all appeared to belong to another, less relevant age.[2]

His airships, on the other hand, belonged very much to the present. In the summer of 1900 he had launched his first lighter-than-air vessel, LZ-1, an ungainly 420-foot-long fusion of oddball technologies that lumbered into the air for a few minutes, then failed to respond to controls and dropped back into the lake. Critics judged her useless. She was dismantled and sold for scrap. In 1906 the count was back again, this time with LZ-2, a new and improved version of his first airship. After a promising liftoff, LZ-2 struggled and shot unbidden up to an altitude of fifteen hundred feet, where her transmission broke, her rudder jammed, and her engines stalled, sending her free-ballooning off toward the Bavarian mountains. She crash-landed. That night, while anchored to the ground by cables, the wind tore her to pieces.

The German press now responded more viciously. The count was mocked, derided as a crazy and reckless dreamer whose "pathetic career," in one account, had led him to sacrifice "his estate and his fortune, after reducing his wife to destitution and his only daughter to penury."[3] The German air minister told him that what he was doing was "pure Jules Verne." The minister did not mean that as a compliment.

Von Zeppelin had indeed invested much of his own money in his obsession with lighter-than-air vehicles. Born in 1838, he had become interested in balloons—the original lighter-than-air concept—which had been around since the eighteenth century. But balloons had a serious limitation: you couldn't steer or control them. When a balloon ascended, it went where God or the wind wanted it to go. A balloon made more sense anchored to the ground as a military observation post.

In 1852 Frenchman Henri Giffard changed all that. He made the first powered and controlled flight in a 144-foot-long balloon filled with hydrogen, traveling seventeen miles from Paris to the town of Élancourt.[4] He had thus *directed it* to go where he wanted it to, though he could only accomplish a one-way flight. The French verb for "to direct" is *diriger.* A balloon that was controllable was *dirigeable.* Thus, *dirigible.* The count found Giffard's work inspirational. But what turned inspiration to obsession was the 1884 round-trip flight of *La France*, an odd-looking contraption with a strangely shaped balloon and inadequate engines that still managed to be the first fully controllable airship.

Though a mere 15 mph wind would have caused the underpowered *La France* to fly backward, the count saw something larger and, to him, far more important in the achievement. *La France* was not just a nifty-though-flawed piece of technology. It was a *weapon*, at least potentially, a weapon now possessed by Germany's archenemy that could be used to rain down fire and death on German cities.* The count, a career army officer with the rank of brigadier general, saw everything in military terms. Germany would, he concluded, need technology like this.

The German airship he envisioned—this was his great stroke of brilliance—would have to carry much more weight in fuel and crew and armaments and would thus have to be much, much bigger. To be bigger it could not be a blimp like *La France*, which was essentially a frameless gasbag with an engine attached to it, a more sophisticated version of a balloon. The problem with blimps or balloons was that, in the absence of superstructure, they tended to collapse upon themselves. This greatly limited their size and speed, which meant they could lift little cargo, human or otherwise.

---

* France and Germany had fought a major war, the Franco-Prussian War, in 1870 and 1871. National memories of the war were still fresh.

Von Zeppelin's flying weapon, he decided, would have a skeleton, a hard metal frame able to hold large gasbags. It would be a *rigid* airship, the first of its kind, and would be vastly larger than anything that had flown before. He had learned a useful scientific principle: the lifting capacity of an airship increased with the cube of its dimensions. Which meant that small dimensional changes yielded exponential increases in the weight carried.[5] In practical terms, an increase of a mere three feet in a ship's diameter produced more than three tons of additional lift. Three tons, say, of bombs.

This was the startling, revolutionary truth of LZ-1, though no one else understood it at the time. The ship may have been a practical failure, but the concept was not. With airships, size was *everything*. The lifting gas was hydrogen, the lightest atom in the universe and the element that had lifted most early balloons and airship prototypes. It was cheap and relatively easy to make through various chemical reactions, the simplest of which was to pass steam over heated iron, decomposing the water into its elements: hydrogen and oxygen.

Undiscouraged by his failures, the count pressed on. When the German Ministry of War offered a prize for the best airship in the form of large government contracts, he saw his chance. To win the competition, which pitted his rigid airship against much-smaller blimps, entrants had to fly continuously for twenty-four hours and cover 435 miles. He took his first step toward that prize in September 1907, when his LZ-3 made a record-setting seven-hour, fifty-four-minute flight. Unaccountably, and to the complete surprise of the German government, newspapers, and public, the batty little count's airship idea had actually worked. For the first time the German press and public showed enthusiasm for what he was doing. After so much failure and obloquy, he was becoming famous. Investment money flowed into his factory.

This allowed him to build his supership, LZ-4.

On July 1, 1908, the count dazzled the world again. For LZ-4's final trial, he flew from Friedrichshafen to Zurich and back with twelve people on board, setting world single-flight aviation records of twelve hours and 236 miles. Now he was a *global* sensation. The international press, which had once mocked him, breathlessly covered his every word and deed. He received a thousand telegrams and a gold medal from the king of Württemberg.[6]

Which brings us back to the German Ministry of War's twenty-four-hour endurance contest. Unfortunately the smooth sailing—along with the cheering, weeping, and cannonading—would not last. The ship's troubles started in early afternoon near Mainz, the journey's turnaround point, when an engine broke down. The count landed and made repairs. The problems continued after midnight when a melted crankshaft caused another engine to shut down. The ship was forced to land again, this time in a field near the town of Echterdingen, just south of Stuttgart, sending terrified sheep and cattle running for safety. LZ-4 was secured to a buried wagon. Before long thousands of people had gathered in the field. The airship was so huge, so stunning, so utterly unlike anything they had ever seen, that they surged forward to inspect and try to touch her. Soldiers held them off while Daimler mechanics worked on the engines. The count dozed peacefully in the gondola. At noon he went to the inn in Echterdingen for lunch.

His goal was still in sight.

Then the weather changed. In midafternoon a storm blew up and a high wind hit the airship's giant sail-like surface like a freight train, snapping the mooring cable and carrying the ship off with three hapless crew members aboard. Wind was a mortal enemy of rigid airships. "The crowd faded away beneath me," said one crew member later, who'd tried frantically to vent hydrogen gas. The ship traveled half a mile, came briefly to earth, hit a clump of trees, then resumed its wild downwind ride.

A few moments later it caught fire. Sparks also were a mortal enemy of rigid airships. While this was no secret, watching what happened when a spark of static electricity from the ship's rubberized cotton gasbags encountered 530,000 cubic feet of hydrogen gas was something different altogether. A great surge of flame engulfed the ship, followed by a series of reverberating booms as the gas cells exploded. "Flames shot up from the hull," wrote one journalist who witnessed it. "A column of fire rose to the sky, immense, horrible, as if the earth had opened up, releasing the flames from Hell. Huge flames ate their way up the balloon, piece by piece."[7]

The hydrogen fireball was brief and spectacular and quickly consumed nearly everything on the ship that wasn't made of metal, leaving behind a glowing skeleton. Somehow the three crew members, badly singed, got out alive. As the crowd looked on in silent horror and removed their hats like mourners at a funeral, the count, who had seen the fire destroy his ship, made his way gravely forward to inspect the wreckage. He stared at it, then turned and walked away, not only from his smoking vessel but from his career as an airship builder. He had failed again.

Then something strange happened.

The crowd, which had been quiet, began to sing, at first softly, then with greater and greater volume until strains of the "Deutschlandlied," the German national hymn, with its refrain, *Deutschland über alles*, were booming out across the river valley.[8] As the old count walked to his car, the mass of people surged around him, singing, cheering, and applauding as though he had just accomplished the most wonderful thing.

Then something even stranger happened.

Within twenty-four hours money began to arrive at the count's office. Lots of it, in cash, postal orders, and telegrams. By the end of the first day, he had received several hundred thousand marks. That was just the beginning. Soon campaigns by newspapers, cities, and corporations produced hundreds of thousands more, and soon the count had over 6 million marks—some $30 million in today's currency.[9] Along with the money came so much mail from his fellow citizens that the local post office stopped trying to sort it. He received every kind of gift: bottles of liquor and wine, sausages, whole hams, socks, poems, and songs. The press called this outpouring of love and currency "the Miracle of Echter-dingen." What happened was incomprehensible to most outsiders, and even Germans had trouble articulating it. How had the count's horrific failure been turned, almost instantly, to glorious triumph?

The answer lay somewhere deep in the German heart, where national pride came before everything else and dauntless courage in the face of great obstacles counted for something. The count was instantly perceived as a symbol of German patriotism, national pride, honor, and resourcefulness. His ship may have burned, but hadn't he flown farther and longer than anyone else? Hadn't he taken risks that no one else would? And wasn't his miraculous technology 100 percent *German*? The nation was suddenly in the grip of what the papers called "Zeppelin Mania." Streets and squares and even a chrysanthemum were named for him. Newspapers clamored for quotes from him—anything, it did not matter. Shops sold all manner of count-endorsed, Zeppelin-related goods: candy, clothing, pocket watches, cigarettes and cigars, yachting caps, detergent, cheese, shoe polish, suspenders, gingerbread, and other items. The greatest gift of all was the buy-in of the German government. In exchange for his failure in the endurance test, the count received a fat subsidy. Soaring, romantic nationalism had trumped actual performance—a phenomenon that would repeat itself many times in the history of rigid airships.

In the same month as LZ-4's fiery crash, Wilbur Wright astonished a French crowd in Le Mans by executing a complete turn in a thirty-yard radius, a maneuver most people had thought impossible. In the next few months he broke all existing heavier-than-air flying records. By December he proved he could stay in the air for more than two hours. Like Count von Zeppelin, the Wrights were now world-famous. But they had competition. In France alone by May 1909 fifteen different factories were building airplanes.[10] The brothers already had patent fights on their hands.

The count, now a full-blown folk hero in his native land, had a global monopoly on rigid airships.

In September, barely a month after the disaster at Echterdingen, he had enough money to establish a new airship construction company, Luftschiffbau Zeppelin (Zeppelin Airship Construction Company), and to buy a piece of land in Friedrichshafen where future *zeppelins*—as they were now known—would be built.

At the age of seventy he was the newest and hottest entrepreneur in Europe.

THE COUNT SAW his rigid airships as more than just aircraft that could shoot bullets and drop bombs. He also conceived of them, from the beginning, as *terror weapons.* A cannon could blow things up and knock things down. But a giant airship could sow panic and demoralize whole populations. A fleet of rigid airships, attacking from the dark skies over London or Paris and unopposed by anything else in the air, could cause sovereign governments to sue for peace. This was the count's fantasy. His thinking was in line with the German martial culture of his day.

In 1907 the German author Dr. Rudolf Martin wrote a bestselling science fiction novel called *Berlin–Baghdad: The German World Empire in the Age of the Airship, 1910–1931.* In it he theorized that four hundred German airships flying at an altitude of 29,500 feet could inflict immense damage on enemy cities, enabling Germany to conquer Europe and the Middle East. He wrote that German airships would soon be capable of transporting 350,000 soldiers across the North Sea to invade England.[11] He called the ships *Wunderwaffen*—"wonder weapons."[12] Two years later, in his bestselling *World War in the Air*, he featured a fictionalized Count von Zeppelin leading an airship attack on Paris, which set the city on fire. The real count found Martin's bloody visions cogent and thoughtful.[13] So, apparently, did the German people. In the war's first year in the book, German schoolchildren were already singing a song that included the verse "Fly, Zeppelin! Fly to England! England shall be destroyed by fire!"[14]

But the count still had to persuade the War Ministry to buy his airships. Though he hated the idea of commerce, he set up a small commercial airline called the German Airship Transportation Company, or DELAG, as a means of demonstrating his products and thus winning military contracts.*

DELAG, like his first zeppelin projects, failed immediately and spectacularly.

The company's first airship, *Deutschland*, offered passengers, in an era of noisy, oil-splattered airplanes, what seemed astounding luxury: a carpeted lounge with wicker chairs, mahogany-veneer walls and ceilings, and a full luncheon service. On June 28, 1910, what was supposed to be a three-hour flight carrying twenty journalists became a nine-hour, wind-tortured ordeal during which the ship was often flying backward and the crew admitted to passengers that they had no idea what to do. "The swerving, driving, rain-beaten airship fought inch by inch," wrote one of the terrified passengers, "sloping steeply first forward and then aft as we rose and fell in the storm."[15] Unable to cope with the high winds, *Deutschland* ran out of fuel and crash-landed in a forest of tall trees, which impaled the ship as it descended. The passengers managed to climb down a grapnel-rope ladder thirty feet through the trees to safety. The ship was a total loss. The passengers and crew were lucky to be alive.

On September 14, 1910, a raging hydrogen fire destroyed DELAG's other ship, LZ-6A, in its hangar.

On May 16, 1911, a successor ship, *Deutschland II*, took off in a high wind and was blown away from the three hundred men who were

---

* The company's name in German was Deutsche Luftschiffahrts-Aktienegesellschaft, thus the acronym DELAG.

holding her down. She hit her hangar and broke in half. Passengers and crew escaped by means of a long ladder. DELAG's safety record was frightening, even in a world where air crashes were common. *Deutschland I* had lasted only a week, LZ-6A three weeks, and *Deutschland II* five weeks.

At this point in the Zeppelin company's troubled history, an heir to Count von Zeppelin emerged: Hugo Eckener. A stout, undistinguished economics writer, he had covered the early zeppelin flights and had finally become hooked on the count's ideas. As DELAG's flight director, he not only made a point of learning how to handle the big ships but set precise rules and protocols for flying. He insisted on extensive crew training, and training for ground handlers. He also organized his own weather-forecasting service. He learned from the crash of *Deutschland II* that he should never let the company be pressured into flying in adverse weather—and he never again did. Thus began a relatively crash-free period that saved the count's struggling company.

What Eckener had really figured out was how to improve the company's public relations, which meant convincing the world that his airships, against all evidence, were safe. He made sure that his new airship, *Schwaben*, flew only in summer, only in clear weather, and only in light winds.[16] She made only short-duration flights. She was more of an airborne amusement park than an authentic airline, a vehicle for brief joyrides, two-thirds of which were given free. Over the next year *Schwaben* made 218 flights and carried 1,553 passengers, as DELAG loudly proclaimed, *without passenger injury*. *Schwaben* thus became the world's first commercially successful passenger airliner. The company's promotional materials neglected to mention that a year after her debut *Schwaben* exploded in a giant fireball outside her hangar, injuring thirty-four soldiers.[17] The cause was the same as that of the LZ-4 crash: static electricity from the gasbags.

DELAG persisted. Eckener's fly-only-in-perfect-weather ploy worked. From 1910 to 1914, using three ships, DELAG carried more than thirty-four thousand passengers without injury, which convinced the German government to order nine airships for use as weapons—a gigantic boost for the company.

The first two airships delivered by Luftschiffbau Zeppelin to the Germany navy were, like most of the company's other airships, disasters. LZ-14 plunged into the North Sea in September 1912 after its rudder failed in heavy rain and high wind. Fourteen of the twenty aboard died. The second airship, LZ-18, caught fire in the air, exploded several times, and fell 450 feet to earth. All twenty-eight men aboard were burned alive.

At another time, and in another culture, such a consistently dreadful safety record, built up over more than a decade, might have led to some basic questions about the count's famous technology. Perhaps starting with: Hadn't most of his airships crashed? Did their enormous surface areas make them too vulnerable to wind? Wasn't a hydrogen-based airship a profoundly flawed idea? But no such questions were asked. German public opinion remained overwhelmingly positive. Airplanes, the other new flying technology, crashed often, too—causing five hundred deaths between 1908 and 1914—and the planes often caught fire because gasoline, too, was flammable. Airships and airplanes were still experimental machines. They had always attracted a fringe of risk-takers anyway. Or so the thinking went. Hugo Eckener even took time to deliver a convoluted and ultimately incomprehensible explanation of *why hydrogen wasn't inherently explosive*. It was only *potentially* hazardous, he pointed out, when, as it was expanding from the heat of the sun or from a drop in air pressure, it was valved from the gasbags *and* permitted to accumulate in an unventilated space.[18] Anyone who saw a burning, exploding zeppelin might have wondered if there was any truth at all in what Eckener said.*

---

* Hydrogen gas is very flammable and can explode when mixed with air and its oxygen. There is no scientific debate about this.

But war loomed and so did big new contracts for the builder of Germany's largest killing machines.

IN 1914, the first year of the Great War, German rigid airships became the world's first long-range bombers. They introduced to humankind the notion that it could be annihilated from the sky by something other than a thunderbolt. Because the bombing missions were often aimed at innocent civilians, these airships, most of which were made in the Zeppelin company's now-nationalized factories, were—as Zeppelin had predicted—also the world's first weapons of mass terror. For four years they brought their mechanized terror to seven different countries: Great Britain, Belgium, France, Greece, Poland, Romania, and Russia. Of these, Great Britain suffered by far the largest number of attacks, the largest number of civilians killed, and the most property damage.

It was ironic that Britain, whose navy had ruled the seas for so long, and whose island geography made it both fortresslike and virtually unassailable, should have been so helpless against aerial attack. On January 3, 1915, First Lord of the Admiralty Winston Churchill made this staggering admission in a memorandum to the British War Council: "There is no known means of preventing the airships coming, and not much chance of punishing them on their return. The unavenged destruction of non-combatant life may therefore be very considerable. . . . The Air Department of the Admiralty must make it plain that they are quite powerless to prevent such an attack."[19] No British minister had ever before made such a statement admitting weakness. At the beginning of 1915 the city of London had only twelve guns and thirteen searchlights to defend itself from air attacks.

And on the attacks went. When airships first crossed the English Channel in January 1915, in a raid on Great Yarmouth, they encountered no antiaircraft guns, no searchlights, no fighter planes. They dropped their bombs on the city and returned safely home. In April zeppelins hit industrial and commercial sites in England almost every day, with little effective resistance. In May a zeppelin attacked London for the first time, dropping 154 bombs on the city, killing seven, injuring thirty-five, and damaging buildings. Bigger raids with bigger bombs—including a 660-pounder—followed in September and October. The zeppelins always came at night, usually on the dark of the moon. British citizens who had once found them objects of curiosity or even amusement quickly learned to fear the odd clacking of the airships' wooden propellers, which signaled their arrival, and the hiss of falling bombs followed by chains of detonations and screams of people in the streets. Newspapers were filled with news of the "baby killers" who murdered indiscriminately from above.

Meanwhile zeppelin factories ramped up. They were soon able to produce a new ship in only a few weeks. They were building streamlined 535-foot monsters with more than a million cubic feet of hydrogen gas, which meant they could lift bigger engines, more crew, more machine guns, more bombs. They could run at 60 mph and range as far as England's western coast with two tons of bombs. Within four months nearly four thousand officers and men were stationed at nine airship bases, mostly on Germany's north coast. By 1916 Germany was producing "superzeppelins," up to 650 feet long, with 2 million cubic feet of lift. They could climb to thirteen thousand feet and fly at 66 mph, the fastest airship speed recorded, and carry even more bombs.

As the German airships hit targets all over Great Britain, the German press wrote triumphantly of their victories: tens of thousands of British dead, twenty-one thousand in two raids alone in August 2016![20] Factories in the industrial heartland crippled, massive economic damage inflicted. Zeppelin captains reported cities in flames, Britons running in terror through the streets. A million British troops, needed to fight zeppelin attacks, were being kept from the Western Front! All of Germany was thrilled by the zeppelins' success, convinced that they were destroying not only British war-making capacity but the British will to fight.

The problem with such German claims is that they were not true. Most were exaggerations at best. Many were outright lies.

Though German bombs had destroyed *some* buildings and killed *some* people, news of widespread death and devastation in England was false, manufactured by airship commanders, German government press agents, and German newspapers and readily believed by a credulous German public. On January 31, 1916, to take just one example, the German government reported that "large quantities" of bombs had been dropped on factories in Liverpool, Birkenhead, and Manchester, causing "gigantic explosions and serious conflagrations."[21] In fact no German airships had attacked any of those cities, and the "raid" managed only to hit a few buildings and houses elsewhere, causing minimal damage. Zeppelin captains, who were often not sure what or whom they had bombed, were more than happy to report their successes when they returned. The crew of one zeppelin that had been following the river Thames was certain that they had released their bombs on London, imagining the terror and death that were unfolding below them. But they were actually over a canal sixty miles from London, and their bombs had fallen into a swamp.[22] In a typical raid in early 1916, Zeppelin L-19 crossed into England and dropped its bombs on the small town of Tipton, demolishing a pub and killing several farm animals. On its return the ship's engines broke down and it crashed into the North Sea, killing everyone on board.[23]

In truth the zeppelins and their crews were not up to the job of foreign invasion in the dark, of precision bombing in aircraft that were hard to fly and navigate and easy to shoot down. More than one-third lost their way. A significant percentage never even made it across the Channel, victims of cold weather, engine problems, or lack of lift. In one estimate of the war's first twenty months, only 108 of 146 airships successfully crossed into England.[24] During a raid in August 1915, five zeppelins could not find London, the largest city on earth.[25] In 1916 the German airship L-20, at 585 feet the longest airship ever built, attempted to bomb Edinburgh, Scotland. But she became so lost in fog that she instead bombed a castle in the Highlands, 150 miles north. Her crew believed she had bombed a coal mine. Later, L-20 made a soft landing on the ocean next to a German steamer to inquire about her navigational position, only to discover that she was in the far northern latitudes of the Orkney Islands, more than two hundred miles from the original target. She lost an engine and was blown helplessly across the North Sea, crash-landed in a fjord in Norway, became airborne again in a gust of wind, hit a mountain, and broke in half while crash-landing again in another fjord.[26] Miraculously no fire broke out, though three crew members died. So many bombs fell in fields that the British began to believe that the zeppelins were deliberately attacking crops and livestock.[27] The commanders' reports were not all lies. Many zeppelin commanders honestly thought they had hit industrial targets when they had destroyed only a stable and a few donkeys. But it was bad information all the same.

Something about the idea of German crews laughing exultantly while they released hellfire upon innocent civilians—when all they had done was destroy a few melons in a farmer's field—was grimly comical, too.

During the war zeppelins made fifty-one raids over England and dropped five thousand bombs. They managed to kill only 557 people and injure 1,358.[28] Those numbers were so small as to be rounding errors in a war that killed and wounded millions. By comparison, a single U-boat torpedo fired at the *Lusitania* in 1915 caused more than twice the casualties inflicted by zeppelins in four years of war.[29] (The number of British soldiers kept from the front to defend against German air attacks was about seventeen thousand.[30])

Still, the zeppelins came.

But navigation, weather, and engine problems were just the beginning of their troubles. The British learned quickly how to fight back. Their early defenses consisted mainly of searchlights and antiaircraft guns. These were not always effective, but when they were, they offered a sight that Londoners would not soon forget. A single searchlight would find a ship and then a dozen others would find her, too, and the sky became brilliant with searching white fingers of light as a hundred guns opened fire and the stricken zeppelin, unable to stop the loss of gas caused by the shells, sank to her destruction.

By 1916 the British had discovered another major truth of anti-zeppelin warfare: that fighter planes firing incendiary bullets could set the giant airships on fire.* Several million cubic feet of hydrogen, enclosed in a series of gigantic gasbags stretching for more than five hundred feet, presented an enormous target. Not every incendiary bullet that hit a gasbag caused a hydrogen explosion; on the other hand, all it took was one of them, one small spark in the right place, and the airship and its crew would be destroyed in seconds. The experience of killing one was at once horrific and, for many pilots, richly satisfying.

Just how effective British fighters could be was evident on the night of September 2, 1916, when German naval airship chief Peter Strasser sent sixteen airships against England. They were intended to be a definitive blow to British morale. Instead, the fleet met high-flying, incendiary-bullet-armed British fighter planes. The first victim—a 570-foot-long airship built by Zeppelin competitor Schütte-Lanz (SL-11)—was hit by an incendiary bullet from a tiny British B.E.2c biplane and was quickly engulfed in an inferno so bright that it could be seen sixty miles away. From below, the show was spectacular. Londoners gathered to watch. The zeppelin fell slowly to earth, her crew burned alive by the incandescent white flames. From the air—the point of view of the other German crews—the sight was terrifying. Since they did not have parachutes—too much weight, their superiors said—they knew that even the smallest fire meant death, and they

---

* The British used different types of incendiary rounds. One contained phosphorus, which ignited on firing and left a tracer trail of blue smoke. Another was the "Pomeroy" bullet, which exploded on impact with a zeppelin's outer cover.

would have only a few seconds to choose between burning alive and jumping. (Only three soldiers ever survived a burning zeppelin.) In one of the most remarkable retreats in the war, all the other raiders turned and headed back to Germany. In the next four months, eight more zeppelins were shot down by British planes, all ending in dazzling hydrogen fireballs.

Thus began a lethal competition between German airships, which initially had the advantage of altitude, enabling them to fly above their enemies unmolested, and British fighters, who began to contest it. The fights pitted one national technology against the other and the physical endurance of airshipmen against that of fighter pilots. On its most basic level, the race was purely scientific: who could fly higher. The Germans mounted a frantic effort to increase size and lift and strip out weight. Girders were shaved down, engines discarded, crew quarters removed, fuel and bomb loads reduced by half. The British kept pace. In 1915 it took a British fighter forty minutes to get to 10,000 feet—well below the 13,000 feet that zeppelins could reach. By 1917 improvements in zeppelins allowed them to reach 18,000 feet. But the latest British fighter, the Sopwith Camel, was able to fly at 17,300 feet.[31]

While these advances produced striking improvements in the performance of planes and airships, the higher altitudes had horrific effects on the unprotected humans flying them. The cold was intense, often thirty degrees below zero or worse. Men suffered from frostbite. They went unconscious from lack of oxygen. Long periods of time at high altitude could cause lungs to fill with fluid and the brain to swell, resulting in loss of coordination and paralysis. Though fighter pilots also suffered from the exposure to cold and thin air, they spent much briefer periods at the higher altitudes. Both sides experienced inevitable hardware problems: controls malfunctioning, compasses freezing, oil lines snapping, windows cracking.

The new generation of German airships, which debuted in 1917, known as "heightclimbers," were Germany's last and best chance to win the air war over Britain. But by the middle of that year even they could no longer compete with airplanes.

One of the best examples of this shift was the story of L-48, which in June 1917 was the newest airship in the German Navy. The account is from an officer named Otto Mieth, one of the three crew members ever to survive a burning zeppelin.[32] On the night of June 17, the six-hundred-foot-long L-48 crossed the English coast flying at eighteen thousand feet—about a hundred miles north of London—and headed for the heart of that city. Engine problems meant she would never get there. A frozen compass made it difficult for her crew to even understand where she was.

The airship's attack began around 2:00 a.m. She dropped three bombs, which did nothing but break several panes of glass. A searchlight found her, and soon twenty to thirty of them were arcing across the sky. Then the big guns on the ground opened up, firing what was later estimated to be 569 rounds. "Their flashes twinkl[ed] like fireflies in the blackness beneath," Mieth later wrote. "Shells whizzed past us and exploded. Shrapnel flew. Rockets sang past us . . . like a great pack of hounds at the heels of a stag." Somehow the airship made it through the flak field and dropped more bombs, including a six-hundred-pounder, which blew some roof tiles off a barn.

In full flight from the guns, L-48 headed north—mistakenly, for east was where safety lay. She was losing altitude. She dropped to sixteen thousand feet, then below fourteen thousand feet. The British fighters closed in. The 350-yard range of their guns meant that they had to fly close—within range of the belt-fed zeppelin machine guns. At around 3:30 a.m., tracer bullets from one of the fighters set the airship on fire, and, according to Mieth, "almost instantly 600 feet of hydrogen were ablaze." The ship fell slowly, burning, to earth, from a height of ten thousand feet, a spectacle witnessed by people on a lightship sixty-five miles away. Mieth's survival and the survival of another crew member were miracles.

By the end of the war this story, or some version of it, had been repeated over and over. One of the last of the high-flying superzeps to go down was L-70, which carried the legendary German airship master Peter Strasser, and was shot down by a fighter plane off the coast of England on August 5, 1918. Strasser, unwilling to be burned alive, jumped to his death.

Germany's own record of what became of 125 zeppelins showed why they had been such a sensationally bad idea:

DESTROYED BY GUNFIRE	46
DESTROYED BY STORMS	8
DESTROYED BY FIRE IN SHEDS	15
WRECKED IN FORCED LANDINGS	12
SCRAPPED AND BROKEN UP	32
GIVEN TO ALLIES AT WAR'S END	12[33]

In 1917 the Germans began the switch to Gotha bombers—airplanes—which inflicted more casualties in a single raid than did all of the zeppelin raids combined.[34]

Why did the German airships continue to raid? Because the German government never stopped believing its own disinformation. It believed that the raids were having a ruinous effect on British morale and British industry. A better question, perhaps, is why, knowing exactly how vulnerable zeppelins were, and how little damage they really did, the British government decided in midwar to embark on a costly program of airship building to compete with them. The British, too, had bought into the lie, though a slightly different version of it.[35] They believed that the zeppelins had performed brilliantly as scouts at the Battle of Jutland, the war's largest sea battle, in which the British lost fourteen ships and over six thousand men. This was not true. The German airships had performed marginally as scouts and had no role at Jutland. The British believed, enviously and irrationally, that the technology was valuable. Their building program produced only a few uncompetitive vessels—knockoffs of outmoded zeppelins—which did not fly until near the end of the war or until after it.

But those ambitions did lead to the buildup of the industrial town of Cardington, which laid the groundwork for R101, a grand-scale airship that was a transparent attempt not only to keep up with the Germans, but to beat them at their own game.

CHAPTER THREE

NIGHT AND STORM

As R101 slipped into the rain-swept darkness on the night of October 4, 1930, Christopher Thomson was getting his wish. The storm was rising. He was riding it. He had flown in an airship only once before, on one of R101's first trials, in perfect, nearly windless weather. He had experienced that serene, gravity-defying feeling of buoyancy in the air, of levitating high above the earth and watching forests and farm fields and towns pass below. He had loved it. He thought he was seeing the future. Now there was rain and wind and darkness and the ship shifting and bumping about. That was fine with him. He held to the unshakable belief that R101 was an "all-weather" aircraft. He had made the remarkable statement that his airship was "safe in any weather she is likely to encounter"—which would have included thunderstorms, line squalls, and gale-force winds. He had insisted that she was "safe as a house but for the millionth chance."[1]

By contrast Lord Thomson had considerable experience with airplanes. As secretary of state for air he oversaw the Royal Air Force as well as all British civil aviation. He had flown in all manner of heavier-than-air machines, some more dangerous than others. He was no stranger to grass fields, open cockpits, flying boats, troop carriers, and flights in which something went wrong. He had flown practice bombing runs. In 1924 he had traveled from England to Egypt and Iraq and back in a Vickers Vernon biplane—a six-thousand-mile round trip by air at a time when no one but the military was flying over Middle Eastern deserts.[2] From all accounts, he was fearless.

Anyway, he didn't believe that this voyage to India would be anything but pleasant and uneventful, in addition to being epic and historic. He had brought his valet and his ministerial papers and his fancy rug with him. This would be a working trip. For this purpose he had been given an extra berth.

But he wouldn't be doing any state business tonight. Tonight he would be joining the other passengers and nonduty officers for drinks in the lounge and dining room followed by dinner on Royal Airship Works–crested china. Thomson, a veteran of five wars and a noted raconteur, would tell his tales of the conquest of Jerusalem, fighting Boers in South Africa, burning Romanian oil fields, meeting Leon Trotsky and Vladimir Lenin in Russia, dodging bombs in Bucharest. His friend civil aviation chief Sefton Brancker would do his trick of swallowing his monocle, leaving his astonished companions to wonder what would become of it.[3] Thomson had no other on-board responsibilities. In spite of his leading position in the British airship world, he was just a passenger. He was along for the ride.

His fifty-three shipmates—five officers, thirty-seven crew, and eleven other passengers—included many of the elect of the British airship establishment: Reginald Colmore, who reigned over the Cardington airship works and supervised the building of R101, as well as his lieutenants Vincent Richmond, the airship's chief designer, and, as mentioned, George Herbert Scott, Britain's leading airshipman, in charge of airship flying. There, too, were the ship's captain, Carmichael "Bird" Irwin, navigator Ernest Johnston, and First Officer Noel Atherstone, all with considerable airship experience. There were VIPs: Brancker, Chief Inspector of Aircraft Percy Bishop, and empire officials from Australia and India.

All were packed tightly into an interior space whose complexity would have astounded the observers on the ground. They could see only the opaque, almost entirely windowless hull and, slung below it, the five metallic engine pods and the twenty-foot-long control car, which held only a handful of duty crew.[4] Traditional airships and especially zeppelins had located most of the human infrastructure *outside* the hull, in suspended gondolas. But R101's designers had stuffed most of the people and their accommodations *inside* the ship, within that dark bulk, whose eyes on the world, other than from the control car, consisted only of long slits of windows provided for the entertainment of passengers in the ship's lounge.

The unseen interior was a fantastic tangle of the latest in engineering and materials science: circular stainless steel and duralumin (aluminum alloy) frames stretching 130 feet across, longitudinal girders running the length of the ship, miles of tubing and harnesses and electrical and bracing wire, sprawling complexes of fuel lines, water lines, tanks, and compressors.[5] The human accommodations included fifty sleeping berths on two floors, bathrooms, cooking and dining facilities, wireless and chart rooms, and staircases, all tucked into the inner darkness. The total floor area, all invisible from the outside, was 7,780 square feet, the equivalent of a large country house.[6]

Nor could outsiders see the fifteen gigantic gasbags, which held 5.5 million cubic feet of hydrogen and took up by far the largest part of R101's inner space. They rocked and billowed just a few feet above the berths where Thomson and his shipmates slept. The bags looked like monstrous cheese wheels, tipped on end, lined up bow to stern, and held in place with equally monstrous harnesses. The largest bags were as big as ten-story buildings. Amazingly— considering their scale—they were made of cattle intestines, known as goldbeater's skins, which resembled sausage casings. What were cattle intestines doing in the midst of so much ultramodern technology? They were less permeable than anything else the engineers could dream up in 1930. Their purpose was to contain the smallest and lightest element in the universe and also one of the most explosive, and permeability was important. Hydrogen inside gasbags was dangerous. Hydrogen leaking into the vessel's envelope was wildly dangerous. The bags were supposedly sparkproof, too. They didn't generate static electricity like the rubberized cotton bags that doomed LZ-4 at Echterdingen.

The trade-off was fragility. These cells were so thin you could put your finger through them. They were so easily torn that contact with a single metal bolt could produce a tear. A man losing his balance could—and did, on at least two occasions—fall clear through the bag and out the other side.[7] And he might keep right on falling through the thin layer of linen of the ship's outer cover. This was the oddity of all rigid airships, from the turn of the century forward: they were large, heavy (160 tons in the case of R101) steel-and-duralumin-framed and piston-driven objects that were also made of acres of fabric. They were weirdly insubstantial. For those who chose to think about it, life aboard R101 was like being crammed into a large, windowless building with fabric-thin walls while millions of cubic feet of hydrogen in membrane-thin, intestine-lined sacs billowed and surged about you. The asbestos firewall in the smoking lounge and the fire extinguishers positioned every ten yards were meant to reassure passengers of the airship's safety.[8] They were also, unavoidably, reminders of the element that was all around them.

R101'S START FOR INDIA had seemed oddly hesitant. Instead of heading straight for the English Channel, she had taken off on a looping farewell tour of Bedford and its suburbs, where many of her crew and builders lived. She flew low, at six hundred feet, so everyone could see her, and everyone did see her and knew she was outward bound for India, and they were enormously proud. They were all going to make history. Such an airborne tip of the hat was in keeping with tradition. But circling Bedford for more than forty minutes, traveling nearly thirty miles without going anywhere in rapidly worsening weather, seemed a perplexing choice.[9] The wind was rising. What would the crew decide to do? Push on into the bad weather to France, the Mediterranean, and Egypt? Or wait it out?

That question had been on the mind of Major Herbert Scott all day. Though Scott was in charge of flying on all British airships, he was not officially part of R101's crew. He was not the captain. He was a passenger, one of the Royal Airship Works managers who was along for the ride. Yet as the country's preeminent airship pilot, he had been given the authority to decide whether R101 would fly, and if she did, what route she would take. This appeared to many people, including Captain Irwin, to give Scott actual command of the ship, a notion that Scott himself quite liked. He had shown up for the flight wearing an officer's uniform and insisted to an aviation reporter, "I am officer in command of the flight and that is why I am wearing a uniform." He said that Irwin was "responsible for carrying out my orders."[10]

Neither statement was true. Irwin had been told that Scott had the status of an admiral who was a guest on one of his fleet's vessels.[11] But no one really knew. Least of all Scott and Irwin. Nor was this debate new. The ship's first officer, Noel Atherstone, had complained eleven months before about the confusion in rank and function between Scott and Irwin.[12] In a crisis, with the ship's safety on the line and everything at stake and mere seconds to make life-or-death decisions, who would give the commands? The problem was not theoretical. Scott had once jumped command on another airship flight, overriding the captain and ordering him to fly through instead of around a thunderstorm, with near-disastrous consequences.[13]

To discuss the urgent problem of weather, Scott had met that morning with Chief Meteorological Officer Maurice Giblett, one of the most important men in the airship establishment. The big rigids were preternaturally vulnerable to weather. Though their hulls had been made more streamlined over the years, they were exactly what they looked like: multi-acre sails that were easily knocked about by crosswinds and vertical drafts. The size that gave them their lift also made them dangerous. The greatest threat was near the ground, where even a moderate wind could smash an airship to pieces. At higher elevations, unstable air could propel the vessel helplessly upward four thousand feet in less than a minute and could cause her to fall just as fast. Rain caused problems for airships, too. It soaked their cloth outer covers and added many tons to their weight.

Giblett, a gifted young mathematician with a talent for organization, had been hired in 1925 because Lord Thomson and the other authors of the Imperial Airship Scheme knew that, to fly great distances on a regular schedule, weather information on a much larger scale than had ever before been attempted would be needed. An *oceanic* scale. A *global* scale. Nothing like that had existed before the 1920s. In World War I most aviators had not had the benefit of forecasts. They had looked out their windows to check the weather and trusted the rest to luck. The belief persisted that since God made the weather, only God could predict it.

Giblett helped change all that. In the five years that followed his hiring he became a key figure in the transformation of weather forecasting from a marginally useful Edwardian pastime to a serious operational science.

To prepare for empire-spanning flights he took a world tour, traveling routes from the United Kingdom to Canada, South Africa, India, Australia, and New Zealand. He and his colleagues became experts on low-level winds and barometric gradients, air masses and fronts, troughs and depressions. They developed original techniques for predicting weather over large oceanic areas that later came into wide use in general aviation.[14] Under Giblett's supervision, Great Britain set up forecasting centers in Cardington, Malta, Ismailia (in Egypt), and Karachi, and systems for retrieving information in France, Italy, and North Africa. Then he helped devise the means of getting the information to the airships, pioneering the transmission of synoptic data—which showed simultaneous weather patterns over a large area—by wireless telegraph that would allow airship navigators to create their own weather charts.[15] All of this was in the service of the imperial plan, meant to allow British airships to know the weather hundreds or even thousands of miles in front of them in ways that had not been possible.

On the morning of the ship's scheduled departure, Giblett, who would be flying to India as R101's meteorological officer, already had doubts about the weather. He was so certain of deteriorating conditions that he had told his wife before leaving home, "Don't worry, we won't be going."[16] He had seen a depression riding in from the North Atlantic, the early outlines of which appeared on a report issued by his own office in Cardington at 9:09 a.m.

By midday his fears had been confirmed: the depression was spreading eastward much faster than anyone had anticipated. Reporting stations in Ireland were already affected. Clouds were coming in thicker and lower. The wind was rising and would continue to rise. Rain would be falling when R101 left the mast. Giblett's system was working, but it was producing bad news. By 5:00 p.m. Scott was so concerned that he was pushing hard for an early departure. "The glass is falling," he reminded everyone, referring to the liquid in the barometer.[17]

By 6:00 p.m. the true contours of the storm came into view.[18] The monster was fully visible.[19] By this time Giblett was almost certainly advising his bosses against going, if he had not done so before. But it wasn't his decision to make.

Scott finally made the call. At 7:19 p.m., over the tiny medieval village of Clophill, the ship turned decisively away from Bedford and toward London, the first crossing point on the way south.

IF ONE WERE TO ADD UP R101's assets and liabilities at the moment of her departure for India, Major George Herbert Scott, CBE, AFC, would have figured prominently in both columns. He was a national hero, so well loved that in recordings of R101's departure on her first trial flight, voices from the ground can be heard shouting "Good luck, Scottie!" and "Well done, Scottie!"[20] Newspapers celebrated his dashing "press-on-regardless" attitude.* He was still the name and face of the airship service. Unbeknownst to his adoring public, as R101 slipped her mast that night, he was also in the middle of a tragic personal decline.

Scott was born in London in 1888, the oldest of five children of a successful civil engineer, and raised mostly in Plymouth. He was known as Bertie as a young boy and then Bert when he attended the Richmond School in Yorkshire. He was popular and good at everything, including math, sailing, track, and rugby. While he excelled in school and his father prospered building docks, his mother, Margaret, descended into chronic alcoholism. Scott's sister later wrote that their mother's secret drinking transformed her from a "slim and beautiful" woman into a "very fat" person who often "looked stupid" and seemed a stranger to them. "We felt ashamed and humiliated, as well as desperately unhappy and afraid." After a serious accident, Margaret became paralyzed from the waist down and was bedridden until her death in 1910.[21] Scott's father, George, had his own foibles. Though he had a flourishing career, he had a reckless streak and sometimes took foolish risks. He lost large sums of money on several questionable investment schemes. He once bought thousands of acres of land in Bolivia that turned out to be worthless.[22]

Scott was undeterred by his mother's illness. He attended the Royal Naval Engineering College, made high marks, and took a civil engineering job in Spain, working on docks like his father. After the war began in 1914, Scott joined the airship division of the Royal Naval Air Service and began flying hydrogen-filled, nonrigid airships known as

---

* "Press on regardless" was an unofficial motto of the Royal Air Force, occasionally used satirically to describe someone who took irrational risks. The RAF's actual motto was *Per ardua ad astra*—"Through adversity to the stars." Somehow the informal version had morphed into a nickname: Press-On Scott.

Sea Scouts—small, primitive-looking contraptions in which an airplane fuselage was suspended beneath a lumpy, bamboo-reinforced balloon that looked like a pregnant slug and was kept inflated by air forced into it by the ship's propeller.[23] The pilots were fully exposed. The three-man crew navigated by dead reckoning, often in foul weather. The Sea Scouts' British-made engines broke down, on average, every two and a half hours, which meant that the mechanic spent a good deal of time balanced perilously on the car's skids while doing the repair with one hand.[24] After the mechanic fixed the engine, working high above the earth and exposed to wind and weather, his job was also to swing the propeller.[25] Even when the seventy-five-horsepower engines worked, they were often no match for a strong headwind, which meant that Sea Scout crews spent many hours free-ballooning over inhospitable places such as the North Sea. They also suffered the chronic problem of hydrogen airships: they exploded.

But the "battle bags," as they were affectionately known, soon became important airborne scouts. They were useful in tracking U-boats, which had to surface to fire. Scott later gained fame as the pilot of a more advanced, 150-foot-long Parseval blimp, scouting for the ships that ferried men of the British Expeditionary Force across the English Channel. His vigilance kept the U-boats underwater. "I have met soldiers who were thus escorted," wrote former airship pilot George Meager, "who told me that when they saw an airship overhead they felt safe and could go below and get some sleep; otherwise they stayed up all night with their life belts on."[26]

Scott was soon a crucial part of Great Britain's move into airships. He commanded No. 9, Britain's first practical rigid airship. He designed the world's first successful mooring tower, an innovation that for once put the British ahead of the Germans in airship technology. The mast reduced the number of ground handlers for landings from four hundred to twenty.[27] Scott held several key design patents.[28]

In early 1919 he took charge of a brand-new British rigid airship,

R34. She had an interesting lineage. During the war British engineers, facing an insurmountable German lead in airship technology, had been forced to steal ideas from crashed zeppelins. They had worked hard at this. In September 1916 they had gotten lucky. The German super-zeppelin L-33 had been on a bombing run over the London area when she had been hit by fire from both antiaircraft guns and a fighter plane. She lost gas and landed in the town of Little Wigborough, in Essex. The crew burned the ship, but were only partly successful. Most of the frame was intact; the engines were in working order. The ship was technically far superior to anything the British could at that time even imagine. For the next five months British engineers crawled all over L-33, trying to learn her secrets.* At that time not a single British rigid airship had flown.[29]

R34 was the product of the engineers' work and was thus in most ways a straight zeppelin knockoff. The main problem with such tech-nology theft was that British engineers and designers needed time to turn it into an airship. Unfortunately, by the time R34 was finished, the war was over. Which meant that Great Britain possessed a useless and instantly outdated zeppelin built for short, high-altitude bombing runs when no war existed.

On the other hand, she was a perfectly good airship. The boffins in Whitehall had an inspiration: Why not use her to fly the Atlantic?[30] The idea was breathtakingly ambitious. At that time—late 1918—no aircraft of any kind had crossed the ocean. Lindbergh's first crossing was eight years off. The only precedent was the strange 1917 voyage of the 743-foot German airship L-59. She had somehow managed to fly from Bulgaria to Sudan in North Africa on a mission to resupply German troops. When the mission was aborted, the airship had turned around, without landing, and returned home, having covered forty-two

* The British got lucky again when the heightclimber L-49 went down virtually intact in France in June 1918.

hundred miles in four days with a crew of twenty, a nearly unthinkable achievement.[31] The Germans had done something with an airship that no other nation could even approach.

But of course R34 *was* German. She mimicked the design of superzeppelins and heightclimbers and even featured German engines. Why couldn't a 643-foot "British" zeppelin fly long distances, too? British designers and builders were unaware of how harrowingly difficult and dangerous L-59's flight had been. That flight included near crashes due to heat turbulence, wild swings in heat and air density that caused unwanted climbs and precipitous dives. Her engines failed several times. Twice the airship stalled and fell several thousand feet. To avoid crashing at various critical moments L-59 was forced to drop more than seventeen thousand pounds of ballast and cargo.[32] Nor were the British, who had little experience building or flying airships, aware that L-59's immediate predecessor, L-57, the airship that was supposed to make the voyage to Africa, had been torn from its mast, then hurled about the countryside in a succession of spectacular fires and explosions.[33] Nor did they understand that R34 was a wildly inappropriate vessel to undertake the first crossing of the Atlantic.

What they knew for sure was that they had a perfectly good piece of German technology and the redoubtable Bert Scott to pilot her. So they went ahead with their plans: an Atlantic crossing was planned for the earliest possible date. What might have seemed daylight madness was just ignorance. Political dithering and test flights delayed the ship's departure from spring 1919 to summer 1919.

Still, no one else had crossed the ocean by air.

Unfortunately R34's competitors had their own plans. In May the U.S. Navy's flying boat NC-4 became the first aircraft to cross the Atlantic, flying from Rockaway Beach, New York, to Plymouth, England. But she had required twenty-four days and five stops to do it. In the "crossing" of the ocean the Curtiss-built aircraft flew from Newfoundland to the Azores (1,800 miles) and then on to Lisbon (another 920 miles) in two stops.[34] That achievement was almost instantly eclipsed by British pilots John Alcock and Arthur Brown, who two weeks later flew a converted Vickers Vimy bomber nonstop from Newfoundland to Galway, Ireland, 1,880 miles, thereby winning the prize offered by the British *Daily Mail* "for the first aeroplane to cross the Atlantic in less than 72 consecutive hours."

Though R34 was an airship and not an airplane and not eligible for the prize, Scott and his crew considered Alcock and Brown's triumph a bitter disappointment.[35]

R34, meanwhile, which would attempt to fly much farther than Alcock and Brown, had barely been tested at all. Several of her trials had come close to disaster. On her second flight, in March 1919, the controls for the elevator flaps had jammed, sending the airship dangerously out of control. With the crew clinging desperately to any surface they could, a calm, unrattled Scott assumed command and barked out the orders to bring the ship back in trim.[36] In June, while R34 was returning from a test flight over the North Sea, she encountered a gale that caused her to fly backward over the sea for eight hours. What should have been a routine reconnaissance flight required a harrowing fifty-seven hours to return home.[37]

The transatlantic flight went ahead anyway. In July 1919, two weeks after the Alcock and Brown flight, R34, with Scott as captain, became the first aircraft to cross the Atlantic from east to west and the first to make a double crossing. Alcock and Brown, flying west to east, had flown 1,880 miles in 16 hours. Scott, flying from Scotland to Long Island, New York, *against* the prevailing breeze, had flown 3,180 miles in 108 hours. The achievement was magnificent and unprecedented and all the more glorious for having been done in an airship that had never been designed to do any such thing.

The east-west voyage over open ocean—where crashing or engine failure was certain death—was a catalog of near catastrophes. The almost comically unreliable engines did not deliver half their rated power. R34 lost first one of them, then three of them. Against a strong headwind the ship made only 41 mph and was dead stopped for hours over the ocean. Scott discovered that her great length meant that her front half responded to up and down currents differently from the back half, leading sometimes to twenty-four degrees of inclination—so steep that crew members had to hang on to avoid falling out.[38] Once, unable to outrun a severe squall, the ship rose seven hundred feet in a single bump. There were violent up and down currents all the way across.[39] "The ship," according to one passenger, "is first lifted 400 feet and then dropped 500 feet. Scott, who has his head out of a window in the forward car . . . saw the tail of the ship bend under the strain."[40] Meanwhile R34's hydrogen gas was subject to superheating—once hitting 105 degrees when the outside air was only 40 degrees—making the ship wildly unstable. Thundersqualls over Nova Scotia burned out her radio receivers. Her outer cover—the only protection for the gasbags—lost most of its waterproofing and leaked terribly. When she arrived in New York, she had only forty minutes of gasoline left—a perilous situation that had led units of the U.S. Navy to put to sea for a likely rescue.[41] If her mooring connector had not jammed on Long Island, she would likely have been blown away after her tail shot upward at a forty-five-degree angle.[42] The list of troubles went on.

Scott returned home to a full-blown hero's welcome, though the public had no concept of how truly perilous the flight had been. Few people then or later understood the danger of crossing the ocean in a minimally tested faux-German heightclimber or the nerve it took to do it. Scott was, at thirty-one, an instant celebrity. He was made a Commander of the British Empire (CBE). Britons saw him as an empire type: fearless, unflappable, charming, modest in person, and daring in action.[43] When it later became public that his crew had fixed a cracked cylinder using a piece of copper sheeting and the crew's entire supply of chewing gum, this seemed of a piece with Scott himself: doughty, resourceful, willing to do whatever it took.*

Just how lucky Scott had been became apparent a year and a half later when R34 crashed into a twelve-hundred-foot-high hill in Yorkshire, lost two engines, became airborne again, and was blown out over the North Sea, where she was stranded for hours, unable to make headway against the wind. When the gale finally subsided, she tried to land, only to come crashing to earth. The ordeal wasn't over. The wind dragged her over the land; she rose one hundred feet and smashed down again, whereupon the entire terrified crew jumped out. Later her mooring wire tore a great hole in the bow. She collapsed and partially broke up. She never flew again. Such were the risks of rigid airships.[44]

Like the Alcock and Brown flight, R34's historic crossing has been largely overwritten by Lindbergh's solo flight eight years later.

As with so many other heroes, Scott's opening act was difficult to follow. In the ensuing years, the ups and downs of the British airship business often left him with little to do. R38 had temporarily killed the program, which had idled its most famous captain. During the six years of R101's construction, Scott often found himself on the sidelines, responsible for flying and crew training at a time when no flying was being done. Though he was an experienced engineer with airship patents and had been involved in the early design of R101, as the decade of the 1920s passed, engineering was less and less in his job description.

So he languished. And like his mother before him, he began to drink. Or perhaps it is better to say that he began to drink more than he had before. He had come out of the airship division of the Royal Naval Air Service, a clubby, hard-drinking brotherhood if ever there was one— one, moreover, that thought of itself as special and a bit esoteric, like

---

* On board R34 also was Edward Maitland, noted balloonist, parachutist, and airshipman and one of the most colorful officers of the early British airship era. A brigadier general at the time of the flight (he was later an air commodore), he was the ranking man on the airship but was officially a passenger: Scott was R34's commander.

submariners, paratroopers, and other military subspecialties. The men liked being outsiders and liked their booze-sodden parties.

Some, like Scott, never quite grew out of them. It was perhaps not a coincidence that a son whose mother was a chronic drinker and whose father made foolish investments grew up to be a habitual risk-taker who was inordinately fond of alcohol.

He married Jessie Campbell, the attractive, engaging daughter of the manager of the William Beardmore and Company's shipyard, and raised a son and three daughters. Together Bert and Jessie plunged into the hectic social whirl of the 1920s. Everybody liked Scottie. He was the modest hero who told jokes and puffed on his pipe and got along with officers and noncoms alike and who loved throwing parties.[45] He was a regular at the local watering holes, too, such as the Bell bar in the Bedford suburb of Cotton End, and the Bridge Hotel in Bedford. His favorite drinking buddies were R101's navigator, Ernest Johnston, and Second Officer Maurice Steff.

As the decade progressed, Scott's drinking took on a darker aspect. By 1929 he was drinking so much that most of his colleagues believed that after lunch—often a long, bibulous affair with friends at the Bridge— he was too inebriated to be effective.[46] A colleague's wife complained about how much Scott and his wife drank when they visited: "She and he drank two whiskeys and soda and three cocktails before the meal, a stiff whiskey at the meal, a liqueur after it, and another whiskey after the pictures. She drank all that as well as he. They cost us a small fortune in drinks when they come."[47] He also began to have affairs with women, to the point where fellow employees felt sorry for his wife and would avoid the places he and his mistresses went to drink.[48]

His work habits, never fastidious in the first place, declined. His tardiness was legendary, as was his refusal to wear a watch and his hatred of paperwork. His staff often had trouble getting him to do anything at all.[49] In June 1930, three months before R101's flight, Lord Thomson personally addressed these issues with his chief of flying. He "had Scott on the carpet and read the riot act," said the wife of R101's first officer. Thomson told Scott that if the ship wasn't ready by September, he would be looking for a job. The secretary was speaking only of Scott's slapdash work habits, not his drinking. The evidence suggests that Thomson had not been told about that. The airship culture could close ranks. Scott's physical appearance changed, too. He put on weight. His once-bright eyes were now puffy and ringed with black circles. He no longer looked the part of the swashbuckling young airman.

On the day of R101's departure for India, Scott had fit in one of his wet lunches at the Bridge Hotel with Johnston and Steff. In spite of Scott's attendance that day at several weather meetings and his supervision of the loading, one eyewitness, *Flight* magazine editor Major F. A. de V. Robertson, thought Scott was drunk just before the ship left. Robertson said later that while Scott was inaccurately describing his role as officer-in-command of the flight, he was slurring his words.[50]

AT 7:30 P.M. the men on board R101, who had dressed for dinner in their berths, descended the ornate staircase to the gilt-trimmed dining room—a civilized ritual that was not at all incidental. Comfort, luxury, and relaxation were what the British government was selling—all in opposition to the noisy, bumpy, nerve-rattling discomfort that was the hallmark of so much short-hop airplane travel. The men were seated at white-linen-covered tables for what the Royal Airship Works press office billed as a "delectable" cold dinner preceded by hot soup and presented by two uniformed stewards and a galley boy. Wine would be served, followed by port, and later by cigars, as the airship glided tranquilly into the night. Or perhaps not quite tranquilly. Tonight the weather was causing R101's bow to move up and down and the entire vessel to roll on its axis far more than usual—though not enough to cause glasses to fall or men to clutch railings.[51] The guests would have noted it, perhaps, and gone back to their claret and conversation. Downstairs in the stripped-down, ungilded, and promenade-less crew quarters, the rank and file dined on bread, cheese, and pickles, accompanied by hot cocoa.

R101's greatest luxury was its smoking lounge. In a world where the majority of men smoked, a multiday nonsmoking voyage such as R34's Atlantic crossing had been a cruel deprivation. Officers and crew had complained. They wanted their cigarettes and pipes, especially after meals, and they could not have them. On R101, by contrast, they could nip off into the asbestos-insulated smoking room, with the added thrill of knowing that, while they ignited open flames and puffed away, millions of cubic feet of hydrogen swelled just a few feet above them.

The guests moved freely between lounge, promenade, dining room, and smoking room. Or we can assume they did. We cannot be certain. Much of their movement that night, and much of what was said between them, must remain conjectural. We can see what took place on board R101's flight that night only in flashes: a handful of interviews from crew members, a dossier compiled from the ship's wireless messages, the evidence of witnesses and onlookers, and the behavior of the ship itself. We can't know exactly who came to cocktails and dinner, though staying behind in a cramped, poorly lighted, nicotine-and-booze-free berth would not have been an attractive alternative.

At 8:00 p.m. R101 reached London and in spite of the rainy weather caused a sensation. She was flying low, at 600 feet, only 235 feet higher than St Paul's Cathedral, the tallest building in London, and 177 feet shorter than the ship's overall length, which made it seem to some observers that R101 was preparing to land. Her flight attitude seemed odd, too. As the wind stiffened, it drove against the six acres of her cover, pushing her off course. To counteract this, the ship's coxswain had to point R101's bow almost eighty degrees off the actual track she was following. She was flying sideways across London.[52] Such crab-like movement was a known characteristic of the big rigids.

The rumble of R101's engines brought thousands of Londoners out into the streets. Most would remember the sight for the rest of their lives:

her cabin and promenade windows brilliantly illuminated; passengers at dinner silhouetted by the shades of the table lamps; the clacking noise of the huge propellers reverberating through the city streets.

Inside the airship, the wireless operator was tapping out R101's first message to Cardington. Such air-to-ground communication was still in its infancy in 1930, made possible by the advent of radio, which in those early days—the first BBC radio broadcast had taken place only in 1922—was universally called "the wireless" because of the apparent miracle of invisible radio waves. In the case of R101, "wireless radio" meant that operators used keys to send radio messages via Morse code—dots and dashes standing for letters and numbers. When airships and airplanes began to outdistance the wireless range—as R101 would soon be doing—their operators "bounced" messages from air station to air station.

At 8:21 p.m., R101 sent this message to Cardington:

Over London. All well. Moderate rain. Base of low cloud 1,500 feet. Wind 240 degrees. 25 mph. Course now set for Paris. Intend to proceed via Paris, Tours, Toulouse, and Narbonne.

That did not sound so bad. But only eighteen minutes later R101's wireless operator received news from Giblett's weather team that would completely alter this anodyne view of the world:

18.00 GMT Situation. Trough of low pressure along coasts of British Isles, moving East. Ridge of high pressure over Southern France. Forecast for next twelve hours of flight. SE England, Channel, and Northern France. Wind at 2,000 feet from about 240 degrees, 40 to 50 miles an hour. Much low cloud with rain. . . .

The piece of information that would have made hearts race in R101's chart room was the wind speed: *40 to 50 miles an hour*, what mariners call a strong gale. That was more wind than any British airship, including R101, had ever encountered over land.[53] There was no precedent for it, no way for the crew to know how the ship might respond.

The forecast begged the question again: To go or not to go? They were still over London. Wait out the weather by hanging out over the English Channel, then moor, and start again the next day? From R101's wireless message the decision had clearly been made—probably by Scott, Irwin, and Johnston—to fly to Paris then head due south to Narbonne on the Mediterranean coast. But now that second leg looked to be virtually dead into the forecast wind, possibly doubling the time and fuel it took to cross France and causing Thomson to miss his state dinner at the mooring mast in Ismailia.[54]

Just how worried R101's officers were became apparent in the message they sent to the meteorological office in Cardington at 9:19, inquiring about the weather farther west, in Dijon, Lyon, and Marseille. They were looking for a way around the brutal headwind, a route that pushed eastward beyond Paris, then turned south down the Rhône Valley.

This alternative route was in their minds and was probably why Scott decided to stick to his decision: they would cross the English Channel in spite of the wind. They would head to Paris. As one prominent airship historian wrote, there must have been "some tightening of faces" in the chart room when Scott made "the decision to press on."[55] Though this is pure speculation, we might wonder just what condition he was in at 9:00 p.m. that evening. Because he had no role in flying the airship, he would almost certainly have been at cocktails and dinner with Thomson and the others, meaning that he had had an additional hour and a half to drink on top of whatever he had had that caused him to slur his words at the mast. But we will never know.

Scott may have had another possibility in mind, too. At his request, in the days before R101's departure, he had secured from the French government a promise to make available a shed at Orly Airport in Paris large enough to hold R101. He also arranged for over four hundred men on the ground to help her land and facilities for taking on fuel and hydrogen.[56] This seemed like a reasonable precaution. But Orly had no mooring mast, and taking a 777-foot-long airship into a hangar in a 50 mph wind was an impossibility. (So was mooring.) Which meant, if Scott had thought about it, which he almost certainly did, R101 could not head home to her mast at Cardington, either. Nor was there any precedent for landing an airship on the ground (as the Germans did) in such a wind. At Orly, or in Cardington, she would be smashed to pieces. It is noteworthy that Scott had taken the trouble to arrange this at Orly—meaning that on some level he expected he might have to abort his mission before it was ten hours old.

Scott himself had once written of this predicament—facing a strong headwind—in a technical paper in 1923:

> Except in very rare circumstances, such as when the base at which the pilot wishes to land is in the bad weather zone, a pilot should never beat directly into a strong wind, and even in the above case it often pays to lie off for a few hours, as the movement of the centre of the depression will move the area of strong wind away from the base.[57]

However Scott thought of his dilemma, drunk or sober, it illustrated one of the startling weaknesses of rigid airships: there was nowhere to go in a storm, no safe harbor. In heavy weather oceangoing ships made for port, airplanes for either a runway or a flat, open place to land. But airships could not go down; in a high wind they were most vulnerable near the ground. Member of Parliament Joseph Kenworthy (Central Hull) described on the floor of the House of Commons what he called "the helplessness of an airship, if through some miscalculation as to weather, or some accident, such as an engine breakdown, she finds herself caught in a gale, or in adverse weather conditions of any kind, far away from her shed and far away from a mast." Even if R101 could manage a mooring at a mast—something that had never been done in such weather—there were hardly any masts in existence. In the five thousand miles between London and Karachi there were exactly two: one in Egypt, one in India, both built for R101. "She cannot anchor like a ship," Kenworthy stated. "She cannot come down into a wide-open space like an aeroplane; she cannot land on the surface of the sea like a flying boat or a seaplane. She must ride out the storm or run the gauntlet, and she may find herself with her ballast exhausted and her fuel exhausted miles from her mast."[58]

In 1927 Lord Thomson had written a treatise on airship safety that took as its premise the notion that "a long series of disasters to airships has . . . discouraged the public and the constructors of these vessels." In the treatise, which was published as a book, he painstakingly chronicled that list of airship disasters. While pushing the idea of "safety first," he insisted on the absolute necessity of "terminal stations, with one or more sheds, intermediate stations with mooring masts, emergency landing grounds, all equipped with repair shops and manned by skilled mechanics." These accommodations, he wrote, "are as indispensable to airships as dockyards and harbours are to ocean-going steamers. The analogy is almost exact." He concluded, *"The absence of ground arrangements will almost surely cause disaster."*[59] He even used an example: the crash of the French airship *Dixmude* four years earlier. Thomson was imagining a world of the future that never came to pass.

Scott's best option might have been the one he had suggested: lie off, probably over the North Sea, use the engines to hold position on the wind, and wait for the storm to pass, then moor again, refuel, reprovision, and start over. Of course that meant that Thomson would miss both of his parties. He wouldn't make it back from India in time for the Imperial Conference. And the future of the entire airship program would be in doubt. So Bert Scott, Scott of the Atlantic, Lucky Breeze Scott, lived up to his reputation. He pressed on.

There was another factor, too, in Scott's decision. For men of his generation, veterans of World War I, the notion of danger was different from what it was later on. "It now appears reckless that he should have pressed on in view of this forecast," wrote Nevil Shute, a bestselling British author and former airshipman who knew Scott well. "It is, however, easy to be wise after the event, and especially 24 years after." Nowadays, he wrote in 1954, "a pilot who turns back and lands because he considers it dangerous to go on is likely to receive praise and advancement in his profession. . . . But that was by no means the mental atmosphere in 1930. In those days a pilot was expected to be brave and resolute, a daredevil who was not afraid to take risks. One imagines that the weather forecast must have been discussed quietly in the corner with long faces, but the ship went on."[60]

R101's coxswain swung the wheel, and the great airborne ship pointed for the cliffs of Hastings on the Channel coast, and beyond, toward Paris.

CHAPTER FOUR

FLYING DEATH TRAP

The British airship R38 was a beauty. Everyone said so. She was enormous by the standards of the day. At 699 feet in length and 88.5 feet in diameter, with 2.7 million cubic feet of hydrogen gas, she was the largest object that had ever flown. She was streamlined, too, which meant she was wider, more rounded, and sleeker than the earlier generations of airships, which had looked like giant flying pencils. She had the speed, endurance, and climbing ability of the German superzeppelins, which had terrorized Europe during the war. More important than any single statistic, she was a British-built ship. She was of such exceptional quality that she had been sold to the Americans, who badly wanted her for their own fledgling airship program and who were going to fly her across the Atlantic. When R38 emerged from her shed for trials in June 1921—two years after R34's Atlantic crossing—the British press came out to gawk and admire and write breathlessly about what a miraculous piece of technology she was and the great things she was bound to do, albeit in American hands.

R38 was about something else, too. Nationalism had always been the driving force behind the big rigids. They were equal parts engineering and ideology. Count von Zeppelin had seen them as weapons but also and primarily as vehicles of national glory, of victory, of the triumph of *das Vaterland.* This had allowed him to rise from the ashes of the Echterdingen crash. Despite their many failures in the war, Germans still saw zeppelins in those terms. No other nation had been able to match their technologies. None had even come close. But now the British had done precisely that, or so it seemed. On paper R38 was the most capable airship ever built. She represented a long-sought and hard-won moment of national pride. *Flight* magazine wrote admiringly that she was "the first ship of purely British design."[1] This was not exactly true, but just then no one was in a mood to challenge it.

Nearly three years removed from the 1918 armistice that ended World War I, a defeated Germany was no longer the center of the airship world. Germany was not even a player. The war had consumed almost all of its production of lighter-than-air ships. Her remaining zeppelins had either been given away as war reparations or destroyed by their own crews, and the "reparations" airships, with few exceptions, had either been scrapped or were destined for the junkyard. Even the two small passenger zeppelins built by Hugo Eckener after the war—the ostensibly harmless *Bodensee*, a well-engineered smaller airship that had made 103 flights between 1919 and 1921 including a wild, uncontrolled, hundred-mile, balloon-like drift with twenty-nine passengers, and its sister ship, *Nordstern*—had been seized by Allied governments. Which left only a handful of operational airships in the world. Great Britain had four left. One of those, R36, had just been badly damaged in a ground accident and would never fly again.[2]

Now the most advanced ship of that tiny group of airships, R38, was in American hands, and the reason was not a happy one. After a financially ruinous war, Great Britain was unwilling to finance more airship construction. Government orders for new ships had been canceled. Which meant, objectively, that the British were selling off one of the last of a swiftly dying breed of aircraft. Except for the American interest—the U.S. Navy, which had no airships, planned to use them to patrol the tactical vastness of the Pacific Ocean—one might have said that this was the end of the large rigids. The reasons seemed clear enough: they were too slow, too clumsy near the ground and too difficult to moor, too dependent on fair weather, too prone to wildly variable lift from changes in temperature, atmospheric density, and pressure, and built from ephemeral, ultrafragile materials such as cow intestines and spun linen.[3] They were wildly expensive. They also had a dismaying record of exploding in flames. In wartime they had failed as scouts and as weapons. That Britain's relatively primitive, nonrigid "battle bags" had succeeded as submarine spotters only underscored the problem.

Airships had, moreover, made scant progress compared to heavier-than-air machines. Though the rigids were still thought to have long-range potential that airplanes did not—R34's Atlantic crossing and the German L-59's wild ride to Sudan seemed to bear this out—they had mostly proved nothing but their own weaknesses. In retrospect, DELAG's short-duration, summertime-only, fair-weather tourist flights in prewar Germany marked the only time airships had been consistently successful. (For years to come, DELAG's casualty-free flights would be cited over and over as proof that airships were practical.) In the postwar years, as the number of active airships in the world dwindled to a tiny handful, commercial airliners made steady advances. Three-engine, twenty-passenger commercial airplanes had already proven their ability to fly regular routes, even in challenging weather. The first commercial flight from London to Paris, carrying two passengers, had taken place in 1919. By the end of 1920 airplanes had flown 2,270,000 miles over the scheduled air routes of the world. In 1921, the year R38 made its trials, fledgling commercial airlines flew 4,300,000 miles.[4]

Still, there was hope, however slight. A successful new airship cross-ing the Atlantic might change minds. The world of the air was still new and wildly uncertain. Lindbergh's epochal flight was six years in the future.

On August 23, 1921, R38—now bearing her new American regis-tration, ZR-2—was walked out of her shed at Howden, in Yorkshire, by hundreds of ground handlers and pointed into the light breeze. At 7:10 a.m. the order to let go was issued, and the men gave the enormous ship a collective push, and she was away. On board were forty-nine passengers and crew, including twenty-seven members of the Royal Air

Force and seventeen U.S. Navy personnel. She headed east, out over the North Sea, where she would make the last of her trials before departing for the United States.[5]

As the crew and passengers glided through the warm, gentle air that morning, they hadn't the remotest idea of the strange fate that awaited them. Nor could they have had any notion of the massive change that R38 would cause in the world of airship aviation. That change included the creation of R101, an airship modeled quite precisely on the lessons learned from R38. R101 was her direct lineal descendant. R101 existed, in her ultimate form, because of R38. Every girder and joint in R101 was designed with R38 in mind—though not in the way the latter's designers would have intended.

That was because most of R38's lessons were negative. They flashed like warning lights for the next generation, and their message was "Don't do this."

IN THE SUMMER OF 1921 Charles Ivor Rae Campbell was by general consent the leading authority outside Germany on lighter-than-air vessels. He had graduated with highest honors from the Royal Naval Engineering College and was considered one of the most talented engineers of his generation. Like many early airship builders, the engaging forty-three-year-old Campbell came from the world of submarines.[6] In 1915 he was appointed head of the British Navy's airship design and construction department, a job he would hold, in one configuration or another, for the next six years.

Those were the early years of British airship building. The country's first ship, the *Mayfly*—Winston Churchill called her *Won't Fly*—had been built on the sketchiest of jury-rigged submarine technology and early zeppelin design.* She broke in half in 1911 without ever flying

---

* Campbell observed the construction of the *Mayfly* but had no active role.

and grounded the British airship program for the next five years.[7] Production resumed, under Campbell, only after the zeppelin bombers' success in the early days of the war.

The first seven British ships to fly, from 1916 to 1918, were remarkable achievements considering how little technical information their designers had to work with.[8] Outside Germany, airship design was a dark art. German constructors and designers made sure it stayed that way. Campbell and his early design teams had as models only grainy photos of early zeppelins, girder rubbings, secret measurements taken by a British industrial spy before the war, and a few hasty sketches from a forced landing made by a German airship in France in 1913. But this information—snapshots taken of the products of several decades of German experimentation—came only in bits and pieces. By the time the British got the raw data and used it to build an airship, the Germans were already years ahead. Campbell did his best. All seven ships—built by four different contractors—were above five hundred feet in length, with ever more sophisticated engines, increased bomb loads, expanded bays, and propeller modifications. They spent an average of 222 hours in the air.[9] But they were greatly inferior to their German counterparts. They were not as big, not as fast, not as reliable. They were unable to fly as high or as far or carry as much weight. They were, inevitably, years behind. By 1921 Britain had flown a total of 14 airships, including R34. The Germans had flown 138.[10]

But the last four ships built in England—of which R38 was the ultimate—were far more sophisticated than those early tries.[11] This was because Campbell, an enthusiastic proselytizer for the airship cause, had understood that the quickest way for Britain to move forward was to copy downed zeppelins. He had personally led the team that had deconstructed the German L-33 after its crash landing in Essex in 1916. When L-48 went down in England in 1917, Campbell made sure its design elements were incorporated into his own airships. His R38 design team also had the benefit of a late-war zeppelin crash: L-70, a

German airship that was shot down on August 6, 1918, off the Norfolk coast. She was one of the last of the great heightclimbers, a 692-foot technological marvel that could hit twenty thousand feet and travel at more than 80 mph. R38 resembled her closely in size and appearance. Like L-70, R38 had been built using the lightest-possible materials, and engines with the largest-possible horsepower. British engineers did not—as would soon become apparent—learn all of the zeppelin secrets in the years following the war.[12] But by the time they finished R38 at the Royal Airship Works in Cardington in 1921, they knew more than ever before.

Like all rigid airship designers before him, Campbell used hydrogen as R38's lifting gas. Why, when the war offered proof of how dangerous it was? Because helium, the only alternative, was at that moment no alternative at all. It had been found in natural gas deposits on the American Great Plains in 1905, but for the next decade the world's supply of helium had remained on a shelf at the University of Kansas in three small flasks. As late as 1919, the United States' total exportable helium gas would only have filled a small weather balloon. Quantity was just part of the problem. The price of helium was dauntingly high, as were the costs of transporting it in steel canisters and specially built trains.* There were other problems, too. Even if one could secure it, helium provided only half the lifting power of hydrogen. Reduced lift in an airship meant that it had to carry less fuel. Using helium meant a 40 percent reduction in range.[13] Perhaps because R38's designers had no other choice, they convinced themselves—as had Hugo Eckener and his staff in Germany—that the risks of hydrogen were manageable.

By spring 1921 Charles Campbell's prize project, the synthesis of everything he had learned from the war, the world's biggest and most

---

* Americans later became more focused on the strategic value of helium. But during World War I and the years just after its end, production quantities were too small to have been practical for large airships.

advanced airship, was finally ready to be tested. But nothing would ever be easy about R38. The officer in charge of trials, thirty-one-year-old J. E. M. "Jack" Pritchard, had recommended three flights totaling 150 hours, including flying in rough weather, to prove the reliability of the ship.* This seemed reasonable to the crew and designers. But Pritchard was almost immediately overruled by the Air Ministry's director of research, Henry Brooke-Popham, an "aeroplane man," who wrote a blistering annotation of Pritchard's report, disagreeing with almost everything and insisting on a mere fifty hours of tests and an August departure. Brooke-Popham was bowing to political pressure. The Americans wanted their airship, which was already a year late. The British wanted to be free of the costs of building airships. And they wanted their money.[14] The airship would do a rushed fifty hours of testing, then depart for the United States.

On June 23, 1921, R38 took off from Cardington on her initial trial. Almost from the first moment, things went wrong. Her overfilled gasbags expanded in the sun's heat and snapped twenty circumferential steel wires.[15] She was difficult and sometimes impossible to steer. Her elevators and rudders were balky as their control chains jammed and jumped sprockets.[16] As a result the ship, whose top speed should have been 72 mph, could fly no faster than 46 mph. She suffered minor girder damage.[17] None of these defects was reported to the Air Ministry or the Admiralty.[18] The second flight revealed worse elevator and rudder problems, and a postflight inspection showed structural weakness in her fins. The third flight brought even more trouble, though of a different and more serious sort. When the ship accelerated, it now began "hunting"—climbing and diving—over a range of five hundred feet, a porpoising action that put great strains on the frame. Girders in the middle of the ship buckled. The ship limped home at reduced speed.

---

* Pritchard had famously parachuted from R34 as she made landfall in the United States to help the American landing crew.

Campbell gave orders to repair the damaged girders and strengthen others.

Pritchard once again insisted that R38 be put through longer and more vigorous trials. He wrote his superiors at the Air Ministry, "It should be clearly recognised that when R38 was designed, she was lightened in every way to provide the greatest performance . . . and it therefore must be recognized that the factors of safety have been cut down in many directions." The concept is central to aeronautical engineering. A "safety factor" expresses how much stronger a system is than it needs to be for an intended load. The Germans, aware that lightening their ships made them structurally weak, had tested them only at altitudes of seven thousand to ten thousand feet, where the air was far less dense and the stresses far lower. "Keeping these factors in mind," Pritchard continued, "I feel that a very unjustifiable risk was taken with R38 and I most strongly urge that before R38 is flown again, the question of the height at which she should be flown at various speeds should be very carefully considered and far more definite orders put forward for the guidance of the captain of the ship."[19]

On August 11, Pritchard, whose title was "officer-in-charge / airship flying trials," raised the alarm again with the Air Ministry, asking now for a "definitive ruling" on the flying height of the ship's fourth trial. "The ship has not been put up to full speed and has never been flown in disturbed air conditions," he wrote. "The trials so far carried out are of little value."[20]

Others were worried, too. Air Commodore Edward Maitland, who had been aboard the R34 on her transatlantic voyage and would be flying on R38 to the United States, also urged that speed trials be conducted at higher altitudes. U.S. Navy admiral Robert S. Griffin wrote the U.S. chief of naval operations to say how upset he was that, in spite of the failure of the girders on her third trial, R38/ZR-2 was still scheduled to fly the ocean after just one more flight.[21] Major George Herbert Scott, Great Britain's leading airshipman, added his support for longer trials.[22] (It is noteworthy that "Press-On" Scott was, at this point in his career, advising caution.)

They were ignored. The bosses simply did not believe in the danger. They could not see R38 for what she really was—an experimental prototype—and they would never treat her that way. Trials were a formality to be gotten through. Charles Campbell, consumed by his two jobs as Royal Airship Works manager and chief airship designer, was too distracted to focus on this rising drumbeat of protest. He wasn't paying attention.

He, too, along with Pritchard and Maitland, would be on R38's next flight.

TWELVE DAYS AFTER Pritchard's blistering report, R38 was aloft for her fourth and final trial, conducting a series of relatively mild tests at low speeds. She spent that night out over the North Sea, cruising easily up and down the coast. The following day, August 24, the trials became more intense. In late afternoon R38 underwent a series of basic tests that included flying her at full speed of 72 mph. She appeared to pass. The weather was fair, the sky overcast as a light breeze blew across the river Humber near the city of Hull, two hundred miles north of London near England's east coast, where R38 flew.

Shortly after 5:00 p.m., the great ship broke through the clouds over the city, flying in a southwesterly direction at an altitude of twenty-five hundred feet. The roar of her engines attracted the attention of factory workers who were heading home for the day. A large crowd gathered on an observation pier to watch her implausibly long, silvery, fishlike form pass. She was a splendid sight, especially for those who had never before seen a big airship. She was cruising at about 60 mph.

Then, in full view of thousands of spectators, R38 did precisely what Pritchard and Maitland and others had said she must not do: *turning trials at high speeds and low altitude.* The ship's coxswain was not simply turning. He was driving R38's rudders from hard-over on one side to hard-over on the other, apparently trying to simulate the effects of rough weather. The danger should have been apparent. The strains on the ship caused by turns at twenty-five hundred feet were *twice* what they would be at seventy-five hundred feet.

R38 had crossed the city of Hull and was passing over the river Humber when an extraordinary—and to witnesses inexplicable— change occurred in the silvery magnificence of R38's outer cover. A great diagonal crease appeared in the fabric of the 699-foot-long ship. Wrinkles and folds became visible in long, vertical lines. Bow and stern sagged. Within seconds she had been transformed from an apparently flawless piece of engineering into what looked "like a twisted and rolled newspaper," according to one eyewitness.[23] Then the giant ship cracked open like an egg. The noise of her engines persisted for a few moments, then stopped altogether. In the weird silence that followed, time seemed to slow down. The broken airship began to fall in a languid motion, spewing out streams of gasoline and water, while men, fuel tanks, and other matériel fell out of the gaping rupture.

As she fell toward the Humber, R38 parted into two distinct pieces. The rearward section drifted, broken and crumpled but intact, gently down and away. The forward section caught fire, and the fire ignited the mixed hydrogen and oxygen gases inside the hull, causing two immense explosions, five seconds apart, so powerful they shattered plate-glass windows all over the city of Hull, knocked people down in the streets, and were felt twenty-five miles away. Then followed the by now familiar sight of an airship being engulfed in flames. The forward section plunged flaming into the river, igniting the gasoline floating on the water. The crowd watched in silent horror as a parachutist dropped slowly to his death in the spreading flames.

A few moments later, the aft section of the ship, which had not caught fire, fluttered to earth and came to rest in three feet of water on a sandbar, where four crew members stepped off, were swamped in gasoline, and were rescued just before the flames reached them. In the front half of the ship all but one of the crew burned to death, either in the vessel or in the flaming river. In all, forty-four of the forty-nine crew members of R38 died—sixteen Americans and twenty-eight Britons. That number included many of the elite of the British airship service: Charles Campbell, Edward Maitland, Jack Pritchard, John Pannell of the National Physical Laboratory (NPL), and five qualified pilots.

The entire event had lasted fifteen seconds. Unlike the familiar zeppelin fireballs, which had lit up the nighttime skies in the war, this horror took place in full daylight.

After the crash, funerals and memorial services were held in Hull and London. Amid a vast outpouring of national grief, the dead were laid in a mass grave. A succession of inquiries looked into the causes. Their findings were appalling. They suggested an almost unthinkable negligence on the part of R38's designers. The investigators, who included Major Herbert Scott and three others who later played large roles in the building of R101, concluded that for all of R38's advanced engineering and precise building specifications, and the extraordinary time and money and manpower that had been put into her, Campbell and his team had paid little or no attention to the airship's aerodynamic loads in flight. They had instead calculated only the *static* stresses, as might occur in a ship cruising slowly in calm air and in level flight.

The absurdity of that failure was lost on no one. "It was inexpressibly shocking to me," wrote British airship engineer Nevil Shute, "that before building the vast and costly structure of R38 the civil servants had made no attempt to calculate the aerodynamic forces acting upon the ship."[24] They failed in spite of the existence of at least ten major papers on aerodynamic forces on airships (including one by Gustave Eiffel, of Tower fame), none of which they had read or consulted.[25] They had assumed, since no British airships had ever collapsed in the air, that such an event could not happen. They had also assumed that the Germans had never experienced problems with aerodynamics. They were wrong. The Germans, in their quest to fly ever higher and faster with ever lighter airships, worried obsessively about stresses and loads. Though R38 was bigger and faster than earlier British airships, and with bigger engines, she had been built with *only half* of the previous ships' factors of strength and safety. That was because the British had copied a German airship that had been designed with absolute minimum factors of safety—acceptable in wartime but absurdly dangerous for civil and commercial travel. The British had also assumed that each generation's zeppelin was better in terms of structure and performance than the previous generation. But in this case the Germans, desperate to fly above the British fighters, had purpose-built L-70 to fly higher than any other aircraft in history; *flying high* was what mattered, not operational strength. Though built a bit stronger than L-70, R38 was nowhere near as structurally sound as she should have been.

What of the ship's inspectors, who were supposed to make sure that such mistakes of calculation did not happen? The inquiry pointed out that the airship works at Cardington, which had built R38, was the same organization that inspected her, a violation of the most basic separation of duties in engineering practice.

The final, chilling conclusion of the inquiries was that even if R38 had made it through her rushed English trials, she would have crashed in the first bad weather, possibly in the middle of the Atlantic Ocean. She was deeply unstable. Her structure was inherently weak.

The crash of R38 destroyed what was left of the British airship program. A prolonged fight ensued between the British Admiralty and the Air Ministry over who deserved the blame. Both were responsible. But it didn't matter. Within a few months all British airship activities stopped. The three remaining ships were put into storage. The manufacturers—Vickers, Armstrong Whitworth, and Beardmore—wrote off their interests in airships.[26] Britain had scrapped its two zeppelins.

France still had two "reparations" zeppelins and Italy had one, but neither country had plans for future production. There was simply no money left for airships. More telling was that there was no real use for them, no purpose. The rigid airship era, inaugurated by Count Ferdinand von Zeppelin in the early years of the twentieth century, was apparently at an end.

CHAPTER FIVE

"THE FEELING OF UTTER LONELINESS"

R101 reached the English coastline at 9:30 p.m. She crossed some four miles east of the town of Hastings, site of the battle, in 1066, that began the Norman conquest of England. She was flying at an altitude of fifteen hundred feet on a southeasterly heading of 141 degrees, aimed at Paris. Witnesses on the sea cliffs below remembered the throb of her engines and the sidewise way she flew, her bow pointing well off her actual line of travel. Flying at an altitude of roughly twice her length made her seem even larger than she was.[1] Watchers recalled seeing the brilliantly lit windows of her lounge and promenades. She was so low they could see the shapes of the passengers in silhouette.

If this wasn't dreamlike or phantasmic enough for English country people on a stormy night in the autumn of 1930, they could hear *dance music* descending from the sky. R101's builders had thoughtfully mounted loudspeakers in both the lounge and dining room. The speakers had been hooked into the airship's wireless receiver, which was tuned to the BBC, where Ambrose and His Orchestra were just beginning their regular Saturday broadcast from London's May Fair Hotel, playing the fox-trot "My Baby Just Cares for Me."[2] The people on the ground knew exactly what they were hearing. They were part of a radio craze that had seized England for a decade, resulting in the purchase of radios on an unprecedented scale. While we cannot know with any precision what was taking place in R101's lounge at that hour, we can guess that the passengers and off-duty officers were having a jolly good time.

A few minutes later R101 sent the following message to her Cardington home base:

> Crossing coast in vicinity of Hastings. It is raining hard and there is
> a strong southwesterly wind. Cloud base is at 1500 feet. . . . Engines
> running well at cruising speed giving 54.2 knots [62.37 mph].
> Reached London at 2000 hrs then set course for Paris. . . . Ship is
> behaving well generally and we have already begun to recover ballast.[3]

So all was well, considering the weather. Or was it? R101 was rolling from side to side in ways several crew members had never seen. Her bow was rising and falling hundreds of feet. Though all the big rigids did this to some degree, correcting such "hunting" was still exhausting work. The ship was laboring, too, fighting a 40-plus mph southwest wind. Later, when R101 turned due south toward Tours, Toulouse, Narbonne, and the Mediterranean, the wind would be even more of an obstacle. The wire did mention, curiously, that the ship had begun to *recover ballast* from rainwater collection points in her outer cover. Curious because the crew had never admitted losing four and a half tons of water ballast in the first place, which meant that if more ballast had to be dropped in the forward part of the airship, it would have to be done manually by sending a man forward.[4] Having so little ballast, relative to gross weight, did not meet basic airworthiness standards. In this condition, R101's crew would likely have to dump fuel in an emergency, and no one wanted to do that.*

Flying in an aircraft of any kind over the ocean at night was something most people in 1930 had never experienced. Many found it unsettling. Having made the English Channel, the view from R101 changed radically. In place of the lambent glow of the city of London

---

* Officially, the amount of droppable ballast had to be 10 percent of gross lift, and half of that had to be capable of being dropped rapidly. That meant sixteen tons of total ballast, and eight quickly droppable. *Minutes of Proceedings at Public Inquiry into the Loss of Airship R.101*, 1:29.

and delicate fairylands of light in the small towns, there was nothing but the opaque night: black water below them, dense cloud above. The inhabited earth and whatever ideas of comfort and safety came with it vanished completely. The airship glided through ink-black space and would do so for many hours to come, crossing France and all those darkly unimaginable lands below, as the equally inconceivable journey across the Mediterranean to Egypt loomed ahead. Air Commodore Edward Maitland, who flew on R34 across the Atlantic and lost his life aboard R38, wrote of this feeling on his R34 flight:

> When flying at night, possibly on account of the darkness, there is always the feeling of utter loneliness directly one loses sight of the ground. We feel this loneliness very much tonight, possibly owing to the fact that we are bound for a totally unknown destination.[5]

Did the rhythmical swing of Ambrose and His Orchestra, the fashionable dinner, port, cigars, and splendid company blot out such feelings as R101 shouldered forward into the storm-tossed Channel? We will never know. From eyewitnesses on the cliffs, we do know that some of the passengers were on the promenade, presumably gazing out of the windows into that consuming darkness.

Whatever they thought, they were all aware that the fate of the ship that night was in the hands of Major George Herbert Scott, hero of R34, the man who would, in his own words, decide R101's "height, speed, and course flown." This was perhaps a comfort to some of them, but worrisome to the Royal Airship Works people who knew about Scott's drinking. It had been his call—with the wind rising and Giblett's predictions coming alarmingly true—to push on into the worst weather R101 had ever encountered.[6] "The combination of high, gusting winds, heavy rain, and low-level turbulence, all maintained for hours on end," wrote airship historian Peter Masefield, ". . . was possibly never exceeded in airship experience, even taking account of the substantial total of some 61,000 hours flown by German rigid airships."[7] Scott had decided not only to challenge the wind and rain. He would fly faster, as measured by air speed, than R101 had ever flown for an unbroken time. That speed, and into a wind expected to hit 50 mph, would create enormous and unprecedented strains on the airship's thin outer cover of doped linen, which protected the ultrathin, cotton-backed cattle intestines of the gasbags.

Since pressing on had been Scott's call, it is worth looking at his actual record of flying airships, which was not what the public thought it was. In his early career, he had shown courage and resourcefulness. A good example was the test flight of the British airship R36 on April 3, 1921. When the ship went into a sudden nosedive, dropping eighteen hundred feet in forty-five seconds, Scott, who was not in the control car, came swinging forward, using columns to break his fall and "looking like Tarzan of the apes."[8] He stopped the dive by ordering crew members to various points on the ship's keel, fore and aft, thus redistributing the weight, then slowing and alternating R36's speed.[9] He brought the ship in at Pulham naval station for a perfect landing. He had been the pilot of R34's jaw-dropping, high-risk double crossing of the Atlantic.

But Scott had another side as a pilot, marked more by ham-handedness and poor judgment than swashbuckling and invention. Early in the war he had run his Sea Scout nonrigid airship into a mountainside. He had hit the top of a shed in a nonrigid Beta and had been in command of Parseval No. 4 blimp when it collided with an airship shed.[10] He had two significant accidents while in charge of the big rigid R33 in 1926, smashing gondola cars, struts, and girders on one occasion and slamming into the airship-shed doors on what would prove to be her last flight.[11] During R101's trials he had twice pulled rank on Captain Carmichael "Bird" Irwin as the airship was mooring at Cardington, in one case dangerously and unnecessarily discharging ballast, and in another colliding with the mooring mast and damaging girders that kept the airship's cover taut.[12] By the time R101 finished her flying trials in the summer of 1930, Irwin and First Officer Noel Atherstone were furious with Scott over these interventions. Atherstone viewed Scott's judgment with outright contempt. Scott's alcoholism almost certainly figured in these incidents—though to what extent is not known.

IN SCOTT'S DEFENSE, flying an airship was not easy to do, drunk or sober. It was considerably more difficult than flying an airplane, with many more elements to keep track of and many more opportunities for things to go wrong. The slow speed and gracefulness of the big rigids belied their danger, quite apart from the problem of hydrogen's explosiveness. Airplanes had their problems and suffered many crashes. But their fundamental design—as history would show—was sound and easily improvable. The concept of the rigid airship was, in ways that we have already seen, deeply flawed and ill adapted to change. History would prove that, too, and sooner than anyone thought. One of the airship's flaws, perhaps its major flaw, was that flying one was dangerously complex, requiring the hands of experienced airship officers—a small group, most of whom were German. "While the record of the airship has been marked by a number of disasters," wrote former airship pilot T. B. Williams, "each of them appears to have been either due to errors in navigation or airmanship . . . or to a serious miscomprehension of the capacities of the airship. The operation of airships is a highly specialized art, requiring long experience and the highest order of skill."[13]

Airship flight is based on two principles. The first is that lighter-than-air gas rises, and thus lighter-than-air gas trapped inside an airship causes the airship to rise. In this sense, it is an *aerostat*, floating in its medium like a child's helium balloon. But an airship can also fly according to the same principle—Bernoulli's—that causes airplanes to fly. When flying nose up, the air flows faster over the top of the airship than underneath it; the higher air pressure under the hull pushes it up. The reverse is true when the nose is down. Using the huge elevators on the tail, a pilot can thus fly the ship as an *aerodyne*—carrying its weight more like an airplane. To take off or land, the airship must be a pure aerostat, floating in approximate static equilibrium. But as we will see, she could employ both principles in flight.

The main worry for airship pilots was "lift"—how much weight the hydrogen in the ship's gasbags could carry. This would seem a simple enough idea. But it was astonishingly complex. That was because the lifting power of the gas wasn't constant. It was affected by a range of different factors, including changes in temperature, barometric pressure, humidity, gas temperature, and gas purity. The lift was greater with high density—cold temperatures and high barometric pressure—and less in high temperatures and low pressure. An increase of temperature of one degree Fahrenheit was equivalent to a loss of a third of a ton of lift. Airships could carry significantly more weight on a cold winter day than on a hot summer one. All airships leaked hydrogen, which reduced lift. All suffered from hydrogen impurity—the diffusion of air into the bags—which also reduced lift. Lift was affected by altitude. As an airship ascended, the gas in the bags expanded. Once the ship reached what was known as its pressure height—where its gasbags were at maximum capacity—automatic valves kicked in, blowing out hydrogen to prevent the bags from rupturing. For every three hundred feet R101 rose above her pressure height, she lost a ton of lift.[14] Phenomena known as superheating and supercooling—impossible-to-predict conditions in which the temperature of the gas in the bags was hotter or colder than the air outside—had large and destabilizing effects on an airship's buoyancy. During trials in the summer of 1930, for example, R101 left her mast in Cardington at 4:00 p.m. in sunny weather with superheated gas. Five hours later she returned in much cooler weather and with so much less lift that she had to drop two tons of ballast just to land.[15]

But lift, or buoyancy, was just one of the concerns in airship flight. There was the issue of actual weight. At takeoff, the captain had to make sure that the total weight carried was equal to the lift. The ship would sink to the ground if too heavy, shoot up into the sky if too light. The weight had to be properly arranged, too. Crew, fuel, ballast, and cargo all had to be spaced evenly over the length of the ship, lest she fly nose heavy or stern heavy. Rain, which soaked the outer cover, caused the ship to gain weight, and a heavy rain could increase R101's weight by as much as seven tons.[16] Using up gasoline in flight had the reverse effect, causing the ship to become lighter. On her trip to Egypt, R101 would burn enough fuel to become *twenty-one tons lighter*, fully 13 percent of her gross weight. A ship's crew tracked such changes with precision and had to know exactly how much weight was lost or gained and how to compensate for it.

To control the ship's whimsical buoyancy—as measured by her variometer (which measured rate of climb or descent), inclinometer (which measured the angle of slope/tilt), and barometric altimeter—the captain had two main tools at his disposal: ballast and gas. Airships carried up to 10 percent of their gross weight in water ballast, which could quickly be dropped, making the ship lighter. Up to one-third of its fuel was carried in tanks that could quickly be emptied.[17] Easily jettisoned ballast—water or fuel—was a falling airship's ultimate defense against coming to ground.

Ballast had other functions, too. If the ship was down by either the bow or stern, water ballast could be pumped to different locations along the keel using compressed air, thus "trimming" the vessel. Ballast was used, too, to help a ship come into equilibrium when leaving or returning to its mooring. When R101's crew dropped that giant, four-and-a-half-ton waterfall of ballast from her forward section on her departure for India, it was because the ship had been too heavy to take off, and specifically too heavy by the bow. The now lightened ship was then able to rise slowly from the mooring, engage her engines, and fly off—minus the safety of the ballast.

A vessel that was too light could valve gas from the gasbags, which could be done from the control car.

There were other, less conventional techniques to deal with lift or lack of it. While piloting R34, Scott once found that the gas in his superheated gasbags had hit 106 degrees, while the air remained at 40. The ship was suddenly rising fast and would have to valve precious gas. Scott solved the problem by flying into a wet cloud bank, which equalized the temperatures.[18] Such primitive, seat-of-the-pants solutions were common in airship flight.

Finally, a captain could use aerodynamics to compensate if an airship was either heavy or light. If R101 gained five tons of weight from a heavy rain, this would normally cause her to sink and eventually hit the ground. The captain could drop ballast, stop the fall, and bring the ship back into equilibrium. But he could save his ballast by flying aerodynamically with the airship's nose, say, four or five degrees up.[19] R101 could be flown this way when she was up to *thirteen tons heavy*, as long as she moved forward at speed. If she lost her engines in that condition, she would sink like a stone. She could save herself only by dropping water and fuel ballast in large quantities. If she had to, she could drop cargo, too.

So many weight-and-lift-related situations could occur. When a large ship flew at 60 mph, the weather at the nose took about nine seconds to arrive at the tail, which could lead to very different conditions around the same aircraft. By the time the conditions in the tail caught up with those at the nose, the nose could be in different conditions again.[20] A light ship could be flown nose down to keep from rising. But if engines on a light ship were lost, the only way to keep the ship from rising uncontrollably was to release gas. An airship that flew above her pressure height, thus automatically losing gas, would instantly become heavy and have to drop ballast or use dynamic flight to compensate. Flying low conserved hydrogen gas, but the airship still burned gasoline, which meant that she became lighter by the hour and would eventually have to compensate by valving gas. A ship coming in for a landing light or heavy would have no choice but to valve gas or drop ballast to regain static equilibrium.

And so on. The possibilities were staggering. Nothing on an airship was simple.

For some situations there were no solutions at all. The big rigids' enormous surface areas made them vulnerable to vertical air currents produced by storms. They could rise or fall wildly and uncontrollably, sometimes thousands of feet in seconds or minutes. For the same reason, even a light wind near the ground was a lethal threat.

The British airship R34 and the German L-59 offer examples of how the quirky science of airship flight played out in practice. During its four-day trip from Bulgaria to Sudan and back, L-59 burned so much gasoline and oil that she became lighter by 27,071 pounds. To counteract this, she had to release 930,000 cubic feet of gas, an astounding 38 percent of the total hydrogen she started with. Over the Egyptian desert, her supercooled gas caused the ship to fall. The captain saved her only by dropping 4,400 pounds of ballast. On another occasion the captain tried to compensate for L-59's heaviness by flying nose up. This worked fine until the engines broke down, causing the airship to fall precipitously from thirty-one hundred feet. She was saved from crashing by dropping another sixty-two hundred pounds of ballast and cargo.

During R34's Atlantic crossing, after sunrise one morning she superheated and had to valve off hydrogen. After sunset, that same day, the superheating effect disappeared, leaving the ship three tons heavy due to the loss of gas at sunrise. She was made even heavier by fog and low-lying clouds. Mitigating these losses was the weight of the fuel burned during the day. The crew estimated that the net loss of buoyancy that day was four to five tons—so much that the ship had to be flown ten degrees up by the bow with all of her engines at cruising speed. "Otherwise ballast in the form of petrol would have had to be jettisoned to prevent the ship from descending into the sea," wrote Air Commodore Edward Maitland.[21]

Such were the technical complications of life aboard an airship. As

R101 crab-walked forward into the rainy darkness, she was getting heavier (rain on her cover) and lighter (expended fuel) at the same time. She was probably four tons heavy, flying with her nose slightly up to compensate. Perhaps the crew of R101 were too busy just keeping the ship on an even keel to think about what might happen to her when she encountered the heat, humidity, thin air, and squalls of the tropical zones that lay ahead. The only airship that had ever tried to fly in those conditions was L-59. In retrospect, it was a miracle that the German ship ever made it back.

THE IDEA THAT WOULD NOT DIE

The crash of R38 in 1921 was a national disaster. There was no excuse for it, no way to defend it. The horror at so many gruesome deaths was attended by shame for the ineptitude that had caused it. The great airship was supposed to be the best that British know-how could build. And that was the problem: the suspicion that the incompetently designed R38 was the best that Great Britain could do.

R38 put a stop to the British airship program, but its destruction had little effect on two other nations—France and the United States—that were still flying large-scale, lighter-than-air craft.

Six months after the R38 crash, the 410-foot-long American airship *Roma*, filled with a million cubic feet of hydrogen, took off from Norfolk, Virginia, on a training flight. She had been built in Italy and sold to the U.S. Army in 1921. A semirigid airship, she lacked a full-scale rigid skeleton like R38; her gasbag envelope was bolstered by a stiff ventral keel and a metal-ribbed bow. With forty-five souls on board, she was flying over the Norfolk Naval Station when her bow flattened and she began to dive. Her keel buckled. Her tail assembly came apart. The crew frantically tried to slow her descent by throwing everything they could find overboard including tools, engine parts, and furniture. The ship continued to dive. When she came to ground, she hit a high-voltage line. She exploded, setting off the gas tanks, and the whole apparatus went up in what was by now the regrettably familiar sight of an airship and its helpless crew consumed by a hydrogen-fueled firestorm. Thirty-four men died, the greatest disaster in the history of American aeronautics

at the time.[1] *Roma* inspired a sharp helium-versus-hydrogen debate in
the United States and marked the end of all American attempts to fly
hydrogen airships.[2]

The horrors persisted. In December 1923 the German heightclimber L-72, given to the French government as a war reparation
and renamed *Dixmude*, took off from the south coast of France, bound
for Algeria in North Africa. She was among the last and most technologically advanced of the superzeppelins, originally designed to cross
the Atlantic and bomb New York City. This huge war machine was
743 feet long with a volume of 2.4 million cubic feet of hydrogen,
capable of flying at 26,200 feet and at a speed of 74 mph. Like the
German ship L-70, on which R38 had been modeled, L-72's metal
frame was extremely fragile at lower altitudes. At just after 2:00 a.m.
on December 23, *Dixmude* wired that she was taking in her radio
antenna because of thunderstorms. Twenty minutes later workers in
a railway yard on the coast of Sicily saw a great fire "like an Aurora
Borealis" descending in the west. Later, pieces of *Dixmude* were found
nearby, along with the body of her inexperienced young captain,
Lieutenant Jean du Duplessis de Grenédan, who was found six miles
offshore by fishermen. In his career he had flown mostly on small,
nonrigid airships.[3] All fifty-two on board perished, presumably by
fire or by jumping to avoid the fire. Not enough was left of the ship
to figure out what had gone wrong.[4]

If R38 had not proven disastrous enough to kill airships once and for
all, then surely the grisly *Dixmude* disaster—involving top-of-the-line
German technology in peacetime—should have done it.[5]

And yet.

In spite of what appears in retrospect to be excruciatingly obvious—
the lethal impracticality of the big rigids—the idea did not die, and
airships did not disappear. By 1923 an idea for a new set of British
airships—which would eventually include R101—would rapidly gain
acceptance in the corridors of Whitehall. By 1924 a fully fledged plan

was in place. Why, with so much evidence against it? For Great Britain the question could be answered with a single word: *empire*. After World War I the small island country held the largest imperial domain in human history, containing some 25 percent of the world's landmass and 23 percent of its population—412 million people. Germany's old colonies in the Pacific were now under the imperial hand. Britain had swallowed whole chunks of the vanquished Ottoman Empire, including Iraq, Transjordan, and Palestine. Persia was under its control. India, the colonial crown jewel, was now connected to Egypt and the Mediterranean by an unbroken chain of British-dominated sovereign lands, which in turn were part of a British-controlled strip of contiguous terrain that stretched all the way to the tip of South Africa. All this was added to the old self-governing British dominions: Australia, Canada, Newfoundland, New Zealand, and South Africa. The sun, indeed, did not set on the British Empire.

But by the early 1920s it was showing persistent and uncharacteristic weakness. The main reason: its subjects were pursuing self-determination as never before. In South Africa the British had been forced to deploy half a million soldiers to suppress a ragtag guerrilla army of Afrikaans-speaking Boer farmers, which, at the end, numbered no more than twenty thousand. In British-ruled Ireland, the 1916 Easter uprising led to a war of independence and the founding of the Irish Free State in 1922. The world war had taken a gigantic toll. Many of Great Britain's roughly 3 million casualties had been recruited from her colonies and dominions. Those countries, which had supplied 2.5 million soldiers to the war, wanted something in return for their blood.[6] In India, a major supplier of troops, the 1919 Amritsar massacre of civilians by British troops was a signal event in that country's swelling movement for self-rule. A 1920 rebellion in Iraq had to be brutally put down. The chinks in the imperial armor multiplied. Even on the high seas, where Britain had ruled for centuries, she was no longer the definitive naval power in the world. Her postwar strength was now determined by a "ratio" of sea power that governed the wartime Allies and locked Britain into parity with the United States.[7]

Into this strange imperial half-world strode a new breed of imperialist, every bit as gung ho as their Victorian counterparts but without the old military punch. Like their predecessors, they believed that their empire was just, virtuous, benevolently paternalistic, and devoted to the advancement of civilization—though it was rarely any of these things and often their reverse. They saw an inevitability to the empire, a rightness that every football-playing Harrovian could immediately grasp. They believed, despite what was happening all around them, that history would remain resolutely Anglocentric. The notion that it would all come crashing down in blood and bitterness in a few decades would have been considered preposterous.

These forward-thinking men had been looking for ways to use the medium of the air to link the far-flung pieces of their domain—to reduce the time to cross it from oceangoing weeks to airborne days. They could thus change the nature of empire itself. They could improve it, bind it more tightly together, make it stronger. Airplanes were considered, but there was no evidence yet that they would ever be practical for long distances: they were still slow, uncomfortable, and dangerous and required constant refueling. Even in the latter 1920s many aeronautical experts still believed that 110 miles per hour would be the commercial airplane's maximum speed, its range no more than two thousand miles.[8] (They were also very wrong about how much lift a fixed wing could provide.) This allowed the airship crowd to assert that, by maintaining, say, 60 mph through twenty-four hours a day—thus, 1,440 miles—airships could cover far greater distances with more cargo and fewer stops than airplanes.[9]

So British eyes came to rest on what appeared to be the perfect solution: rigid airships and their proven ability to cross great global distances. The empire had been built on violence and subjugation, but also, critically, on science, invention, and expertise, on being able to build what others could not. Airships—technologically advanced versions such as R34 and L-59 that had flown thousands of miles without crashing—offered the chance to revive that old industrial dominance. Airships could reduce the time that the prime minister of Australia spent traveling to the Imperial Conference in England from a month to *eleven days*. India could be reached in five days, Canada in two and a half.[10] These were tantalizing, world-shifting ideas. Communication was making quantum leaps in speed and distance. Travel would do the same.

The messy details of airship history were, as usual, conveniently overlooked.

Who were these new men of empire? In the immediate postwar years, they resided primarily in two places: within the Admiralty—the government department in charge of the British Navy—and in the remote dominions. The navy because it persisted in seeing military value in airships as scouts, especially over water, and most especially when they could take the place of costly light warships. The dominions because the premiers, diplomats, and technocrats in places such as New Zealand and South Africa were tired of spending so much time at sea to attend Imperial Conferences in London. The first proposal for an empire-wide airship service came, perhaps predictably, from the agent-general of the government of Tasmania. To inhabitants of a far-off British outpost, eleven thousand miles from England, cutting transcontinental travel time by 60 or 70 percent seemed like a marvelous idea.

By far the most important of the new airship boosters was a driven, flamboyant former naval officer named Charles Dennistoun Burney. His father, Admiral Cecil Burney, a baronet, had been second-in-command of the British Grand Fleet under John Jellicoe at the Battle of Jutland. Young Dennis Burney had distinguished himself in the navy as a resourceful inventor. In 1911, at the age of twenty-three, he designed a seaplane with a hydrofoil undercarriage, though it was never produced. In 1923 he wrote a visionary article in *Naval Review* that accurately predicted, years in advance, the use of airpower against submarines.[11]

Early in the world war he invented a device called a paravane, which was towed from a ship's bow and could cut the anchors of moored mines. The paravane worked brilliantly. Burney was soon under contract with the Admiralty, orchestrating a complex engineering project that would save countless tons of shipping. His paravane patents earned him an astounding £350,000—roughly $15 million in 2020 dollars. He retired from the navy in 1920, took a consulting contract with Vickers Ltd., which was then the largest engineering company in the world, ran for Parliament and won, and continued to hatch big ideas.[12]

The biggest of those involved airships. Though Burney had never even seen an airship and had no precise idea of how they flew, he understood the deep national interest in what the British blandly called "improving imperial communications." As early as 1918 Vickers had proposed a London–New York service with a then record-size airship—3.5 million cubic feet of volume.[13] It was Burney who finally united the two streams of support—the navy and the dominions—behind a single idea that appealed to both them and to the British government.[14]

In March 1922 he presented a proposal for a single large airship, 760 feet long, with a gas volume of 5 million cubic feet. The airship would provide weekly service to India, would be able to fly at 80 mph for three thousand miles and carry two hundred passengers, cargo, and ten tons of mail. To the navy he offered full use of the airship in wartime, carrying extra fuel so that her range would be twelve thousand miles at 80 mph or, if the navy so desired, twenty-four thousand miles—the circumference of the earth—at 40 mph. She could go three weeks without landing! Circle the globe! Burney even added a bit of filigree: the ship could be converted to duty as an aircraft carrier, carrying fighter and torpedo planes.[15] He argued, moreover, in an opinion piece for the *Daily Telegraph* that "16 airships of 5 million cubic feet, each equipped with three fighters and two torpedo bombers, could be built for the cost of one battleship." Vickers would build the ship, and in exchange the company would receive a government subsidy and Britain's four existing airships, and the old wartime airship stations at Cardington and Pulham. Ultimately Vickers would build six airships that would make twice-weekly voyages to India and later Australia.

This idea quickly became known as the Burney Scheme or the Imperial Airship Scheme.

Practically, Burney's ideas were preposterous. No airship of that size could possibly carry that many passengers for three thousand miles at such a speed. There wasn't even a market for that level of intercontinental human travel. Staying aloft for three weeks in remote parts of the world defied imagination, technical or otherwise. His carrier ideas, which involved fighter planes stored inside the airship hull, then launched and retrieved on a sort of trapeze, were unproven and would never become operational.[16] Burney's models for regular long-distance travel were the flawed R34, which was lucky to have survived its transatlantic crossings, and Hugo Eckener's DELAG short-haul airship service. Using the latter as an exemplar of global airship service was like basing a long sea voyage on a cruise around a bay. Burney had not even looked at the tropical weather between London and Karachi, with its wild and unpredictable effect on lift, which had caused so much havoc with the German L-59. He didn't know what he was talking about.

Under Burney's plan the first airship would be followed in close order by five more airships of similar size. Together they would provide twice-a-week service to Egypt and India, and later to Rangoon, Singapore, and Perth. All this was at best prodigiously optimistic thinking and at worst pure fantasy.[17] Meanwhile Burney was selling his costly idea to a financially strapped government that was mired in war debt and already struggling to subsidize cross-Channel airlines. Winston Churchill, who opposed the plan, protested, "The government cannot hope the money can be repaid."[18] Nevertheless, Burney had powerful allies. His proposal was taken seriously and closely studied.

The scheme soon became mired in studies in a variety of committees and in the national debate about which service—the navy, the army, or the RAF—would control British airpower. But Burney, whose high opinion of himself was exceeded only by his extravagant salesmanship, kept pushing. In 1923 a panel was set up under the Air Ministry to evaluate the idea. It included a number of key officials but also, crucially, two unusual choices. One was Burney himself. Why shouldn't he help review his own plan? The other was a retired middle-aged brigadier, twice-failed Labour Party candidate for Parliament, and struggling freelance writer named Christopher Birdwood Thomson. His only apparent qualification to sit on such a panel was his friendship with Air Minister Samuel Hoare. Thomson knew nothing of airships. A left-wing Labour politician, he was there mainly to counterbalance the bumptious, ultraconservative Burney.

By summer's end Burney's plan had been approved in principle, even though a majority of the advisory panel, including Thomson, had found it flawed. They liked the concept of linking up the empire but did not like Burney or the way he went about it. Negotiations were underway when on December 6, 1923, a bolt of lightning hit national politics: Britain elected the first Labour Party government in its history. In the economic hard times that followed the war, Labour had advocated massive and historic change—socialism, essentially—which included the nationalization of railways, mines, shipping, and all electrical power. The socialists had prevailed.

The new government's secretary of state for air—promoted to that position by his best friend and close confidant, Prime Minister Ramsay MacDonald—was, to the surprise of Whitehall and everyone else, Christopher Birdwood Thomson.

Thomson's interest in—and eventual obsession with—an imperial scheme to fly to India was no coincidence. India was deep in his blood. India was his legacy and his birthright. His family, on both sides, had played leading roles in the conquest, buildup, and maintenance of Great Britain's most prized imperial possession. Birdwoods and Thomsons had taken the British Empire, quite literally, as their vocation.

Thomson, known as Kit to his family, was born on April 13, 1875, at Nasik in Bombay Province, a small Indian Army garrison town in mangrove swamps one hundred miles northeast of Bombay. His father was Major General David Thomson of the Royal Engineers, a division of the army that had historically been responsible for building much of the British colonial infrastructure of India. Kit's paternal grandfather, Harry Thomson, had sailed from Portsmouth to Bombay in 1799, at the age of nineteen, to join the British East India Company's service. He went on to become a general in command of the Bengal Light Cavalry in the Maratha War of 1803–5. Kit's mother, Emily Lydia Thomson, was a Birdwood, from one of Anglo-India's most eminent families.[19] Her great-grandfather Richard Birdwood had been mayor of Plymouth and agent for the British East India Company. Her father, Major General Christopher Birdwood, commanded a division in the Indian Army and was known as Birdwood Maharaj.[20] Two of her brothers were generals in India, another the acting governor of Bombay, and a fourth brother one of Anglo-India's most prominent writers and naturalists. Her nephew, Thomson's first cousin William R. Birdwood, commanded the Australian and New Zealand troops at Gallipoli in World War I. He later commanded the British Fifth Army. In 1925 he would become commander in chief of the Indian Army.

Thomson grew up in a time and place where the idea of empire, its scope, its achievements, and its preeminence were relentlessly drummed into British subjects. School prayers included blessings for the queen empress and her subjects. Sermons stressed imperial duty. In churches throughout the empire people sang hymns in which patriotic and religious themes were seamlessly intertwined. Songs such as "Land of Hope and Glory" were unabashed appeals for British power, addressed to God. They spoke of blessings that were dispensed only to England. Maps of the world, ubiquitous in homes and schools, showed the astonishing scope of Britain's holdings, colored in with bold imperial-red ink. All of this conveyed the message that the empire was both invincible and God ordained.[21]

When Thomson was five years old, his father, General David Thomson, retired after twenty-five years of service in the Indian Army and moved the family back to England. Why leave after his family's eighty-year presence there? David had been educated in England from the age of ten to twenty and knew the country well. At forty-five he found himself with a family of eight children (two by a first wife who died in childbirth) and wanted a more tolerable climate in which to bring them up. The oldest two were already in England, residing with his brother. With his second wife, Emily Lydia Birdwood, the daughter of fellow army officer General William Birdwood, David settled in Cheltenham. In short order the retired general, barely at middle age, designed and built a splendid Victorian residence, known as Underwood, fathered two more children, hired a governess, several nannies, a cook, and two housemaids—for a total household establishment of eighteen. He then took up painting as his main pursuit.[22] Where the money came from to fund such a patrician lifestyle is unclear. But he wasn't finished. He soon moved out of the house, apparently seeking "peace and quiet" to work on his paintings, but more likely because his wife, Emily, had taken up with a conservative evangelical sect known as the Plymouth Brethren. From that moment forward, Kit's mother became the dominant influence in his life. The family had moved into its new home and its cheerful, noisy, and rambunctious—albeit soon to be fatherless—atmosphere when Kit was eleven years old.

Thomson attended Cheltenham College, one of the leading British public schools of the Victorian era, as a day boy. An excellent student, he could quote passages from Matthew Arnold, Edward Bulwer-Lytton, Shakespeare, and Keats. He ranked first in French. He was not above mischief. At age fourteen he was caught kissing the headmaster's daughter behind the cricket pavilion. From Cheltenham he went to the Royal Military Academy at Woolwich and received a commission in the Royal Engineers. Thus began a long career in the army, much of it in outposts of the empire. He, too, took the empire as his vocation.

He served under Britain's greatest military legends: fighting Boers in South Africa with General Herbert Kitchener; capturing Jerusalem from the Ottoman Turks with General Edmund Allenby; crushing the Matabele rebellion with General Frederick Carrington. Thomson became the youngest major in the army, one of Kitchener's favorites.[23] In the gaps in Thomson's empire work he held staff positions in the peacetime army in England. When World War I began, he went to France with the British Expeditionary Force. He was thirty-nine years old. A year later, in 1915, he was assigned to Romania, first as military attaché, and later as head of the British Mission. His two years in Bucharest were a turning point in his career, and the first time his considerable diplomatic and personal talents came fully into focus.

In some ways Thomson could seem almost a public-school stereotype: handsome, cheerful, urbane, clubbable, fond of conversation and long dinner parties, and, as one friend put it, "a keen follower of the chase, throwing his heart over fences, a good cricketer, and a useful man at golf."[24] He was all of those things, but was a great deal more than a hail-fellow-well-met at the officers' mess. The most striking thing about Thomson was his ability with languages. He spoke three in addition to English—French, Russian, and German—and spoke French more fluently than any other officer on the general staff, a skill the British army put to considerable use. He read widely in the classics and astonished his friends by quoting works in French and English at length. He wrote poetry. He was a competent journalist and nonfiction writer. He was passionate about music. Perhaps the weight of his family's martial history explains how such a refined soul could have chosen an army career, how a man who was so comfortable in a literary salon could spend nearly three decades in barracks. "[His] connoisseur-like attitude to life was suggested by his very appearance," wrote his friend Basil Liddell Hart. "In his finely chiselled features, his essentially aristocratic bearing, and, above all, his expressive hands, the hands of an artist, with tapering fingers, perfectly kept, that had a blended sensitiveness and strength. In his air, too, of natural dignity, with sometimes a trace of hauteur, that would gradually or suddenly melt into irresistible charm."[25] It was part of the mystery of Thomson, as was his eventual embrace of socialism, which surprised and dismayed many friends and acquaintances. He was never easy to categorize.

He also had a hard edge to his personality that was at odds with the image of the charming socialite. He had a quick temper. He liked to argue, sometimes to a fault. He was not afraid of challenging authority. When he first went to France with the British First Army, he clashed so forcefully with General Douglas Haig's chief of staff that Thomson had to be transferred. In Romania he opposed the Allied policy to bring that country into the war. He believed—and told his military superiors repeatedly—that Romania had been lied to and goaded into a war it could not win. In his highly critical 1922 book, *Old Europe's Suicide*, he called the major powers' behavior "a carnival of mendacity and intrigue" that sacrificed "the public interest to the designs of a few ambitious men."[26] He had the misfortune of being right. Romania entered the war and was soon overrun by Germany. Thomson was appalled when, as the German Army advanced, he was charged with the task of burning Romania's Ploiesti oil fields, to keep them from German hands. "I felt like a hired assassin," he later wrote. After the war some of Thomson's critics decided his opinions had been sound after all. "Had {Thomson's} advice been accepted," former British prime minister David Lloyd George admitted much later in the House of Commons, ". . . a very considerable tragedy might have been averted."[27]

But in 1916 Thomson's heated criticism of Allied policy mainly won him enemies. He was soon banished from the civilized comforts of Europe to the hot, dusty military backwater of Palestine, a career retrogression that was clearly a punishment.[28] "I am in the black books of the War Office," he wrote.[29] His undiplomatic behavior was not the only reason for his exile to the Middle East. There was a moral component, too. "The more orthodox soldiers," wrote Thomson's friend, politician, and cabinet member Samuel Hoare, "were shocked at his gay life in the Roumanian capital."[30] The reference may have been in part due to Thomson's place as a fixture on the Bucharest dinner-party circuit. He loved wine and good food and smart conversation and was immensely popular. He did not care for money and was unfailingly generous with it.[31] (He was unmarried.) But his chief sin was more likely his very public infatuation with a dazzlingly beautiful Romanian princess named Marthe Bibesco, who was married.

She was born Marthe Lucy Lahovary to one of Romania's most accomplished and influential families. The Lahovarys were generals, judges, bank presidents, directors of mines, cabinet ministers, and the owners of major national newspapers.[32] Her father was at various times the leader of the Romanian conservative party, foreign minister, and minister of agriculture. The language of the Lahovary house was French, though young Marthe soon became fluent in German and English, in addition to her native Romanian. At the age of sixteen, already considered one of Romania's great beauties, she married Prince George Valentine Bibesco, the scion of an old and immensely wealthy Romanian family. She had a child a year later. The marriage didn't work. Her husband ignored her, chasing other women and spending time with what he really loved: racing automobiles, motorcycles, airplanes, and boats. "The physical union of two people is like murder," Marthe recalled with a shudder. "All at once one is obliterated; no identity remains except pain." Years later in her book *Où tombe la foudre*, she proclaimed, "Giving a virgin to a man is like giving a Stradivarius to a monkey. . . . In spite of the best will in the world, I could not find any pleasure in yielding to my husband's demands." Gradually she formed the conviction that physical pleasures "are a slightly obscene and overrated pastime, unremarkable when compared with the sublime delights of intellectual pursuit." To make matters worse, she spent little time with her young daughter, whom she did not like.[33]

At twenty-two Marthe published a travel book in French, *Les huits paradis*, which was an immediate critical and commercial success. With her striking looks, obvious literary talent, aristocratic rank, and full fluency in French, she quickly became the toast of Belle Époque Paris, an era of rapid change that featured modernity in all of its novelty and excitement: subways, automobiles, telephones, men in bowler hats escorting women in flowing, tight-waisted dresses to Fouquet's or Maxim's. She literally stepped off the Orient Express and into a world that immediately loved her. Marcel Proust wrote a poem to her. In a note, written just as he was beginning À *la recherche du temps perdu*, he wrote, "You are not only a splendid writer, Princess, but a sculptor of words, a musician, a purveyor of scents, a poet." André Gide and Jean Cocteau were admirers. She was dressed by top Parisian couturiers, painted by famed society portraitist Giovanni Boldini. In 1910 she published another critically successful book, *Alexandre asiatique*. While her husband pursued his hobbies, and neglected his beautiful wife, she embarked on a series of progressively more serious dalliances with European royalty. Crown Prince Wilhelm, heir to the German empire, fell in love with her, as did the dashing Charles-Louis de Beauvau-Craon, the scion of an old French aristocratic family and the most eligible man in Europe. Their tempestuous affair was an open secret in Paris. Her husband didn't care.[34]

Though she was widely celebrated for her looks—languorous brown-green eyes, light English complexion, cascades of chestnut hair—contemporaneous accounts suggest that she was a strikingly engaging personality. Her knowledge of art and literature was varied and deep, her memory for people, events, and books prodigious. She could quote widely and effortlessly in several languages. Perhaps Thomson himself captured her best, writing later, "With Marthe one enjoys a rare companionship wherein romance and mental stimulus are combined. She listens, laughs at British jokes, suggests their parallels in French, makes stupid men with dull, fagged brains feel brilliant, draws out the best one has to give."[35]

She could also be haughty and dismissive. Not everyone liked her.

She inspired jealousy in other women with what one of her rivals called her *airs de l'imperatrice*.

In March 1915 she was at a concert at the royal palace in Bucharest, wearing a black velvet dress offset by emeralds, and accompanied by the king of Romania, when she met Christopher Thomson, who had just arrived from London. She found him smart, cultured, and engaging. He fell immediately and completely in love with her. He had seen her before. In a diary entry written in 1902, thirteen years earlier, he noted he had seen the sixteen-year-old Marthe in an open carriage in the rue de Rivoli beside the Tuileries Garden in Paris. He found her "radiant" and "entrancing" and even claimed to have exchanged glances.[36] Now, to the sensitive and romantically inclined Thomson, she was like a vision fulfilled: a real-life fairy-tale princess from a remote mountain kingdom with not one but two castles at her disposal and a reputation as one of Europe's brightest literary stars.

It would be inaccurate to say that she fell as hard for him. She was still in love with Beauvau-Craon. She was still married to the prince. An army colonel such as Thomson was far below her in Europe's social ranks. She was attracted to power and wealth, and he had neither. He was an amusement. But she accepted his affections, without commitment. She called him Kit. He called her Smaranda, after a Byzantine princess. They spent many evenings together at Mogoşoaia, Marthe's eighteenth-century Venetian-style palace. She consoled him when a German zeppelin dropped a bomb on the house where he was living, partially destroying it and wounding two of his orderlies.[37] When the German Army occupied Romania, Marthe fled to Paris, while Thomson went into his exile in Palestine. They would not see each other until the Versailles Peace Conference, more than two years later, when Thomson served on the staff of the Supreme War Council.[38]

Thomson, who had by then been decorated for his service in the Middle East and promoted to brigadier general, was still besotted. But in the whirl of 1919 Paris, Marthe, who was now keeping company with such celebrities as Winston Churchill, Georges Clemenceau, David Lloyd George, Maynard Keynes, Colette, and Marcel Proust, had far less time for Thomson. Though she would soon end her long affair with Beauvau-Craon, a few years later she would begin another with the editor of *Le Matin*, the most influential French daily. Along the way, she was courted by Spanish king Alfonso XIII. Thomson, who sent her ever more ineffectual love letters, was left out.[39] "Here in Paris," he wrote later, "I sometimes feel an accessory and not a fact."[40] Their love affair existed mostly in Thomson's mind.

But it had a great deal to do with the next phase of his life. In 1919, when he was forty-four, he astounded his friends and fellow soldiers by leaving the army. He had little money saved—he wrote that he regretted spending it on so many dinner parties—and a small army pension. Even more uncharacteristically, he decided to run for Parliament as a Labour Party candidate, "a party whose creed and personnel," Ramsay MacDonald later wrote, "were anathema in those circles in which he had hitherto moved."[41] His decision led to three years of difficult work and two successive election losses.

Why did he decide to change his life? Was it "rare courage" as one friend suggested, or something else? Thomson himself provided a succinct answer: he wanted to do something that was worthy of Marthe Bibesco. He said as much in the roman à clef, *Smaranda*, which he wrote a few years later about her and his time in the Balkans. "She hoped at one time that I would be a successful general, one of the heroes of the war," he wrote. "It must have required effort on her part to remain loyal to a failure."[42] He loved her more desperately than ever and knew that as a career officer he could never have her. He confessed as much to her in a letter: "It is entirely because of you that I continue to spend money and, what is more important, my nervous energy on politics. I would give up all this political mud if it weren't for the fact that I am determined to prove to you—before it is too late—that I am not a failure."[43] His plans had misfired. He had not faded away entirely. In

1921 he traveled to Russia as a member of the executive of the Save the Children Fund and had tea with Lenin at his country house.[44]

But by 1923, at the age of forty-eight and with few resources, he looked more like a failure than ever—a humble freelance writer with limited prospects. Many of his old friends, who didn't like Labour politics, had turned a cold shoulder to him.[45]

What saved him was simple friendship. During his attempts to win elected office, Thomson had met Labour Party leader Ramsay MacDonald. Implausibly, the Scottish son of a housemaid and farm laborer and the blue-blooded scion of one of India's most prominent families became instant soulmates. "We shook hands, and, like David and Jonathan, that was enough, for ever after, we understood each other," MacDonald later wrote Marthe Bibesco. "It was one of those affections that require no growth. Perhaps, in some other life, we had met; perhaps our harmonies were so perfect that they required no tuning and no testing. We met for the first time as old familiars."[46]

Thomson, the new lord and cabinet minister, immediately sought out the driving force behind his political ambitions: Marthe Bibesco. Though she had kept up a correspondence, she had not seemed much interested in him in the years after he left the army. Recent attempts to meet her in Paris had failed. She was surrounded by a more or less continuous whirl of statesmen, artists, writers, and the Parisian beau monde, leaving little room for a man without resources or position. He had been left to moon over her in his small London apartment, where he worked on *Smaranda*, his autobiographical novel about his time in the Balkans. There is no evidence that he saw any other women. "A poor man should avoid women like Smaranda," he wrote despairingly. "Such women, however human they may be, are lovely pictures and need splendid frames."[47]

Marthe, a self-confessed opportunist who once wrote that she "gravitated toward power," responded quickly to his promotion. She visited him in London in early 1924. She wrote later that she enjoyed "the feeling of being with a man who has finally attained power."[48] She counseled him on the décor of his ministerial office and helped him choose a new apartment near the Houses of Parliament. We do not have a clear picture of their physical relationship. Marthe, who said she didn't like sex, still managed to have plenty of it with other men. The correspondence of the two is curiously free of any language—such as "I long to hold you"—that suggested sex. They had no shortage of opportunities.

In Paris in June 1924, Marthe underwent a hysterectomy. The operation was a success, but complications followed that threatened her life. She asked Thomson to visit her, and he did, spending an afternoon sitting at her bedside. He later wrote, "She has sent for no one else except a few members of her family." His visit moved him deeply: "I have often called her the light of my eyes, but have never realized til now how well the words describe what she was and is to me, present, or absent."[49]

Still, he did not have her full attention.

While she was writing him fond letters, she was in the midst of what was clearly a sexual affair with Henri Bertrand Léon de Jouvenel, the forty-seven-year-old editor of Le Matin, who visited her at her two Romanian palaces, where she and her husband, George—they were still married, and getting along well—entertained guests from all over Europe.[50] Jouvenel had been married to the popular writer Colette for eleven years, but the marriage had failed amid her lesbian affairs and his ongoing infidelities. At one point Marthe and Jouvenel had promised to divorce their spouses and get married. Their relationship would last for three years. At thirty-eight Marthe was still beautiful, still a fixture in literary Paris. The swooning Lord Thomson, who had designed his life and ambition around her, was still on the outside looking in.

AS AIR MINISTER and the prime minister's closest friend, Thomson found himself with enormous influence in Whitehall. He got on well with the other service chiefs, some of whom were old military friends from the Royal Military Academy, the Boer War, and the War Office. To make Thomson a cabinet minister, MacDonald had to arrange for his appointment to the House of Lords. There, as Lord Thomson of Cardington, he was well received, too. The other peers saw him as a mannered, sane, and reasonable sort of socialist, a man they could deal with. Thomson's first appearance before the House of Lords was a tour de force. He engaged in brilliant, witty, often contentious debate with his fellows and gave as good as he got, as though he had been partic- ipating in such debates for years. He was a terrific public speaker. "I have thrice heard him speak," wrote American Nobel Prize–winning novelist Sinclair Lewis, "both as a lecturer and as a politician for a seat in Parliament, and he carried everything before him with his great charm and knowledge. I have talked about him to editors like Garvin of the *Sunday Observer*, to writers like H. G. Wells, to political leaders like Ramsay MacDonald and Sidney Webb, to conservatives like Lord Queensborough, and whether or no they approve his liberal political opinions, they all like and vastly respect him."[51] No one had expected him to do so well.[52]

Thomson used his new power immediately to attack almost every part of Burney's Imperial Airship Scheme. Thomson distrusted capitalism and distrusted capitalists and wanted nothing to do with a plan to give all of the government subsidy to a large engineering conglomerate and allow the company a de facto monopoly on airship production. Thomson was a socialist, and socialists believed in government ownership of important things, and so it was with airships. (At the same time he moved forcefully to protect the fledgling Royal Air Force, order new types of planes under government contract, and expand commercial air service.)

As an alternative to the Burney plan, Thomson came up with his own radically divergent empire air scheme. The British government would build an airship of 5 million cubic feet that could take one hun- dred passengers and their baggage plus sixteen tons of cargo nonstop to Egypt, at 63 mph. She would be twice the size of anything that had ever flown. Though less extreme than Burney's plan, these were still remarkably advanced and entirely unproven concepts. The government itself would be the lead contractor, a role it had not played before. The government would also give a private contract to a Vickers subsidiary, run by Burney, for a ship of identical size and performance specifications. Thus simultaneously two competing airships would be constructed: the "socialist" ship, to be known as R101, and the "capitalist" airship, R100. Docking facilities would be built in Karachi, India; Ismailia, Egypt; and Montreal, Canada, for the use of both ships. The two ships would share a common goal of safety. So that R38's tragedy would not be repeated, R101 and R100 would be made four times as strong as they needed to be.

Thomson's plan was approved in May 1924.

Though the performance requirements were the same for the two ships, the ideas behind them were entirely different. Built under a fixed-price contract, the Vickers airship was to be a fairly orthodox aircraft based on proven zeppelin principles. There was no budget for "research" as such. R101, on the other hand, was meant to be an entirely new thing. She would be brimful with technological innovations. Her contract, as it evolved, was more what we would today call cost-plus. She would have a large budget for research and development and would receive whatever she needed, from diesel engines, which had never been used in airships, to automated controls, a new type of metal frame structure, and gasbag harnesses that were unlike anything before seen in a zeppelin.[53]

Thomson's ambition did not stop there. He wanted nothing less, he told the House of Lords on May 21, 1924, than to make Great Britain "the leading country in the world for the production of airships," to do in effect what von Zeppelin and Eckener had done in Germany, but for a new era.[54] He could fill the skies of the empire with airships, floating majestically over oceans and deserts and mountains, binding all the territories together with British technology. He had chosen the title Lord Thomson of Cardington because Cardington would be the center of this bright new industrial world and because that was how he wanted to be known to history. Once again, the violent specifics of airship history bowed to the high-flown rhetoric of empire. Problems with hydrogen as a lifting gas were set aside, as were difficulties with gasbags and covers and airship maneuvers near the ground. The R38 debacle was seen as an asset: an object lesson in how not to do it. In Thomson's vision, the mishaps of the past, including the many airship crashes in the war, were just the growing pains of a new and highly experimental technology. Airships could be made better. Airships could be made safe. Airships had the potential—as they had from their beginnings in the count's workshops—to bring national glory and triumph. Thomson's vision of a peaceful, air-linked world was romantic and internationalist. But it would be driven by *British* technology.

The lighter-than-air idea had survived, too, because the world in 1924 had not yet fully embraced heavier-than-air machines. In the years after the war some ten thousand British military airplanes had been decommissioned. No one knew quite what to do with them. New passenger airlines struggled, as did airplane makers. British airlines flew only 11,295 passengers in 1924. Airliners carried twenty passengers at best, at bumpy, lower altitudes in unpressurized cabins, and had to land frequently to refuel. Commercial air travel was noisy, cold, and perilous. One of the fixed-wing aircraft's greatest achievements in 1924 was an aerial circumnavigation of the earth by single-engine biplanes. It was astonishing to most people of the day. The details were perhaps more problematic. The 28,425-mile ordeal had taken 175 heroic days and required sixty stops. Two of the four original planes crashed en route. The heroic work of the pilots and engineers also illustrated the airplane's apparently incorrigible weakness.

That same year a German airship—one of only two big rigids then flying in the world—offered a striking contrast to the problematic airplanes. When Germany's small commercial airships *Bodensee* and *Nordstern*, built by the Zeppelin company using loopholes in the Versailles Treaty, had been seized by the Inter-Allied Council in 1920, that appeared to end the possibilities for German production. But the ever-resourceful Hugo Eckener, who had completed his evolution from humble journalist to airship captain and finally to the head of the business by taking over the Zeppelin company, had yet another idea.

He would build the Americans a state-of-the-art machine for free (using German government money), which would neatly take care of the compensation Germany owed the United States for the zeppelins destroyed after the war by sabotage. Thus the new airship was neither a reparation nor a German ship: it was *compensation*, an idea that everyone could understand. The United States had long coveted a European-built airship. The ill-fated *Roma* had been its first attempt. The second ship it wanted, L-72, was instead given to the French, who renamed it *Dixmude.* The United States had then contracted for R38, British built, but from Zeppelin models. Thrice disappointed, the Americans tried again, this time dealing directly with Eckener. With the R38 fiasco in mind, their contract specified that the Germans bore full liability for the new airship until it arrived on American shores.

Thus did Eckener's German factories once again crank into action. When the ship was finished and tested, he and a crew that included his best pilots and officers flew the gleaming LZ-126 across the Atlantic Ocean. On October 15, 1924, they landed it at Lakehurst, New Jersey. The ship—soon to be rechristened *Los Angeles*—had made the first oceanic crossing by air since R34 had done it in 1919. She had made the east-west trip in 81 hours, compared to R34's 108 hours, and had set a world record of 5,060 continuous miles of flight.

The airship's reception in America dwarfed the welcome Herbert Scott had received five years before. Though most of the crew had fought for Germany and many had bombed innocent civilians in Europe, Eckener and his men were treated as heroes. They were given a ticker-tape parade in New York City. When Eckener spoke at the Capitol Theater in Manhattan to a crowd that was one-quarter German American, the orchestra played

the German national anthem for the first time in public in the United
States since the war. Many in the crowd rose to sing along.[55] Eckener
traveled to Washington, where he met President Calvin Coolidge,
before continuing the victory tour in the West. On Eckener's stop in
Ohio, he continued talks with Goodyear about a joint-venture company
with Zeppelin to build airships in the United States. He boasted in an
interview that his company's technology would allow a traveler to fly
from Hamburg to New York in the same time that it would take to
ride the train from New York to Chicago (twenty-five hours).

Eckener became, within weeks, the most celebrated flier in the
world. No one else was even a close second. The world at large had not
yet given up on airships.

That same week another airship made a landmark flight. Like LZ-126's
transatlantic trip, this one, too, seemed to underscore the rightness of
Lord Thomson's grand vision. In 1923 the Americans had finally built
their own rigid airship, one that, like R38, was based on downed or
captured German heightclimbers, in this case mainly L-49, which had
been forced down by French pilots in October 1917 after her crew had
been overcome by altitude sickness. The *Shenandoah*, as she was called,
had been built in Lakehurst for the U.S. Navy. She was 680 feet long,
with a gas volume of 2.1 million cubic feet, and a top speed of 70 mph.
She was in most ways almost amusingly obsolete, built of recycled, six- or
seven-year-old German technology.[56] What was new about her was her
lifting gas. *Shenandoah* was the first rigid airship to use helium instead of
hydrogen. After making a series of successful shorter flights, in October
1924, as Eckener was making his transatlantic trip, the *Shenandoah* flew
from New Jersey to Seattle and back—the first flight of a rigid airship
across North America.

IN A YEAR when airships seemed to be miraculously rising from
the dead, Lord Thomson of Cardington launched the most ambitious

program of airship development in the world. By October, work had already begun to lengthen the enormous hangar in Cardington where R101 would be built. Having done this, and having set the British industrial world on a course that would end with the launch toward India six years later, Thomson almost immediately departed the scene. Nine months after it was elected—the same month that LZ-126 and the *Shenandoah* made their crossings—Ramsay MacDonald's Labour Government fell in a general election that swept Stanley Baldwin and his Conservative Party back into power. Thomson found himself once again unemployed, though still a peer in the House of Lords. The *Times* of London noted approvingly, "He is one of the best brains in the Labour Party—a thinker, a wit and, at the same time, one of the most charming of men."[57] He had not only kick-started the airship scheme. He had succeeded, with support from MacDonald, in preventing the small, financially struggling Royal Air Force from being split in two and merged into the Royal Naval Air Service and the Army Air Corps. Without Thomson, Britain might not have had a Fighter Command to defend itself during the Battle of Britain in 1940, or a Bomber Command to invade Germany.[58] He would not return as air minister for more than four years.

But his socialist airship plan remained fully active and fully funded. In spite of the dreadful track record of rigid airships and the tangled and polarized politics of postwar Britain, R101, savior of empire, lived on.

CHAPTER SEVEN

INDIA SEEMS A VERY LONG WAY

In the darkness over a storm-tossed English Channel, where waves threw enormous plumes of white foam that were visible from the control car and promenade deck, R101 struggled forward.[1] The wind was still rising and veering to the south—the direction R101 was headed on her course from London through Paris to Narbonne on the Mediterranean coast. She now faced a 44 mph gale from almost due southwest. There was no way of knowing how much the wind was gusting since weather instruments from the French stations were not capable of recording individual gusts, which could well have been as high as 70 mph.[2] The airship had started her voyage traveling at a ground speed of more than 60 mph. By the time she crossed the coastline at Hastings, she was running four engines on high throttle and barely making 40 mph. By mid-Channel her speed over ground had dropped to less than 30 mph. Could her ground speed sink to zero, as other airships had experienced? Could she be blown backward? The questions were no longer theoretical. All the while, she continued to simultaneously pitch and roll in ways no one had seen before, her enormous, waterlogged, linen-clad bow rising and dropping hundreds of feet, while she rocked side to side athwart her vertical axis as the wind played havoc with her large surface area. In these conditions, R101's first destination—Ismailia, on the Suez Canal—seemed a startlingly long way off.

Just before 10:00 p.m. the ship's lights went out, not a serious problem, but it meant that the electrician and wireless operator, a reliable ten-year airship service veteran named Arthur Disley, had to haul himself out of bed and into the ship's switch room, where masses of colored wires converged in R101's main junction box. He threw the breaker, and the lights came back on, and with them no doubt the gaiety in the smoking lounge, which had momentarily been pitch-dark. Lord Thomson and the others were enjoying their social evening. Disley then took the short walk to the control room—an interior space located just above the suspended, gondola-style control car—to speak to the on-duty wireless operator. When he got there, Disley observed something unusual: the officer of the watch, Noel Atherstone, was berating the elevator man, Leonard Oughton, whose job was to control the ship's altitude.

Disley later recalled, "I saw him [Commander Atherstone] take the elevator wheel and pull the ship up to this height.[3]

Atherstone admonished Oughton, "Don't let her go below one thousand feet!"[4]

According to Disley, the altimeter reading at the moment Atherstone seized the wheel was nine hundred feet.[5] His colleague foreman engineer Harry Leech, who had been on every flight R101 had ever made, had earlier "judged our height to be no more than eight hundred feet" and possibly "as low as seven hundred feet."[6] With the ship hunting in a four-hundred-foot arc—two hundred feet up and two hundred feet down—both men may have been right.

What was this? Atherstone, the airship's first officer, was probably the most talented airshipman on R101. The son of a Scottish merchant from a titled Polish family, Grabowsky had added his mother-in-law's maiden name to his own when he married and took that as his surname. He was known to everyone as Grabby Atherstone. He had joined the British Navy in 1913. In the early war he had served on cruisers and destroyers. In 1917 he transferred to the airship service and served, as Herbert Scott had, as pilot of a Sea Scout, escorting ship convoys and looking for U-boats.[7]

Atherstone was a natural leader and a gifted pilot of the finicky, fragile battle bags. He quickly distinguished himself. On April 7, 1918, flying Sea Scout Zero 1, based out of Capel Airship Station near Folkestone, he stalked, bombed, and destroyed a German U-boat.[8] He had leaned over the side of his gondola with a bomb in his hand and dropped it.[9] He was the only nonrigid airship pilot in the war credited with a submarine kill. He later moved up to larger North Sea–class blimps and toward the end of the war served as first officer on the 539-foot-long, Charles Campbell–designed rigid airship R29.[10] His commanding officer on that airship was Carmichael "Bird" Irwin, the tall, red-haired Irishman who would, eleven years later, command R101. Atherstone was tough, hard-nosed, coolheaded, and smart. After the war he moved to Victoria, Australia, to take up pig farming. He returned to England in 1926 when, on the recommendation of his old shipmate Bird Irwin, he was offered the chance to help fly the world's biggest aircraft to India.[11]

In R101's control car Atherstone was justifiably upset at the coxswain, but only for his lack of precision. Flying at low altitudes—fifteen hundred feet or less and often less than a thousand feet—was built into the very concept of peacetime rigid airships. Since their lifting capacity depended on how much hydrogen they contained, and since gas would automatically be vented if they climbed too high, they were flown as low as possible. To carry the 160 tons that R101 absolutely had to carry, fully laden, when fully inflated, she had a low pressure height: fifteen hundred feet.[12] (On October 4 the rain had added even more weight—as much as several tons, net of fuel burned.[13]) R101 would lose one ton of lift for every two hundred feet of rise, and a disastrous five tons for every thousand feet.[14]

What, then, of the high-flying wartime German zeppelins? Though they were structurally roughly similar to R101, they were adapted to serve a different purpose. R101 needed to bear as much weight as it could for a long distance. Zeppelins had to fly higher than fighter planes in order to survive, thus German engineers stripped out every bit of weight that wasn't necessary—including parachutes—so that the ship was so light she would easily rise with her hydrogen bags half-full. As elevation was gained, the hydrogen would expand but not hit the "pressure height"—when the bags would be so full they would have to be vented—for many thousands of feet.

For the heavily laden R101 there was no question of climbing even to three thousand feet, even though her captain, the former track star Irwin, told several crew members that he might have wanted to. "Irwin was entirely confident about reaching Ismailia," said Harry Leech, "if only he could get rather higher into steady air conditions, but this he could not do at that time without discharging fuel, which they were very anxious to conserve. All their water ballast forward had gone when leaving the tower."[15] According to Major Archibald Church, speaking in Parliament on the subject in 1931, "Again and again [R101 chief designer] Colonel Richmond and Major Scott told me that their one hope would be that they had exceptionally fine weather in going across France, so they might be able to remain comparatively near the ground, because they did not want to lose too much gas on the way, knowing what they had to confront in the latter part of their journey."[16]

So, flying high was not a choice.

Common sense tells you that flying a 777-foot aircraft at an elevation equal to her length left little margin for error. We can absolve the crew of accusations of poor judgment because they were supposed to fly low and had been trained to fly low. That did not mean it was always a good idea. That did not mean that in a strong gale on the dark, rainy night of October 4, 1930, it was a safe way to fly an unproven airship.

Flying low also assumed that the crew knew exactly how far off the ground they were. But this was rarely the case. The sole instrument they carried telling them how high they were—a barometric altimeter—was just a barometer calibrated for height. The first such products hit the market in 1928. They were nothing more than sensitive barometers, able to measure air pressure and translate that into a distance above sea level. They required constant adjustment based on weather and barometric conditions, so that the indicated altitude was the same as the true altitude. The crew of the German airship *Graf Zeppelin*, which debuted in 1928, used an altimeter but had little confidence in its reliability. "Although such an altimeter might read correctly for a short flight," wrote Harold G. Dick, who made twenty-two transatlantic airship crossings and was at one time a member of the *Graf*'s crew, "it could be in error by as much as 500 feet if, for example, the airship moved from a high pressure area to a low pressure area. Such error could not be tolerated when making a landing maneuver, at night or in thick weather."[17]

To keep its altimeter honest, the *Graf*'s crew (and later the *Hindenburg*'s) used a nonbarometric apparatus known as an Echolot, which featured a gun firing blank cartridges to the ground from a sleeve in the control car, and a device to measure the time until the return of the sound from the ground. Since this tended to annoy passengers, at night the *Graf*'s crew dropped empty water bottles, timing their fall with a stopwatch.[18] They did this obsessively, checking altitude with the Echolot or bottles *every morning, midday, and evening and also just before landing.*[19]

At any given moment, R101 might be flying several hundred feet lower than she thought she was. If she had been flying at, say, three thousand feet, that distance would have meant little. Under one thousand feet was a different matter. There was simply less room for an airship to save itself.[20] An inexperienced crew—which would describe most of R101's flying company—only underscored the dangers of leaving a small margin for flight error. In the year before R101's India flight her crew had done a scant five days of flying trials for a ten-thousand-mile round trip. Prior to that, none of her officers and crew had flown for the previous three years, while First Officer Atherstone had not flown since his assignment to R29 in 1919 and Second Officer Maurice Steff had not flown in an airship at all.[21] Compared to German crews, British airshipmen had little experience: something over three thousand total hours since 1916 against more than fifty thousand hours for the Germans.[22]

The crew in any case had no choice. Low-altitude flying was, along with hydrogen gas, outsize surface areas, fragile gasbags, and ultrathin outer covers, another of the built-in flaws of the descendants of Count von Zeppelin's first rigid airships.

R101 SOLDIERED ON. Because the wind was on her quarter, she naturally drifted from her plotted course. And because knowing how much she was being blown off and how to compensate was important, navigator Ernest Johnston employed a primitive but effective technique. Between ten and eleven o'clock Johnston dropped seven pyrotechnic calcium flares by hand from the open window of the control car. The flares were activated by water and detonated in a pulse of brilliant light when they hit the sea and kept burning. They allowed Johnston to both measure wind speed over the sea and calculate drift. Any passengers watching from the promenade windows would have seen a spectacular sight on the dark surface of the water. It apparently occurred to no one that the conspicuous presence of highly flammable flares in the ship's control car might be a potential problem. At least, there is no record of it, though R101's builders had taken enormous care to ensure that nothing on board could create a spark of any kind. No matches or lighters were allowed outside the hermetically sealed smoking lounge. Precautions had even been taken to ensure that crew members' boots could not create sparks when they touched the ship's girders. Yet R101 carried a large store of highly combustible flares. Presumably designers did not see how flares ignited by water could possibly detonate in the dry interior of the airship. Along with many other incorrect calculations of risk, the notion that water could not penetrate the control car would also turn out to be wrong.

As the ship crossed sixty-six miles of the English Channel, Johnston, regarded as one of the best navigators in Britain of both airplanes and airships, now turned his attention to the airship's immediate future. The storm had changed his calculations. The original plan had been to fly to Paris, then continue south, flying through Tours and Toulouse to Narbonne, where she would take a sharp left at the coast and continue over the Mediterranean toward Egypt. But the wind argued otherwise. The wind on that course meant dead-slow speed, rapid fuel consumption, and the likelihood that Lord Thomson would miss his precious state dinner in Egypt. The breeze was edging ever more toward the south. R101 would be bucking it all the way to the Mediterranean. More of the same labored progress, more of the same weird pitching and rolling.

Then came a wire from the Meteorological Office that seemed to offer the sort of hope that had been missing in earlier forecasts. The message, which was acknowledged by R101's wire room at 9:52 p.m., reported, "Winds over western and central Mediterranean light and variable with fair weather." The eastern Mediterranean, it said, was mainly fair with northerly winds and a few local showers. This must have been good news. One imagines a whoop or two and possibly some words of congratulation. Once through France, R101 should have clear sailing. France was the obstacle.

But how to get through France?

Two minutes later the answer arrived from the heart of Maurice Giblett's reporting system in Cardington:

Serial No. 5. To R101 from Meteor, Airships, Bedford.
Forecast Paris—Dijon—Lyons. Wind westerly, 25 to 30 mph at 2,000 feet. Lyons to Marseille, wind variable and light. Cloudy with cloud base 1,000 to 2,000 feet.

The news suggested that a route taking R101 *east* of Paris, through Dijon and down the Rhône Valley—sweeping around the weather—

would avoid headwinds altogether. By shifting eastward, the ship would have a tailwind to Dijon and comparatively light winds after that. There was just one problem with the new route. Northwest of Dijon lay the famous wine-producing region known as the Cote d'Or, where wooded ridges rose nearly to two thousand feet, and this elevated ground was shrouded in low-lying fog. R101 would have to vent gas, exactly what Scott had said he did not want to do. Thus the choice: low ground and high headwinds on the route from Paris to Narbonne, or tailwinds and fog-draped high ground via the Rhône Valley.[23]

Which meant that Scott had another decision to make. He would have to make it in consultation with Captain Irwin, First Officer Atherstone, and navigator Johnston. But in the end the call would be Scott's. Wire operator Arthur Disley observed the legendary airshipman climbing down into the control car sometime after ten o'clock. Coming from the smoking lounge, which was on the lower level of the airship right next to the control room, Scott did not have far to walk. He was likely asked to respond to the weather reports. What did he think?

Scott was probably well into his cups by then, though just how drunk he was we cannot know for certain. Sir Peter Masefield, a leading figure in Britain's post–World War II aviation industry and the twentieth century's leading authority on R101, was personally acquainted with many of the British airship people and believed he knew. Though he spared Herbert Scott from most criticism in his 1982 book on R101, only obliquely mentioning his drinking problem, Masefield later admitted in his correspondence that he had left out many factual details.*

"By 1929 he had deteriorated seriously and his confreres accepted that, from lunchtime onwards, he was ineffective as a result of drink," Masefield wrote in June 1982 to his friend Lord Frank Beswick, former deputy leader of the House of Lords. "It is a fact that Scott took Ernest Johnston and Maurice Steff off to lunch with him at the Bridge Hotel

---

* Masefield's book was *To Ride the Storm*.

in Bedford at frequent intervals, and that, on the day of the departure for India, they all came back 'the worse for wear.' "[24]

Scott, as noted by the editor of *Flight* magazine, was slurring his words just before R101 departed at 6:36 p.m., many hours after his wet lunch at the Bridge Hotel. He had sat down to dinner with his fellow passengers at 7:30. Dinner came with wine followed by port and brandy. There was no shortage of alcohol on board. By 10:30 p.m. he would have had three additional hours to drink, smoke, and socialize with his peers. There is little reason to suppose he would have abstained.

"As for Johnston and Scott, not only would they both have been dead tired after midnight," said Sir Alfred Pugsley, a technical officer at the Royal Airship Works, in an interview, ". . . but knowing both of them, I am sure that, after a celebratory dinner on board, neither would have been in condition to contribute to the flight further that night. Scott was, I am sorry to say, a complete dipsomaniac by the latter part of 1930."[25] Unlike Scott, Johnston was on duty until 11:00 p.m.

What this meant for the fate of R101 is impossible to know. Would a sober Scott, advised by a sober Johnston, still have decided to challenge the storm? As the weather worsened over the English Channel, would they have held to that decision? Absent the enormous political pressure to meet the Egypt and India deadlines, the sensible thing to do would have been to delay departure. No one who has studied the R101 case in the last ninety years has disagreed with that.

The good news: France loomed just ahead.

More good news: at 10:56 p.m. the engine in the aft car, which had gone out, was fixed and restored to full power.

The ship would need every bit of it.

CHAPTER EIGHT

SHE FLOATS FREE

R101 is making her debut. The date is—mark this—October 2, 1929. That is *five and a half years* from the date she was approved for construction. Five and a half years of what one exasperated member of Parliament calls "an eternity of delays." That is two years and ten months beyond the date she was originally supposed to have flown to India.[1] (For perspective, German workers could build a zeppelin in less than a month during the war.[2]) The delay has so many causes—from labor strikes to balky technology to whimsical policy shifts at Whitehall—that it is impossible to enumerate them all.

So much time has passed that Christopher Birdwood Thomson, out of office for five years, has had time to reinvent himself as chairman of the Royal Aeronautical Society, the center of British private aviation; become an active dissenter in the House of Lords; rekindle his desperately unequal affair with Marthe Bibesco; and, most significant, return to his old job as secretary of state for air in a new Labour government. Labour was back in power because Great Britain was, in the middle and latter 1920s, becalmed in a sea of unemployment. The country's staple industries—shipbuilding, iron and steel, coal mining, and cotton textiles—had never recovered from the devastations of war. In a general strike in 1926, 1.7 million workers went out, shocking the government and everyone else. During Thomson's time out of the cabinet, Charles Lindbergh crossed the Atlantic and touched off a wild expansion in heavier-than-air flying. The giant, helium-filled American airship *Shenandoah* had been torn apart by violent updrafts in an Ohio thunderstorm. She went down in a gruesome, twisting fall from six thousand feet, demonstrating how ill adapted airships are to North American thunderstorms and why helium is not the airship cure-all the Americans thought it might be. So much time has passed that the British people have largely forgotten about British airships. They have forgotten about the touted competition between the "socialist airship" and the "capitalist airship," and even the Imperial Airship Scheme, which was the reason these vessels were supposedly necessary in the first place. The process has been exhausting, infuriating, and expensive.

But here she is, at last, the magnificent R101, floating on her own inside her gargantuan shed at Cardington, a vessel so large that the human beings who witness her for the first time can scarcely comprehend her scale. The Air Ministry has invited the press to view the finished product before she flies, and the press has trooped over, brimming with enthusiasm as though the Shroud of Turin were about to be unveiled. Two hundred of them from national, regional, and overseas papers and magazines have shown up. The ship has been prettied up for the occasion: new paint, linen tablecloths for the dining room, deck chairs for the promenades, ferns, flower arrangements, and thoughtfully placed blotters for the writers.[3]

As the reporters listen, the airship's designer, Vincent Richmond, reviews R101's credentials. Richmond is compact, modest, quiet, and benevolent, with dark hair and dark eyes, and projects an air of solidity, of reliability. Because he did important work in the war in the use of dope (celluloid varnish) on the fabric of nonrigid airships, he is widely known, in a friendly way, as Dope or Dopey. His airship, he explains, is the largest ever constructed: 732 feet long, 132 feet wide.* She is by displacement almost twice the size of the SS *Leviathan* of United States Lines, the largest ocean liner in the world, and twice as fast. Richmond reminds his audience of R101's remit, dating from 1924: she and her sister ship, R100—the latter is in Howden, in Yorkshire—were to have

---

* Note: these measurements were taken before the airship's enlargement in 1930.

1

CHRISTOPHER BIRDWOOD THOMSON, SECRETARY OF STATE FOR AIR: He envisioned a world in which fleets of lighter-than-air ships floated serenely through the skies of the British Empire, linking everything British in a new space-time continuum. R101 would attempt to prove his vision by flying successfully to India and back.

2

GEORGE HERBERT SCOTT (LEFT) AND ERNEST L. JOHNSTON: They were buddies and shipmates, part of the hard-drinking culture of the British naval airship service. Scott was considered to be the best airship commander in England, and Johnston was thought to be the best navigator. Together they plotted R101's course to India.

3

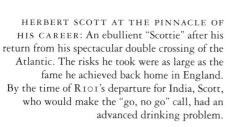

HERBERT SCOTT AT THE PINNACLE OF HIS CAREER: An ebullient "Scottie" after his return from his spectacular double crossing of the Atlantic. The risks he took were as large as the fame he achieved back home in England. By the time of R101's departure for India, Scott, who would make the "go, no go" call, had an advanced drinking problem.

4

ONE OF EUROPE'S GREAT
BEAUTIES: During World War I,
Christopher Thomson met and fell
in love with a real-life fairy-tale
Romanian princess named Marthe
Bibesco. With her striking looks,
sparkling literary talent, aristocratic
rank, and fluency in French, she
became the toast of Belle Époque
Paris. She stepped off the Orient
Express and into a world that
immediately loved her. Marcel
Proust wrote a poem to her.

5

MARTHE BIBESCO AND HER DAUGHTER,
VALENTINA: Though Marthe was married to a
prince and raising a daughter, she managed to have
love affairs with several prominent men in Europe in
addition to her ultimately tragic relationship with
Lord Thomson.

6

THE "SLEEPING WATERS" OF MOGOŞOAIA: Marthe Bibesco's eighteenth-century Venetian
palace in Romania, where she entertained the beau monde of Europe. She restored it herself,
financing the improvements largely with her own substantial earnings from her published books.

7

THE MAN IN CHARGE OF BUILDING AND
FLYING R101: Reginald Colmore was perhaps
more responsible than anyone else for R101's
institutional failures. In the dapper forty-three-
year-old's world, good news was pulsed out in
banner headlines, while bad news was bottled
up, compartmentalized, and buried.

8

BRITISH PRIME MINISTER RAMSAY MACDONALD:
Lord Thomson's best friend and staunch political ally.
MacDonald wanted Thomson to take over as viceroy of
India, the biggest job in the British empire, where he
would rule over 319 million people and live in a 340-room,
200,000-square-foot Edwardian baroque palace in Delhi,
the largest residence of any head of state in the world.

9

MICHAEL ROPE, R101'S TALENTED BUT
INEXPERIENCED DESIGNER: The shy
engineer found that the airship's outer cover was
so badly rotted that he sent an extraordinary
memo to his bosses, telling them bluntly
that the cover's condition meant that "there
is no margin of safety for flight in a rough
atmosphere." He recommended that they delay
the flight. They refused.

THE FIRST GERMAN RIGID AIRSHIP, OVER LAKE CONSTANCE, 1900: The primitive, pencil-shaped ship was ungainly and underpowered. On her first flight her controls failed and she landed back in the lake. Critics judged the first "zeppelin" to be useless.

COUNT FERDINAND VON ZEPPELIN: He intended his radical, metal-framed airships to be used as weapons of war. After several unsuccessful attempts at flight, he was considered a failure. Many would have added modifiers: a clownish, bumbling failure, a caricature of a hopelessly inept inventor. He seemed, too, to be from another world, a place more like a feudal kingdom than Europe of La Belle Époque.

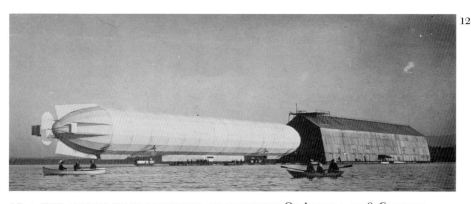

LZ-4, THE AIRSHIP THAT LAUNCHED AN INDUSTRY: On August 4, 1908, Count von Zeppelin attempted to fly LZ-4 continuously for twenty-four hours. But LZ-4 never made it. She was destroyed in a hydrogen-fueled explosion. The German people responded, unaccountably, by making the count a national hero and showering him with money. At age seventy he became the hottest entrepreneur in Europe.

13

SEARCHLIGHTS FIND A ZEPPELIN OVER LONDON: Zeppelins were the world's first long-range bombers. They introduced to humanity the notion that it could be obliterated from the sky by something other than a thunderbolt.

14

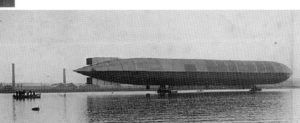

15

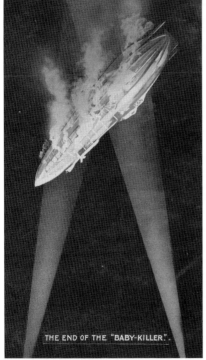

THE ILL-FATED *MAYFLY*: Winston Churchill called the first British airship the *Won't Fly*, and with good reason. Cobbled together from the sketchiest of jury-rigged submarine technology and early zeppelin design, she broke in half on her first flight in 1911 and stalled the British airship program for five years.

16

THE END OF THE "BABY-KILLER".

WARTIME BRITISH POSTER OF A ZEPPELIN IN FLAMES: The long-range zeppelin bombers came at night and released their bombs from great heights, terrorizing people across Europe. Most of their attacks took place in England. The war changed when British fighters learned to shoot the hydrogen-filled German airships down with incendiary bullets.

GERMANY'S BRILLIANT HUGO ECKENER: This stout, undistinguished economics writer became the heir to Count Ferdinand von Zeppelin and the driving force behind the German airship industry. He was acknowledged by all to be the greatest airship pilot in history.

17

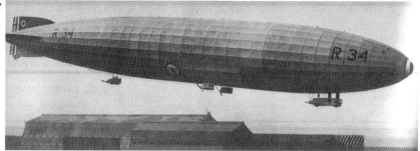

THE LEGENDARY R34: In 1919, with Major Herbert Scott in command, she became only the second aircraft to cross the Atlantic, but the first to cross east to west and the first to make a double crossing. Though she had been built to mimic the German superzeppelins, she was in no way qualified to make such voyages and courted peril all the way.

18

CHARLES IVOR RAE CAMPBELL, GREAT BRITAIN'S GREAT IMITATOR: Unable to keep up with the Germans, British designers under Campbell stole their designs. They studied downed zeppelins and resorted to industrial espionage. Campbell's ultimate project, R38, which supposedly had the speed and climbing ability of the superzeppelins, went down in a horrifying crash.

19

THE TRAGEDY OF R38: She was sleek, rounded, technologically sophisticated, Great Britain's bid for airship glory. But she was terribly flawed. In 1921, over the river Humber, she cracked open like an egg and fell burning into the water, killing forty-four of forty-nine crew.

20

AMERICA'S BID FOR AIRSHIP GLORY: The helium-filled, 785-foot-long *Akron*, launched a year after the crash of R101, was the most technologically advanced airship ever built. She was destroyed in a thunderstorm off the coast of New Jersey, having demonstrated one of the greatest weaknesses of airships: they could not land in a storm. Seventy-three of seventy-six crew died, the greatest airship disaster in history.

THE CRASH OF THE USS *SHENANDOAH*: She was copied from a downed German zeppelin. Though most of her technology was obsolete, she was the first rigid airship to use helium instead of hydrogen. That didn't save her from being torn apart in an Ohio thunderstorm, plummeting in a gruesome, twisting fall from six thousand feet.

THE *GRAF ZEPPELIN* OVER BRAZIL: In the late 1920s the German *Graf* was the airborne symbol of everything the British aspired to and had failed to achieve. While R101 and R100 languished in their sheds, the *Graf* astounded the world with her swashbuckling exploits and globe-spanning flights. Her crew was given a ticker-tape parade in New York City.

23

A "BATTLEBAG": Unlike metal-framed rigid airships, wartime blimps were frameless balloons filled with gas. They could carry only small crews but were useful in spotting U-boats. This one, Parseval No. 4, was once commanded by Herbert Scott, who made a name for himself escorting British ships carrying the British Expeditionary Force across the English Channel.

hydrogen gas volumes of 5 million cubic feet, cruise at 63 mph, and be able to carry up to one hundred passengers on transcontinental flights of up to thirty-six hundred miles. R100 was to be a conventional design, using mostly tried-and-true practices, many directly from zeppelins. R101 was to be experimental, loaded up with new and untested technology, and far more expensive than R100.

The two ships have met those expectations. R100 is a tricked-out version of the past. R101 is the glorious future. Thomson, after all, has not chosen to be Lord *Howden*. Richmond ticks off a list of R101's innovations. They include power-assisted rudder and elevators, pre-doped outer cover, ventilation holes in bow and tail, a backup control room in the tail, deep-V ring transverse frames, double-parachute gasbag restraints, small tail fins, diesel engines, ventilation "gills," rain catchment systems, hinged reefing girders, heated passenger cabins, smoking room, siphon-operated gas valves, stainless steel structure, steam-fed kitchen cooking unit, low-water-consumption toilets, dumbwaiter, and pneumatic fuel and ballast-water distribution systems.[4] He then makes what seems to some of the reporters an odd point: that these huge ships must be flown low to get the best economic results, fifteen hundred feet or lower. Flying higher, he says, means they can't lift as much weight. "One can add," Richmond jokes, "that flying low in an airship offers a splendid view of the ground or the sea." The reporters don't quite understand this, but Richmond goes on anyway. When R101 arrives in Egypt, he says, she will lose about ten tons of lift just due to the lower density of the air.[5] Even the trade press would have trouble quickly calculating the meaning of such a loss.

Richmond moves on to safety, which everyone understands because the reference point is so clearly the colossal British disaster of R38. Concern for safety is the driving force behind the design of R101. The stainless steel skeleton is *four times stronger* than it needs to be. Her diesel engines, the first used in any aircraft, offer an all-new form of safety, too. Fumes from gasoline engines are considered dangerously flammable, especially in hot-weather zones where R101 is going, while diesel fuel—heavy oil—has an extremely high flash point. While those things are true, the danger to airships from gas engines is mostly theoretical, unproven by heavier-than-air flight or any other mechanized process and later completely disproven by the successful flight of thousands of heavier-than-air craft in the tropics.[6] (Also, diesels require gasoline-powered starter motors.) In their hearts Richmond and his boss, Britain's director of airship development, Reggie Colmore, do not believe that diesels are absolutely necessary and later admit as much, saying in a memo to the Air Ministry that they had "no technical objection" to "the use of petrol engines in hot climates" and that "we do not think that there would be any more risk of fire than from the existing petrol tanks in the power cars."[7] But R101 is supposed to be the technological leader, and this is new technology, which is what everyone wants. So they humor the technocrats. The trade-off is weight, and that is the problem: R101's diesels, which have been adapted from railroad locomotives, are a great deal heavier than conventional gasoline-burning engines. The whole idea of taking locomotive diesels and dropping them into weight-sensitive lighter-than-air ships lives on the border between experimental and wildly impractical. In most ways, they are exactly what you would not want.

Richmond brings the subject back to weight. He is obviously thinking about the subject. He is also lying to the assembled press or, if not quite lying, withholding critical information. Less than twenty-four hours earlier he had received what would be, for an airship designer on the eve of a launch, the worst news possible. On September 30, R101 underwent her first "lift and trim" trials. The ship was "ballasted up" to a state of equilibrium—floated inside her shed—and the weights carefully examined. R101's weight goals are relatively straightforward: the ship itself, including the engines, is supposed to weigh 90 tons. Based on her lifting capacity of roughly 150 tons, that leaves some 60 tons available for so-called disposable lift: fuel, water ballast, crew, passengers and baggage, supplies, and cargo.

On the following day, October 1, the results are tallied. To the astonishment of everyone at Cardington, the true weight of the airship is *113.4 tons*, an increase of 23.4 tons—26 percent—over the target weight.[8] Richmond thought the ship would be heavier than expected.[9] But he foresaw nothing like this.[10] R101's actual weight leaves only 38.2 tons for everything that isn't nailed down. With the expected ten-ton loss of lift in the tropics—meaning she could really only lift 28.2 tons—one does not need to be an aeronautical genius to know that R101 is never going to Egypt or India. Either she is going to have to lose fifteen tons of weight or gain that much lift. A third alternative, building another one or two enormously expensive mooring masts along the way—in Gibraltar, Baghdad, or Malta, for instance—seems entirely out of reach. The impact of this engineering disaster, after more than five years and a large expenditure of money, cannot be overstated.[11] Richmond and Colmore would have known immediately that they had failed, at a fundamental level, to fulfill their brief. A great deal more time and money would have to be spent to get R101 to India. They knew, even as the reporters were streaming into the Royal Airship Works on that October morning, and even as Richmond was singing his airship's praises, that the very structure of the ship would have to be changed.

Richmond doesn't breathe a word of this. He is all smiles. The reporters are taken inside the great airship in groups of twenty, where, as Noel Atherstone wrote in his diary, "they swarmed like earwigs all over everything."[12] They ogle the luxury accommodations and the faux–Pullman car trim and the shiny new technology. For anyone who has not seen it before—and that means most of England—the first experience of R101 is pure wonder. In their stories, many of the reporters reflect a deep sense of national pride. They believe that the British government has delivered a well-designed aircraft. "The Press seems to have bought the idea alright," noted Atherstone, "judging from the pictures and columns of journalese which has been let loose."[13]

Other reporters are less taken by the aircraft's obvious allure. "The interior of the airship affords some striking contrasts," according to the correspondent for the *Scotsman*.

> At one moment the eye is confronted with a vista of silver metalwork, girders in crisscross patterns suggesting a contraption evolved with the pieces of a mammoth Meccano set. It all looks like an ambitious toy rather than an airship designed to link continent and continent. This suggestion of the "home-made toy" on a large scale is strengthened by the flimsy look of the outer cover and tangle of wires and balloon nets. . . . The furniture of the lounge and dining room and the fittings of these apartments have an air of great solidity until it is revealed that the handrails are of hollowed wood, the mahogany tops of the tables are of veneer, and the timber used is in fact balsa wood.[14]

The correspondent for the *Dundee Evening Telegraph* dismisses the new ship as underpowered and too slow: "At the outset she is condemned to be the plaything of the elements." He added, "One cannot help feeling that R101 will not justify the large amount of money that has been spent on her."[15]

For the moment—and the moment cannot last long—the weight revelations will remain a secret. A mixture of rumor and fact has been flying for several years about R101's supposed weight problems. As early as August 1927, R101's engineers had discovered that she was five tons too heavy for an overseas flight and suggested major weight reductions.[16] In 1928 the parliamentary gadfly Frank Rose, member of the House of Commons for Aberdeen North, was already asking questions about R101's "fixed weights that are not to exceed ninety tons." He calculated that R101 would weigh "twenty-eight tons more than her gross lift." He was wrong about that, but he had the right idea. The message was, R101 is too heavy. Put another way, and this is far closer to the truth, *R101 does not have enough lift.* As though to authenticate this heresy, Sir Charles Dennistoun Burney this same month—October 1929—publishes a book, *The World, the Air, and the Future*, in which he bizarrely dismisses the value of his own project. He states that the two airships, R100 and R101, are already failures in their mission to fly overseas, and that they can never work commercially. "He says that the only possibility of building an airship with any chance of success," echoed another House of Commons gadfly, Cecil L'Estrange Malone, "is to build an airship twice the size of R100 and R101—an airship of ten million cubic feet capacity."[17]

Which is another way of saying what Reggie Colmore and Dope Richmond and their bosses in the celestial reaches of Whitehall are soon going to have to admit—that R101 does not have nearly enough lift to make it to India.

THE ROAD TO THAT EVENTFUL DAY in the autumn of 1929— and the discovery of such a calamitous engineering error—was long and difficult. When Christopher Thomson replaced Dennistoun Burney's empire scheme with his own back in 1924, he had done it through tense and often bitter negotiations, the end of which was an inspired compromise. The private sector, in the form of the Airship Guarantee Company, a Vickers subsidiary, would get a contract to build R100 and a chance to show what capitalism, free from government meddling, could do. Burney would oversee the ship's construction. In R101 the socialists would get their heavily subsidized experimental prototype. The competition was going to be friendly, Thomson said. Information would be shared. Cooperation between the two staffs would be encouraged. Synergies would spring up. Pints would be consumed in a spirit of brotherhood. When the ships were built and tested, the best components and practices from both prototypes would become the basis for a series of production airships that would fulfill Thomson's ultimate dream: populating the skies of empire with British technology. The new fleet would operate between England and India, Australia, South Africa, and Canada. The plan was quintessential Thomson: a blend of political pragmatism and starry-eyed idealism.

The two sides repaired to their respective factories in Cardington, where R101 would be built, and Howden, 125 miles due north, the home of R100. They began their designs, tests, and calculations. They would spend 1926 and 1927 designing and engineering the ships, and 1928 and 1929 building them.

From the project's earliest days, however, it was apparent that Thomson's grand plan was naïve, impractical, and self-defeating. It was exactly what Great Britain should not have done. Dennistoun Burney's original concept for a single airship prototype, followed later on by five more ships, had contained many individual flaws, which included his exaggerated claims of airship performance and the probability that the British government was handing Vickers an outright monopoly.

Thomson's idea, on the other hand, had one stupendous flaw: by creating two prototypes instead of one, it stretched the already razor-thin ranks of British airship experts to the breaking point and beyond. Britain had produced few airships—14 to German's 150.[18] More problematic still, a large part of the country's airship knowledge and expertise had died aboard R38 with chief designer Charles I. R. Campbell.[19] Engineers had quit when the government nationalized the Short Brothers works at Cardington after the war, and even more quit when the airship program was discontinued in 1921.[20] The few remaining naval constructors who had worked on R38 had the wrong kind of experience.

Which left few people in the country with the physical experience of constructing a large rigid airship. That field of expertise was rapidly vanishing. "The number of available people who could honestly be called experts could be counted on the fingers of two hands," wrote the R101's navigator's son, the airship historian Ernest A. Johnston, who knew some of them personally.[21]

The problem was concentrated in Cardington, where the most difficult technical work would be done. Considering the size, complexity, and cost of the project, the lack of airship-building experience was breathtaking. The director of airship development—the man in charge of both projects—was Group Captain Peregrine Fellowes, who had plenty of air force experience with airplanes but knew nothing at all about airships.[22] His assistant Reginald Colmore had commanded a nonrigid blimp station during the war, but knew nothing of the construction of rigids. R101's chief designer, Vincent Richmond, who would have to sign off on every girder, rivet, and gas cell, had studied physics—not mathematics, which is necessary to design airships—at the Royal College of Science and had worked after graduation building docks. He had made his name in the war as an expert on the cloth covers of small, nonrigid blimps and military balloons. In 1919 he helped an Allied commission oversee the destruction of German military aviation capability, which included the surrender of airships. This experience, plus seeing Eckener's *Bodensee* during its brief commercial career, hooked Richmond on big rigids. After the war he joined the staff of the British Air Ministry and specialized in the study of airships, even as they were being abandoned by his own government. He was soon lecturing on airship design at the Imperial College of Science. He helped write the specifications for R100 and R101. By 1924 he had moved to the center of British airship affairs—a small, depopulated, and demoralized place.[23]

But none of this qualified Richmond to lead R101's design team. He had not studied engineering in college. He had never built an airship. His own staff at Cardington wondered aloud how he had possibly qualified for that job. Richmond's closest associate on the design team, Harold Roxbee Cox, who admired him, described his boss as a likable man and a competent physicist. "He was not, however, an engineer," wrote Cox in his autobiography. "He had been associated with the design of non-rigid airships but had no experience of rigid airship design. . . . To balance gaps in his engineering knowledge he had as his chief assistant a person of great brilliance and charm."[24]

This was Michael Rope, who was indeed bright and talented but, like Richmond, had never built a rigid airship. He had studied engineering at Birmingham University, then worked on locomotives for a railway company. His airship experience was limited to designing small, inexpensive Sea Scout–class blimps during the war, which were assembled in weeks. From 1921 to 1924 he was stationed with the Royal Air Force in Baghdad, a city that had never even seen a rigid airship.[25]

The list of airship novices went on. One of R101's principal outside consultants, Richard Southwell, the well-regarded professor of engineering science at Oxford's Brasenose College, had never built an airship or consulted on one. Nor had engine whiz Thomas Cave-Browne-Cave. Nor had John North, of the subcontractor Boulton & Paul, a mathematician of high ability and a leading expert on metal airplane construction, who would produce all the girders and joints. All of these men were exceptionally talented in their fields, which did not include airship construction. Cox himself was a raw novice with an engineering doctorate. Still, he knew enough to be astounded to find engineers on the R101 project using flexible rulers to analyze the profile of the airship's hull. Cox politely explained to them that he could do that with mathematics.

The R100 project faced the same shortage of talent, but with one enormous difference. The chief designer on R100—Richmond's counterpart—was Barnes Neville Wallis, the man widely regarded in England as the foremost authority on airships and the engineer with the most experience designing and building them. He had gone to school at Christ's Hospital, a leading British public school, and left at the age of seventeen for several apprenticeships in shipbuilding. He joined Vickers in 1913 and was appointed chief airship designer in 1916. He worked on the British airships No. 9 and R23. He also personally designed the smaller scale R80 (535 feet), the first truly streamlined British airship and one that contained a number of uniquely British innovations.[26] (He would later become one of Great Britain's most famous military engineers, inventor of the "bouncing bomb," which the RAF used with spectacular success against the industrial Ruhr Valley.) R80 was not perfect, nor was Wallis. On her first trial flight in 1920, superheating caused R80 to shoot up to four thousand feet, damaging girders and bending the ship in the middle. She was repaired, used briefly to train Americans for R38, then shelved like everything else after the R38 crash.[27] Still, R80 was thought to be the most effective and innovative British airship design.

Wallis was brilliant, difficult, moody, irascible, and uncompromising. He did not suffer fools gladly. He barely even suffered his children. Early in the project he had refused to work with R101's designers because of his contempt for their credentials and abilities. He had been outraged when the government gave Burney's Airship Guarantee Company, and thus Wallis himself, a secondary role in the Imperial Airship Scheme. He did not believe that Vincent Richmond had any aptitude or ability qualifying him to design a large rigid airship. To Wallis, Richmond was a dope and fabric expert, that was all. "I have never been able to understand the mentality of Scott, Richmond, Colmore and Nixon [Sidney, the chief administrative officer at the Royal Airship Works in Cardington]," Wallis wrote to his biographer in later years. "Not one of them had ever built or been responsible for the building of a Rigid Airship. It seems as though they had not the faintest notion that no man can perform a great engineering task successfully unless he has started at the very bottom of the ladder of experience."[28] Wallis had known Scott a long time. Scott had once crashed a nonrigid airship with Wallis aboard, a harrowing experience that Wallis never forgot. Though he had affection for Scott, Wallis also knew exactly how much gin Scott drank and found it distasteful. Though Scott was officially a flier, not a designer, his habits did not improve Wallis's opinion of the R101 project.[29]

Wallis's deep, and mostly unmerited, disdain for R101's designers—a number of them would go on to become prominent engineers—and his belief that collaboration would involve handing over work that belonged to Vickers, meant that virtually no information was shared.[30] He refused to cooperate even when Vincent Richmond and Reggie Colmore offered to share technical information that might have helped R100. In 1927, when Richmond sent Wallis the details of a new automatic valve the R101 team had developed, Wallis replied dismissively, "Naturally I suppose every designer prefers his own ideas and I should not be sincere if on the whole I did not still prefer the arrangement we have worked out for R100."[31] In the five years of construction neither chief designer paid a single visit to the other's works.[32]

Not only was there no cooperation, there was active jealousy, bitterness, and animosity between the two teams, inspired at least in part by Wallis's scornful condescension. This caused constant problems for the Air Ministry. "As construction progressed," wrote Samuel Hoare, who succeeded Thomson in 1924 as secretary of state for air, "what was no doubt intended as a friendly competition tended to become a hindering rivalry. I tried my best to keep the peace and to hold the balance between the two centres of construction, but it was not an easy task. For the next five years there was scarcely a day on which awkward problems connected with the double programme did not arise."[33]

Even worse for brotherly colloquy, R101 got most of the attention along with the lion's share of articles in the British media, much of it generated by Lord Thomson's energetic press office. "At times it seemed that every newspaper we picked up had a column describing the wonders of R101," wrote Nevil Shute Norway, the later-renowned novelist who was Wallis's chief stress calculator, "ending with a brief sentence that R100 was also being built at Howden. Our puny efforts at a counterblast could not compete with the Air Ministry press department."[34] R100's critics in Parliament insisted that R100's staff was leaking "continual propaganda . . . to the press that the Cardington ship was no good."[35]

Since Wallis and his team would not cooperate, R101's technical people were forced to muddle through on their own or with help from outside consultants who had themselves never built an airship. The task must at times have seemed overwhelming. R101's technical people were attempting to build from scratch an airship twice the size of anything that had ever flown, a feat of mechanical engineering that would require calculations that had never before been done on any airship. R101's structural plan would have to allow for unprecedented loads imposed by extensive internal passenger quarters, engines that weighed far more than any ever used on an airship, five external engine cars, fuel tanks, ballast, as well as the stresses caused by the movements of up to 150 people. Her design would have to accommodate the variable lift of the ship's many gas cells, the aerodynamics of its six-acre cover, and the effects of turbulence.[36] That they would not get it right the first time was almost a foregone conclusion.

THUS WORK BEGAN at Howden and Cardington on Great Britain's most ambitious engineering project. The Howden airship station, which had been the launching point for R38 on its ill-fated final flight, had fallen into disrepair since its closure in 1921. By 1925, the enormous shed stood alone on a desolate heath, surrounded by ruins of other sheds—an apt symbol of the airships' fall from grace. The massive building contained two bays—each capable of housing an airship that was 750 feet long and 240 feet wide. When the new occupants arrived, they found "the floor of the great shed littered at one end with the feathers and remains of many hens: a vixen had had her lair for years in the covered concrete trench beneath the floor that had housed the hydrogen and water mains. . . . Rabbits infested the enormous piles of steel and concrete debris formed by the demolition of other hangars; partridges, hares, and duck were common on the aerodrome."[37]

The shed was renovated and new buildings constructed. Soon workers began to flow in from the countryside of East Yorkshire. Many came from farms and were trained to do simple riveting and mass production work. Sixty percent of the workforce were women, whose jobs ranged from stitching and repairing fabric to working as messengers, clerks, and cooks. To the snobbish, Oxford-educated Nevil Shute Norway, these farm girls were "brutish and uncouth, filthy in appearance and habits . . . and incredibly foul-mouthed. We very soon had to employ a welfare worker to look after them because promiscuous intercourse was going on merrily in every dark corner."[38] As work on R100 got underway, the town of Howden soon returned to prosperity and became the destination of all manner of official visitors, curious to see what was taking shape in the "capitalist" camp.[39] They were so numerous that Barnes Wallis and his wife, Molly, complained about having to entertain so many of them.[40]

At Cardington, too, the airship station was reopened after years of lying fallow. Its workforce streamed in from the countryside, many by bicycle, and designers and engineers worked furiously to develop their new airship. But in the latter 1920s, Cardington, not Howden, occupied the center of the airship world. Unlike Howden, Cardington had long been the site of a major airship manufacturing base. In 1916, Short Brothers Engineering, the first company in the world to make production airplanes, won a contract to build two large airships for the Admiralty. Short Brothers soon bought a site two miles from the small village of Cardington for a factory that built the airships R31 and R32, which were knockoffs of plywood-framed models made by the German Schütte-Lanz company. Neither saw wartime service. In 1919 the name of the industrial complex was changed to the Royal Airship Works.

Visitors to Cardington were amazed at the sheer dimensions of the place, starting with its two eight-hundred-foot-long sheds.[41] Each had steel windscreens at either end, as long as the sheds themselves, so that an airship could be walked out without being blown against its shed.[42] Looming nearby was the mooring mast, 202 feet high and 70 feet wide at its base, the first of its kind to be built—a refinement on the mast Herbert Scott had pioneered at Pulham in 1919.[43] Flanking the sheds were an array of buildings that housed manufacturing works. These included the large, glass-roofed "Arcade," in whose cavernous, temperature and humidity-controlled interior the giant gasbags were assembled; gasworks where hydrogen was generated by passing steam over scrap iron; engine test beds; facilities for the construction of girders for R101's frame; and a splendid three-story brick-and-stone administration building, where the men who ran the Royal Airship Works had their offices.[44] Across the street was the housing estate built by Short Brothers in 1917 for the workforce and their families, which still went by the name of Shortstown. By 1928, the workforce at Cardington had grown to 354 people.[45]

Inside the shed where R101 was built, more than five miles of stainless steel girders and tubing were assembled into giant, circular transverse frames, many of them eight to ten stories high, which were then hoisted into vertical position and connected by "longitudinals" to form the ship's skeleton. The men on the shop floor and up in the girders of this colossal Erector Set looked implausibly tiny, like tourists in the Eiffel Tower. It was one thing to be told that R101 was twice as big as the largest German zeppelins, another to see the sweeping sculptural curves of the assembled hull. Inside the shed, Sefton Brancker's comment that the project was "the greatest adventure in construction in our time" seemed quite reasonable. Writers quickly ran out of adjectives to describe R101.

Also of a titanic scale was the so-called fabric shop, populated almost exclusively by women, who stitched and sewed and glued, making canvas covers and gasbags that were as colossal as everything else on the ship. The most unsettling aspect of R101 was that its extraordinarily strong frame should coexist with its extraordinarily thin, weak, and vulnerable gasbags and tenuous doped-linen covering. The most vulnerable parts of R101, by far, were her gasbags, not only because of the risk that the hydrogen they contained could ignite, but because any rupture in them could cause rapid and potentially disastrous deflation and loss of lift.

R100's managers bought their gasbags from Germany.[46] But R101's designers had chosen to fabricate their own. Richmond, who as a fabric man understood that the gasbags were "the least satisfactory" component of R101, had searched since 1925 for material that was thin, strong, and impermeable to hydrogen gas.[47] He and his staff investigated varnished silk and various combinations of rubber, gelatin, glycerin, and latex-covered synthetic fabric. All of them cracked and leaked.

More important, none of those ideas worked nearly as well as the Zeppelin company's low-tech solution, which was to make the bags from a part of a cow's intestine called the cecum—known as goldbeater's skin because of its use in making gold leaf.[48] The making of the bags was unconventional, to say the least. To start, the women unpacked five-gallon pails of cattle ceca that had been shipped from Argentinean slaughterhouses.[49] The ultrathin pieces of intestine, which might normally have been used as sausage casings, measured on average about a square foot. Some half million cattle provided R101 with its gasbags.[50] (Faced with an Allied blockade in World War I, German agents strictly controlled cecum sources in Austria, Poland, and Northern France, forbidding butchers there to make sausages, which required cecum casings.[51])

When the ceca arrived, they were covered in blood and mucus. They reeked. The entire workshop stank of offal. The women soaked the intestines to remove salt crystals used as preservatives, scraped away lumps of fat and grease with a blunt knife, then soaked the intestines again. They spread these pieces out on a large roll of canvas. As the skins dried, they adhered to one another. The canvas roll was then taken to the gluing room, where—in the nearly overwhelming miasma generated by the glue, whose main component other than water was turkey-red oil, made from beans, and which reeked of creosote (a lesser ingredient)—the skins were unpeeled from the canvas in a single transparent sheet resembling parchment paper, then glued to a thin layer of cotton fabric, to which was applied oil varnish, beeswax, and aluminum powder.[52]

The finished product, inflated with hydrogen into a giant, billowing 140-foot-diameter cheese wheel, was smelly, ultralight, and only lost hydrogen slowly. The enormous bags were as fragile as they looked, able to withstand only a twenty-pound load per inch of seam. They were so flimsy that tools routinely fell through and perforated them. One rigger fell clean through the No. 13 bag.[53] According to a British government paper, "If a tear of any considerable length is started, a concentration of stress at its two ends is so great that it must inevitably extend, like a tear in a sail on a ship."[54] To inspect the bags, riggers would climb the girders while whistling or singing continuously. Hydrogen, an odorless and tasteless gas, asphyxiates quickly and without warning. The telltale sign of its presence would be the sudden shrillness of voice or whistle—as happens to the voice of a child who breathes in the contents of a helium balloon at a birthday party.

The men and women who worked in these enormous sheds shared a sense of common purpose and destiny. They understood that they were on the leading edge of British engineering. They believed that what they were doing would change the world. Their culture was as different from other institutional cultures as the odd-looking flying contraption they were building. If they forgot that, someone from the other armed services was always there to remind them with a sneer that they were a second-rate service with second-rate funding. Like early submariners they lived in their own proud and insular world, one made more special by the uncertainties of their business. The British airship program had gone away once before; it could vanish again. For now the Royal Airship Works was the undisputed airship capital of Great Britain, as attested to by the chauffeured cars ferrying from the Cardington train station a procession of celebrities, politicians, reporters, foreign grandees, and ministry men.

One of the hallmarks of the airship culture was drinking. Lots of it, all the time. Alcohol flowed at the social gatherings, parties, and celebrations, sometimes in Cardington but more often in Bedford, the prosperous market town of thirty-five thousand that lay five miles up the road. One such dinner was a reunion party for the crew and friends of the 643-foot-long airship R33. Elaborate invitations had been sent out depicting a cartoonish airship with galleon sails bearing the motto "All Adrift Again." The party took place at the Silver Grill in Bedford, featured steak-and-kidney pudding, baked apples, and custard, and a good deal of booze. Toasts were raised to king, country, crew, airships. The revelers, who had begun the evening at six forty-five, were ferried back home to Shortstown after midnight. One of the attendees, a young airshipman named Granville Watts, had his invitation signed that night by some forty men. They included Vincent Richmond, Herbert Scott, Michael Rope, and the future chief coxswain of R101, "Sky" Hunt.[55] The Swan Hotel in Bedford and the Bridge Hotel in Cardington were often scenes of R101-related revelry. The Swan in particular, nestled by the town bridge over the river Ouse, offered discretion for private affairs.

These were among Herbert Scott's favorite haunts. Scott was a charter member of this culture and an enthusiastic promoter of such activities while he worked in Cardington. Michael Rope, by contrast, found the nonstop partying distressing. The deeply religious young engineer moved some distance away from Bedford and Cardington since he did not want himself or his family swept up in the culture of parties and drinking.

"There was a lot of—what shall we say?—quaffing?" said Mary Stopes-Roe, the daughter of Barnes Wallis. "It was a quaffing, drinking culture at Cardington. You didn't want to go flying with anybody if they were sozzled."[56]

ABOUT A YEAR AFTER that long, boozy evening at the Silver Grill in Bedford, several accidents befell that same airship, the R33. They would serve as a reminder of how vulnerable the big rigids were, and how difficult they were to fly. In 1921 a rigger working high up in the ship's envelope while the R33 was in her shed lost his balance and ripped through a gasbag, causing hydrogen to spill and the stern to fall abruptly. Only an emergency release of ballast saved the ship from crashing.[57]

A bigger mishap lay ahead. Four years later, R33, docked at Pulham air station and manned by a skeleton crew, was hit by a blast of wind that caused the mast's mooring gear and movable arm, which connected it to the airship, to fail, and the airship to break away. Her cover pierced, her forward gasbag deflated, and her bows crumpled, she drifted backward off the mast. She was saved from crashing into a building only by Flight Lieutenant Ralph Booth's order to drop forty-five hundred pounds of ballast. (Booth would later serve as captain on R100 and fly on some trials of R101.)

Fifteen minutes later, according to a description of the event written by Lord Thomson, "The ship . . . cannot make half her proper speed, and she is drifting astern, at a height of 2,000 feet, at the rate of 30 miles an hour, eastward, towards the North Sea, a desolate waste of waters lashed into a fury by the gale."[58]

In a 58 mph wind, R33 continued to fly backward, entirely at the mercy of the weather, and was soon over the North Sea. She was sighted nine hours later crossing the coast of Holland, still flying backward. When the wind abated, R33 struggled back across the coastline. At 4:00 a.m. she encountered another gale and was driven back again, at one point coming so close to crashing into the chilly water that sea spray hit the control car and Booth ordered all surplus gear thrown overboard, including parachutes, fire extinguishers, and hammocks.[59]

Eventually she made forward headway, laboring at dead-slow speed, her bows almost comically smashed and still carrying the busted mooring gear plus two pairs of half-ton artillery wheels that had been used as a counterbalance at the mast. R33 landed at Pulham at 1:50 p.m., after a wild ride of more than thirty hours. Booth and his crew received a hero's welcome. "When over Holland, on that dark stormy night," wrote Thomson later, "the temptation to take refuge in an air station on the far side of the North Sea must have been almost irresistible. To turn one's back on land at nightfall, and face that wild expanse of water in the teeth of a north wester, not only demanded courage and stern resolution, it also needed a high sense of duty based on proper pride."[60]

No one would have argued with Thomson. But Booth and his make-shift crew, it must be said, were extraordinarily lucky.

CHAPTER NINE

TRIAL BY ERROR

On October 14, 1929, R101 flies. She slips her mast at 11:17 a.m. in a light mist and floats off on a 108-mile tour to London and back. She climbs to fifteen hundred feet, hits a respectable top speed of 56 mph. She cruises past Buckingham Palace, Westminster, and St Paul's. She returns to Cardington and safely docks at her mast. There is nothing unusual about the flight, and that is the point. The mere fact of it, of its routineness, is the news. R101 *can* fly and she looks good doing it. The wildest of the rumors about her fitness for flight can be put to rest. Her fourteen passengers include some of the men most responsible for her: John Higgins, the ranking Air Ministry official; Peregrine Fellowes, the former director of airship development; the "big three" from the Royal Airship Works, Reginald Colmore, Herbert Scott, Vincent Richmond; and weatherman Maurice Giblett. (Thomson has a conflict and can't make the flight.) They are all delighted, as they should be. The *Times* is impressed, too, writing, "In what is likely to be a new era in airship construction R.101 has made a good beginning. Her designers have worked well and wisely." The *Times* points out how handsome she looks with her wind tunnel–crafted, aerodynamic lines: "The predominant impression made by the State Airship R101, as she now swings at the masthead at the Royal Airship Works here, silver in colour and imposing in her size and sweeping lines, is that she looks right in a way which the elongated ships of the War period never did."[1] The cheap press, which has recently published sensational material to the effect that R101 was never coming out of her shed, is silenced.[2]

No one is happier than Lord Thomson. At 1:30 p.m. he and Sefton Brancker mount the stairs to the roof of the four-story, eighteenth-century London mansion known as Gwydyr House, where their offices are housed, and watch the silver fish with its lovely streamlined bows drone across Whitehall. Thomson is thrilled. He dashes off a wire to Colmore congratulating him. Thomson says this is the start of a new era for British airships and for the British Empire.

Since his return as secretary of state for air in June, Thomson has been intensely focused on R101. One of his first actions, days after his investiture, was to travel to Cardington, sixty miles north of London. He wanted to see his marvelous airship. On the train ride with his private secretary he spoke excitedly about flying to India.[3] He has visited several times since then. His purview as air minister is broad and deep: he oversees all military aviation, civil and commercial aviation, the development of new aircraft, as well as air races and competitions. He is air minister in a world increasingly dominated by heavier-than-air machines. Still, airships, of which only two are intact in Britain, are the things he loves most.

Sometimes his enthusiasm gets the better of him. "I think it would have a very good effect all round," he writes to John Higgins, whose formal title is air member for supply and research (AMSR) and who ranks second behind Thomson in the Air Ministry, "if it is possible for me to announce in the very early future and before hostile critics start asking questions in the House about weights, that it is proposed at an early date to give up to 100 Members of Parliament an opportunity for making a flight." He adds, "I shall further, in all probability, suggest to some of my colleagues in the Cabinet—particularly the Prime Minister and the Chancellor of the Exchequer—that they should make this flight."[4]

Thomson's suggestion is so far out of line that it is difficult to know, then as now, how to react to it. He is proposing nothing less than taking a substantial chunk of the people who govern Great Britain into the air in an untested, experimental prototype. It seems impossible to believe that the air minister, with his knowledge of airship history—he has written about previous crashes and mishaps—can believe that there is no danger.[5] There *is*. Plenty of it, from many different sources. Much of R101's technology, including her engines, gasbags, and outer cover, is completely untried. Thomson will repeat this error—treating R101 as though she were not the risky new piece of science she is—again and again over the next year. He and his ministry will proceed as though there is no real danger, as though the notion that flying an untested seven-hundred-foot-plus airship, with twice the volume of anything that has ever flown, is not inherently hazardous. No one who wants to take one hundred MPs up for a joyride could think otherwise.[6]

Four days later, Thomson himself is airborne in R101 for her second flight, which covers 210 miles, attains 63 mph, and is marred only by the failure of a condenser pump and one of Herbert Scott's trademark botched landings. Though Scott is not officially the captain of the ship—Bird Irwin is—Scott nonetheless pulls rank as he has before and insists on taking over. Maybe he has been drinking. That isn't clear, though all evidence suggests that he drinks daily, and nightly. He does not take days off from drinking. While Irwin and First Officer Grabby Atherstone look on in horror and disgust, Scott upsets the ship's trim by needlessly dropping ballast, overshoots the mast, and fouls the guy wires. The result: after a five-hour-and-forty-minute flight, mooring her takes another two hours and twenty minutes.[7] Thomson and the other passengers are unaware of any serious problems with the landing.

Irwin, meanwhile, is furious. Scott has once again proven that Irwin is captain in name only, a shocking reordering of rank at a critical moment in R101's life. The red-haired, thirty-five-year-old Irwin is by nature sensitive and given to mood swings. He is quiet and holds himself a bit off from the intensely social crowd in Cardington. All of which seems to run counter to the man's glittering credentials. As a young man in Ireland he became a national track star, specializing in middle and long distances. He represented Great Britain in the 1920

Summer Olympics in Antwerp, placing twelfth in the 5,000 meter (3.1 mile) run. In the war's first year, at the age of twenty-one, he joined the Royal Naval Air Service and flew all types of nonrigid airships around the United Kingdom and the eastern Mediterranean—at one point hunting U-boats in the English Channel with Grabby Atherstone—and quickly distinguished himself as an outstanding pilot. In the years after the war he was given command of a succession of big rigids: R26, R33, and R36.[8] By the late 1920s he emerged as one of Britain's two foremost airship captains, an enormously prestigious place in the world of global aeronautics. In 1926 he married the strikingly pretty Olivia Marjory Macdonald Teacher, a doctor's daughter from Fareham in Hampshire. In spite of his success Irwin is ill-equipped to deal with the political infighting in Cardington and at the Air Ministry. He could have objected to the conduct of the trials, which he had helped to plan, but he didn't. He is both tightly wound and tightly compressed. His complaints about Scott, while generating memorandums from the Air Ministry, have little effect. Somehow in spite of his rank and the power that should have accompanied it, he lacks the personal authority to carry it off.[9]

Back on earth after the flight, Thomson says something nearly as jaw-dropping as his idea to put one hundred MPs plus the prime minister aloft. After saying how much he enjoyed the flight ("There is a feeling of complete detachment and security") and the luncheon and the smoking room (employed for the first time), he tells the assembled press, "I hope it may be possible for me to travel to India in R101 during the parliamentary recess at Christmas." Thomson wants to take a historic and pioneering voyage to India *within two months* in a ship that has done only two short flying trials, both in fair weather. He mentioned a Christmas flight to India before, on his June 19 visit, but in light of the ship's weight problems and the delayed trials, the demand now seems unreasonable. He makes all of the appropriate remarks, about how "the whole policy of the airship programme is 'safety first,' and 'safety second' as well," and "so long as I am in charge, no pressure will be brought to bear on the technical staff or anyone else to undertake any long-distance flights until they are ready," et cetera, et cetera. But in fact he wants a flight with one hundred MPs and he wants to go to India, and like a cranky child he wants them now, and his staff, used to dealing with the sometimes overbearing six-foot-five-inch minister, does not misunderstand that.

Five days later, journalist Charles Grey, writing in the *Aeroplane*, a leading British aeronautical journal, takes Thomson to task:

> Those who are responsible for R.100 and R.101 deserve to be regarded as honest, straightforward experimenters to whom all of us wish success. . . . But the Air Ministry ought to make quite clear to the Press the fact that no sort of performance is expected from R.101 and that she will probably be wrecked in the course of the next few months, either because her engines break down and she alights out of control or because, being 25 tons overweight, she cannot carry enough ballast to save herself in the forced descent.
>
> To let people think that she is going to take a hundred passengers to India in a month's time, or in three months or in six months is simply humbugging the public.
>
> The two ships both have so many original features that they must both be looked on as entirely experimental. If they perform journeys without accident the designers and the constructors and the crew will deserve full credit for their success. If they are wrecked nobody will have any cause to grumble because pure experiments must be expected to wreck themselves.[10]

Grey's commentary is spot-on. Thomson is months if not years ahead of himself. Why is he pushing so hard? The answer may lie in political maneuvering that is not yet known outside Whitehall.

After Thomson resumed his chores as secretary of state for air in June, he was visited in London by Marthe Bibesco. Their relationship has deepened. She has plenty of time for him now. She shifts her schedule to accommodate him. She is forty-three and, though not the knock-out she was in her teens and twenties, is still striking and commands the attention of men. She has recently published another successful, well-received novel, *Catherine-Paris*, and finished the restoration of her stunning Mogoşoaia Palace in Romania, financed largely with her own earnings, where she entertains the beau monde of Europe. What we now define as the interwar period was characterized not only by explosions of democratic culture in the form of movies, mass production, radio, refrigerators, cigarettes, and rayon, but also by a steep decline of the traditional landed aristocracy in Europe. They sold off houses and estates and simply could not afford to live as they had in the prewar years. Marthe seemed to just barrel through all of these changes. The world of shifting politics and war would catch up with her, but not quite yet. During a week in July 1929 the tall, Savile Row–clad cabinet minister and his Romanian princess cut dashing figures in British high society: seated in the Royal Box at Wimbledon; sipping cocktails at Baron Philip Sassoon's lavish country house with the king of Spain and the Marquess and Marchioness of Salisbury; dining at Clarence House with the Duke of Connaught, Queen Victoria's youngest son; taking tea with Prime Minister Ramsay MacDonald at the House of Lords; visiting with Winston Churchill.[11]

During their private conversations, Thomson drops a bomb: the prime minister, he tells Marthe, has asked him if he would "go out into the empire" and accept the job of viceroy of India when the job comes open in 1931. "There is no one else of our party who could take that high office," MacDonald tells him. "You would be a heavy loss to me here, but there is no more vital post than India—especially at this time."[12]

MacDonald is not exaggerating. He is offering his friend what is, in 1929, the most important job in the British Empire. The viceroy rules over 319 million people, including 150,000 of British descent, and one of the world's largest standing armies. The job is indeed "vital"—more so than it has ever been—because India seethes with discontent. India wants independence. Uprisings and civil disobedience are on the rise. So is the power of Mohandas Gandhi and the Indian National Congress. If Thomson accepts—subject to the king's approval, which would almost certainly be forthcoming—these festering problems will fall to him to solve. He would be in the job, quite literally, to save India for the British. For his trouble he would live in nearly unimaginable luxury: a 340-room, two-hundred-thousand-square-foot Edwardian baroque palace in Delhi that is the largest residence of any head of state in the world. During the hottest months he would reside at the spectacular Viceregal Lodge at Shimla, in the foothills of the Himalayas. In a remarkable coincidence, his first cousin Field Marshal William Birdwood, one of the most decorated soldiers of his generation, who led empire troops at Gallipoli in World War I, is commander in chief of the Indian Army, a post he has held since 1925—a Birdwood returning to take up his rightful place in Anglo-Indian history.

For the intensely status-conscious Marthe Bibesco, who is drawn to power as flowers are to sunlight, this is interesting news. She knows that she cannot possibly be Thomson's vicereine. She is still married. She is a foreign national. Even if she divorced, itself highly problematic, such a woman is unlikely to ever be allowed to occupy such a position in the British Empire. She has turned down a request from her husband for a divorce to be accompanied by a large amount of money, on the grounds that it would hurt the marriage prospects of their daughter, Valentina, and that his prospective bride was a joke in high society. So Marthe will never remarry. But marriage has never slowed her down before. There exists a line that she and Thomson cannot cross, and they know where that line is. But Marthe is thinking about it anyway. What could be a more splendid exercise of the sort of power she loves than the magnificent British Raj? "Was it not what from the beginning was bound to happen," she wrote in a biography of Thomson, "what he was born for and had been put into the world to do? India! His great obsession! . . . The immensity of the task and its perils appeared to me to make it worthy of his courage."[13]

"How far would I travel to be where you are?" she says to Thomson, as recorded in her diary. "Kit, I suppose you must accept. But one day perhaps I can come too to join you there."[14]

They are both acutely aware that if R101 succeeds, Thomson is suddenly much closer to Europe and to her—only five days by air. In this smaller world they could carry on. R101 unlocks the future for them. In the fall of 1929, R101 thus means vastly more to Thomson than anyone else suspects. The Imperial Airship Scheme is his past and his future. It solves the thorny time-and-distance equation with Marthe. As much as R101 is the empire's airship, she is Thomson's airship, the key to his destiny.

Two weeks later, Thomson writes Marthe a chatty note in which he says he has made up his mind to go to India:

"MacDonald is sixty-four and enjoying his 'crowded hour of glorious life' and displaying his prodigious powers of work. But someone else is fifty-four and will soon go out into the Empire, rather than plough sand in sterile talk back home—and he is yours, ever and as ever, since 1915. With the very best of love, Kit."[15]

THAT R101 COULD NOT FLY to India without severe modification was for the moment a dark secret, held close by Wing Commander Reginald Blayney Bulteel Colmore, the director of airship development, the number one man in Cardington, and a select few associates. Colmore was the organizational link between the Royal Airship Works (RAW) and the Air Ministry in London. Colmore, and no other, decided what would be passed up the chain of command to Whitehall and what would be disseminated to the media. Though the RAW was a civilian organization, its management and many of its employees had recent military backgrounds. Orders were expected to be obeyed. Lower-downs did not generally dare bypass their immediate supervisors with complaints. The ethic was very Air Service, which meant head down and upper lip stiff and no whingeing allowed. It also meant that Colmore could tell Thomson, AMSR John Higgins, and Thomson's powerful secretary, Louis Reynolds, whatever Colmore wanted. This made him the most powerful man in the British airship program.

Colmore was born in Portsmouth, England, in 1887. He was educated at Stubbington House, a prestigious preparatory school, and in the naval school on the HMS *Britannia*. He joined the navy in 1907. He served with the Royal Navy's Armored Car Division in Antwerp in 1914 and commanded an armored car section at Gallipoli in 1915. He was transferred to the airship section of the Royal Naval Air Service in 1916 and was soon promoted to commander of the airship base at Mullion, in Cornwall, the most active of the nonrigid airship stations. There he invented a system of using airships in combination with airplanes and surface craft to patrol for German submarines, for which he was promoted to chief staff officer of aircraft operations with the commander in chief of the British Grand Fleet. He had been part of the team that assessed the wreck of the zeppelin L-33, which became the basis for British airships R33 and R34. Colmore had come to love airships and stayed with them. After the war he served as staff officer for airships in the Air Ministry and helped draw up the specifications for R100 and R101. He was later appointed deputy director of airship development.[16]

Colmore was a competent administrator. He had a deft political touch that helped him weather the political storms that had coursed through the airship establishment since the start of the Imperial Airship Scheme. He was a team player in both the best and worst senses of the term. He worked well with others. But in his eagerness to get along he was not inclined to deliver bad news to bosses who did not want to hear it. In the world under the dapper forty-two-year-old's thumb, good news was pulsed out to the world in banner headlines, while bad news tended to be bottled up and compartmentalized, if not made to vanish. He could be abrupt and imperious with lower-downs, but always tactful and gracious and accommodating to those above him. He wanted very much to please his superiors, and this was his weakness.

On Colmore's orders, neither the media nor Lord Thomson were told about R101's weight and lift problem. Which meant Thomson still believed that he might soon be going to India. R101's trials would take place as though nothing were wrong. Colmore, Richmond, Scott, and their staffs would gracefully accept all of the praise heaped upon them for a job well done.

The trials proceeded.

On October 21 a forecast of gale-force winds caused R101 to be taken off the mast and walked back into her shed. The RAW team felt this was a reasonable precaution. Lord Thomson was aghast. Having asserted many times that his airships were "all-weather" aircraft, he complained that his employees were being too cautious. He "wished to see the behavior of the airship in rough weather."[17] In return he received an unusually curt memorandum from Higgins explaining why, with experimental engines and an untried outer cover, it would be "culpably foolish to run the risk of having this tried out for the first time in a violent gale."[18] Thomson backed down.

R101's third and fourth trials were both flown in weather described by one passenger as "beautifully fine." No difficult operations were attempted. Clearly no one at Cardington was in the mood to stretch this ship's capacities. "Nothing exceptional was tried," noted George Meager, R100's first officer, of the third flight.[19] The fourth flight, supposed to be a full-throttle test, got nowhere near full speed and did nothing to prove the strength of R101's outer cover.[20] Public relations, on the other hand, were as usual played hard. R101 flew over the royal residence at Sandringham, in Norfolk, where their majesties King George V and Queen Mary came out onto the gravel drive to watch and wave. To show off the brilliant airship, all manner of passengers were along for the ride.

Once again Herbert Scott intervened and botched both landings, threatening the ship's safety and acting outside all normal command protocols.

The ship's crew was, meanwhile, becoming alarmed both by the casualness of the joyriding and the Air Ministry's apparent desire to hurry R101 through her trials. "There is a mad rush and panic on at present to finish the ship at all costs by the end of the month," wrote First Officer Atherstone in his diary on August 13, "and she is to do a flight the moment she can fly."[21] He had nothing but contempt for Scott. Atherstone's diary drips with it. Above all he objected to the continual presence of outsiders, politicians, and dignitaries on R101's flights. He believed the ship was experimental and therefore dangerous and that the danger outweighed the public relations value of such actions. His commentaries cut to the fundamental problem with the R101 project that underlay all other problems, past, present, and future: *she was a raw, minimally tested, experimental aircraft, but was never treated that way.* The project's managers and overseers never believed in the danger. "All these window dressing stunts and joy rides during the ship's trials before she has got an airworthiness certificate are quite wrong," Atherstone wrote on November 6. "But there is no one in the RAW executive who has the guts to put their foot down and insist on trials being free of joy riders."[22]

The "guest" passenger problem was about to get much worse as London-based Air Ministry officials under Thomson pushed ever harder to show the outside world how excellent their airship was and to justify both its production delays and enormous cost. On November 8, R101 left her mast with forty-four crew and forty passengers, the largest number of people ever to fly on any British aircraft. A hard rain overnight and a low barometer had made the airship heavy. She could only fly if ballast and fuel were dumped and her gasbags were filled nearly to 100 percent of capacity. These were extremely risky moves. The airship's pressure height was a scant five hundred feet, meaning that above that elevation she would automatically valve gas and the captain would have to drop more of the already insufficient eight tons of ballast to restore equilibrium. In Atherstone's account the overweight airship "staggered round the vicinity of Bedford and Market Harborough for a couple of hours."[23] The ship's weight, and lack of lift, had left almost no room for error. Lives had been endangered. How, precisely? The passengers could be crushed under the weight of 114 tons of crashing airship. They could be incinerated, per the example of Echterdingen, when von Zeppelin's LZ-4 hit the ground, bounced up, then exploded into fire. They could, like R33, be blown far away. R101's passengers, by all accounts oblivious to any of this, had a splendid time.

On November 14 she flew again, this time with thirty-two guests, including ten members of Parliament, and this time there was trouble. When R101 uncoupled from the mast, her bow shot up into the air, causing her stern to drop twenty-five degrees and resulting in "a hellish din of smashing crockery and of things sliding long distances." Air Ministry officials were splattered with soup. It took an emergency ballast discharge to right the ship. Soon afterward the ship became superheated, and thus superlight, causing considerable gas to be valved. She soon had the opposite problem. R101 was so heavy at the end of her flight that when Captain Irwin approached the mooring mast—mercifully free this time of Scott's interference—he had to drop an astonishing eight tons of water ballast just to get the ship even. Noted Atherstone, "I was in the control car while the ship was being landed and had a horrible feeling of nervous tension owing to the shortage of ballast." Almost no water ballast was left. In airship terms, this was operating on a razor edge of disaster. The ship's final trial once again took place in fine weather with light winds and was mercifully uneventful.

Lord Thomson meanwhile had not forgotten his promise to take one hundred MPs for a ride. The MPs had not forgotten, either. So many wanted to go that a lottery had to be held. That flight had first been scheduled for November 16. To the relief of the flying crew it had been canceled because of rain. But Thomson continued to insist on it, and his minions pushed it forward. Colmore had not told Gwydyr House about the problems of the forty-four-guest flight or the smashing crockery and ballast issues on the thirty-two-guest flight.

The hundred-MP flight was rescheduled for November 23. The flying staff were deeply uneasy. But Colmore and Scott had made sure that such dismay had not gone any farther than the Royal Airship Works. Thomson, who appears in retrospect clueless about the risks that were being taken, was so excited that he wrote Marthe, telling her proudly, "Tomorrow—if weather permits—R101 is taking 150 people up on her eighth flight. . . . It will be the largest number ever taken up in any aircraft."*

The idea was, prima facie, not rational. R101's trials were incomplete. She had not flown at full speed. Her crew had little experience flying her. Under normal circumstances, a new airship had to receive a Certificate of Airworthiness, the key government approval from the Air Ministry that would allow taking on civilian passengers. R101 had received no such approval. First Officer Atherstone, who had been hoping "to prevent this stupid flight," had checked the ship on November 22 and found that she was three and a half tons short of the lift required to fly that many passengers and crew with safety, and safety meant carrying sufficient fuel and ballast. "The whole show is an absolute farce," wrote Atherstone. "and if we fly tomorrow it will be taking an absolutely unjustifiable risk with practically nothing to gain and everything to lose."[24]

---

* Thomson later said he regretted his decision to take up so many members of Parliament. On July 11, 1930, he denied a request from J. J. Astor, MP, for a ride in R101, writing, "Both ships are still doing their experimental flights and the only people who should travel on them are experts, with the possible exception of myself. In a weak moment I once consented to take some Members of Parliament and may have to do so even yet, but I am sure you understand how desirable it is to limit the passenger list as strictly as possible." Source: AIR 2/349.

Still, he and Irwin dutifully prepared the ship for flight. In the RAW's militaristic corporate system, men obeyed orders. They drained the airship of all fuel but a bare minimum of five and a half tons, worth about eighteen hours of flying. They ordered all emergency stores, tinned rations, and all parachutes removed from the ship to save weight.[25] *All parachutes.* By 11:00 a.m. on November 23 a crowd from the Houses of Lords and Commons had assembled at the base of the mooring mast. They were in high spirits. Soon 148 people—passengers and crew— were on board. By then the wind had risen to 45 mph. Heavy rain was expected. Atherstone made the astonishing observation that without the high wind and the dynamic lift it provided to the airship while it was moored at the mast, R101 would have hit the ground. The wind, which soon rose to 50 mph, offered another blessing: the ship could not possibly fly that day. Instead, riding aerodynamically on the stiff breeze at the mooring, 180 feet off the ground, the MPs all stayed for lunch and availed themselves of the smoking lounge afterward. (Having been forced to give up all matches and lighters when boarding, they were provided with flame-free, automatic lighters.[26]) They all had a marvelous time. Collectively they posted two hundred letters on formal R101 stationery provided for the occasion.[27] Many of them got so drunk that, with all the wind and the ship moving around them, they believed they had actually flown.

Atherstone, Irwin, and the other officers were appalled. "The Air Ministry were terribly bucked at having pulled this stunt off," wrote Atherstone. "The whole show was merely stupid. A lot of illegal things were done in order to gain enough lift to carry this load."[28] He added in a later entry, "How close we have been on more than one occasion to wrecking the ship."

Scott pronounced R101's trials an unqualified success. At the conclusion of her final flight he told the assembled reporters in his usual anodyne fashion, "We are entirely pleased. R101 has behaved splendidly. She has finished her acceptance trials after seventy-three hours in the air. Any further trials will be to assemble additional data." Irwin commented that they were all "extraordinarily pleased" with their airship's performance. Scott even added a bit of filigree, saying how much they had all enjoyed their airborne luncheon of "soup, roast chicken, bacon, castle pudding, and cheese."[29]

They were telling partial truths, and they knew better. The ship had flown only in good weather with light winds and had not flown far. She had not done a critically important full-speed trial. She had chronic engine troubles, mooring troubles, superheating troubles. One of the best things she had done, Scott told reporters, did not involve flying at all. On November 9 a full gale was forecast, but instead of hauling the airship back into its shed, as the crew had done in October, R101 was allowed to stay moored to her mast. The reason is not clear, though it would seem as though Thomson's earlier sharp protest had found its mark. The ship remained in place at the mast while a howling gale came roaring down on Cardington on November 10, with wildly shifting winds that routinely topped 60 mph with some gusts over 80 mph, accompanied by rain, hail, and plunging temperatures. Remarkably, the gigantic airship swung easily in the wind. Colmore wrote, "The ship rode comfortably at the tower without violent movement." He acknowledged the ship had rolled slightly, an unusual movement. That was all.[30]

This, surely, was an accomplishment to boast about. The Air Ministry, aided by Scott and Colmore, did so. R101 had withstood the full fury of a storm that had disrupted shipping and caused considerable damage onshore. How strong she must be, was the general message, with a clear nod toward the fatal weakness of R38.

The reality was quite different. As crew members soon discovered, the ship's pronounced rolling motion during the storm had caused the giant gasbags to surge and to chafe against the nuts and sharp corners of the radial frames. This had caused tears and holes in gasbags throughout the ship. "It was observed that, in the case of Nos. 3–14 bags, inclusive [of a total of sixteen bags], a very considerable movement from side to side was taking place," chief coxswain Sky Hunt reported to First Officer Atherstone. Hunt explained that parts of the stainless steel structure "rubbed and chafed the bags, and in places such as No. 8 starboard fore end tore the bag 9 inches in a jagged tear. No. 8 thus became deflated to 60 percent." That was a massive loss of gas from a ten-story gasbag. Hunt noted that the ship's gas valves, which automatically vented gas as the ship climbed, were malfunctioning, opening when they should not, losing even more gas.[31] The outer cover had performed badly, too, letting in "considerable quantities of water due to imperfect sealing."[32] So much water was in the hull that it leaked all through the passenger accommodations.[33]

This was bad news. Anyone who was "entirely pleased" with such results was a fool. The gasbags throughout the ship were full of holes. The leakage during the entire period of the trials was staggering. Fully 4,667,380 cubic feet of "top up" gas had been required—nearly 100 percent of the ship's capacity, a daily rate of 86,433 cubic feet, or the equivalent of 2.6 tons of lift. This meant that another of R101's great innovations, the parachute wire harnesses designed by the engineering wunderkind Michael Rope, had not performed well. They had specifically been designed to prevent the bags from chafing on the structure, suspending the bags in the interior of the ship as though by parachute. Unlike zeppelins, where the bags were held in place by being sandwiched between the transverse rings, Rope's system suspended them in independent wire nets, so that they could move back and forth freely, remaining stable while the ship moved around them. The harnesses were meant to solve the problem created by R101's other major invention, the use of independent, unstressed circular transverse frames. Which meant that all of R101's deliberate departures from zeppelin practice were now suspect.

So, too, with the outer cover. Under the supervision of "Dope" Richmond, one of the war's main authorities on fabric, the cover had been doped in the factory, rather than in place. This "pre-doping" was considered an important innovation that removed the necessity of having workmen suspended in slings applying the dope in the shed. But the pre-doped covers had started showing signs of splitting as early as the second week in August 1929, and in November the cover had let in a large amount of water, which promoted mold and weakness in the cotton-backed goldbeater's skins.

Still, the serious problems unveiled by the trials paled in comparison to the single, transcendent problem of R101's "useful lift." She was simultaneously too heavy and too lacking in lift to fly to India.[34] Everyone at Cardington now knew this. The ship's frame was prodigiously heavy, made to avoid the structural weakness of R38. The ultraheavy diesel engines, weighing eighteen tons, were another supposedly ingenious innovation. "The engines," wrote R101 chief calculator Harold Roxbee Cox, "were an appalling handicap."[35] More weight had been added by the innovative "servo" motors engineered by Rope to make moving the rudders and elevators easier—unnecessarily, as it turned out.

Now it was time for Reggie Colmore to stiffen his resolve and tell Lord Thomson that after more than six years and the expenditure of a great deal of taxpayer money the engineers' calculations had been wrong. The problem was simple: if one subtracted the fixed weights of the ship and the necessary other weights, including crew, passengers, equipment, ballast, and baggage, the total amount left for fuel was around fifteen tons. This was not nearly enough, even under optimum conditions. The weather in the Middle East and South Asia could be expected to cause a massive loss of lift and thus reduce this number even further.

This was a spectacular miscalculation.

The bad news was delivered in a memorandum, written by Colmore and Richmond and signed by Colmore and sent to John Higgins, Thomson's immediate subordinate, who oversaw the airship program. They wrote:

It would be impossible to attempt to operate the ship on the Indian route even for demonstration flights with only this disposable lift available. At Karachi during the mid-summer months the air density is such that there would be a loss of about seven percent of the gross lift to 27 tons. Even if the crew, ballast, etc. were reduced to a minimum the ship could not leave the ground in Karachi with more than, say, seven tons of fuel.[36]

So there it was, the end of Thomson's dream. Richmond followed this with an abject memo in January stating starkly, "What all this comes down to is that a 5 million cu. ft. airship *according to British ideas* is not suitable (inherently) to carry 100 passengers over journeys to the East of 2,500 miles at all times of the year. This may be a serious conclusion in view of what the British public have come to expect, but I do not think the particular airships which have been produced can be blamed."[37] He might have added that such a conclusion, on the basis of evidence, was exactly what this experimental program was supposed to allow the British government to make. But it was not the news anyone wanted to hear.

Having admitted the problem, Colmore and Richmond now proposed, in a spirit of panic and desperation, a solution to gain more lift and lighten the airship. First, they proposed to throw out everything they didn't absolutely need. This included twelve passenger berths, two ballast tanks, the unnecessary "servo" steering gear, various kitchen equipment, two lavatories, and girders meant to hold the cover in place. Plexiglass would replace real glass in the lounge windows. These items added to 3.16 tons.

They still had a long way to go. Another 1.5 tons of weight reduction could be had, they suggested, by substituting a Rolls-Royce Condor gasoline engine for one of the Beardmore Tornado diesels. This idea might have sounded reasonable, but it violated a core principle of the Imperial Airship Scheme: that gasoline engines were far too dangerous to be taken to the tropics. The single most important innovation of R101 was the use of flameproof diesels. Her designers had sacrificed ten tons of weight to install them. Now Colmore and Richmond stated, "There is no technical objection and we do not think that there would be any more risk of fire than from existing petrol tanks [used for diesel starter motors] in the power cars." If this recantation wasn't shocking enough, they also proposed, "If it is decided that petrol carried outside the hull of the ship is permissible as a temporary measure, then there is the still more attractive proposition in making use of two German Maybach engines."[38] They were treating R101's original specifications as little more than political window dressing. They were backing off the very premise of R101.

They turned their attention from weight to lift. Their first proposal was to radically alter another major R101 innovation: Michael Rope's wire harnesses. By letting them out so that they could accommodate a larger volume of gas, another 3.18 tons of lift could be gained. This was an extremely risky idea. It severely compromised Rope's original design, and Rope himself hated it.[39] Those modifications would get them to roughly eight tons. But they needed more. And now they suggested the most radical change of all: cutting the airship open and inserting an entirely new bay with a new gasbag that would hold five hundred thousand cubic feet of gas.[40] That would gain nine more tons of lift. Together with the other savings—a total of seventeen tons—the ship would have fifty-five tons of lift. She could thus fly to India.

Soon after Higgins received this bombshell, he sent Lord Thomson his own note, explaining the problem and the fixes proposed by Colmore and Richmond.[41] There is no record of how Thomson reacted. He had to be deeply disappointed. He sat on the news for a few days, then calmly responded with what would become the blueprint for the immediate future of the airship program:

AMSR:

I am of the opinion that no good and quite possibly some harm might be done by a flight to India in the early months of 1930. The best course would I think be:

a) To make various alterations you suggest in paragraph 3 of your minute.
b) To insert the extra bay.
c) To make every effort for a flight with 55 tons of disposable load to India and back at the end of September 1930.

T.[42]

But this, too, went against common sense, for reasons of weather. Colmore pointed out in a letter to Thomson's secretary Louis Reynolds that September was still monsoon season, with its rains and squalls, and "there is no doubt that late November would be a better time for the flight."[43] Colmore said he was "not quite clear as to the importance attached to the flight taking place during this month." What he did not yet know was that the date had been chosen for public relations reasons. Thomson wanted to arrive back in London just prior to his appearance at the Imperial Conference. He wanted to make a grand entrance, and nothing could be grander than stepping off R101, in her full glory from the ten-thousand-mile round trip, and onto the empire's biggest stage. Such a voyage was the perfect credential for the man who fancied himself viceroy of India.

WE MUST NOT FORGET about R100. Everyone else did. While R101's trials were taking place, R100 sat idle in the shed in Howden, awaiting her turn. Had she been first to trials, she would have been the largest aircraft ever to have flown. (R100 was 720 feet long, compared to 732 for R101.) But she had never been the favored child, and she wasn't now. ("R100 gave me pleasure," Thomson wrote to Marthe. "R101 will, I hope, give me joy."[44]) Since the two ships could not share the single mast at Cardington, she would wait and go second, and she would fly without most of the fanfare that had accompanied the launch of R101. As most of the media construed it, she was inherently less interesting. Destined to be a historical footnote, R100 would forever be overshadowed by her fancier sister.

Which was quite unfair. R100 was and would soon be proven to be the better ship, though by a slight margin. This was partly because Barnes Wallis and his team had stuck with a more traditional and thus proven airship design, including its braced, radial transverse frames, its German-supplied gasbags, and its conventional engines. Though its living quarters were, like R101's, stuck inside the hull, they were far less luxurious and far more practical than her sister ship's. But there were plenty of innovations, including, especially, Wallis's inventive use of only eleven standard components of different sizes to build the ship. He had actually made mass airship production possible.

R100 also had more gas volume, which meant more gross lift (5.2 million cubic feet versus 4.9 million cubic feet, mostly due to the limiting influences of Rope's parachute harnesses). Critically, she had far more disposable lift (fifty-one tons versus thirty-eight tons) than R101. The weight difference was mostly due to the diesels (eight tons versus eighteen tons)—the same engines that Colmore and Richmond were now saying they did not need. R101's innovations were also her problems.

R100 performed better in trials, too, which took place in December 1929 and January 1930 and featured a mere fraction of the guests and dignitaries that had flown on R101. She handled better than R101 and was more responsive to controls.[45] She was much faster, hitting

80.5 mph, which made her, after the zeppelin *Bodensee* (82.4 mph) the second-fastest airship ever to fly.[46] She completed five trial flights lasting 87.5 hours. Though she experienced problems of various sorts with her engines, she had flown well enough.

But her outer cover, like that of R101, had shown alarming weakness, for a specific reason. "In each ship the policy had been adopted of building with relatively few longitudinal girders compared with previous ships in order that the forces in the girders might be calculated more accurately," wrote Nevil Shute Norway in his memoir. "This decision was undoubtedly influenced by the disaster of R38. A ship with few longitudinals, however, must of necessity have larger unsupported panels of outer cover fabric than a ship with many."[47]

From the earliest trial flights the fabric had developed bulges, ripples, deformations, and undulations that worsened with speed.[48] She flapped. During the second flight a large section of the cover had come loose from the ventral fin. The problem was so bad that Colmore hired a Bristol Fighter to fly alongside R100 and verify that the cover was flapping. Later, in places where the cover had flapped and torn, rainwater had leaked into the hull and caused gasbags to split and the electrical system to short out. According to an Air Ministry report from February 7, 1930, "The stretching meant that the holes in the seams were unsealed and the cover leaked very badly; in addition, the dope film was cracked in all directions (probably owing to the movement of the cover in flight), and had lost its waterproofing qualities."[49] The cover was so porous that the gasbags were continuously wet.[50] When R100 was put back into the Cardington shed on January 30, the cover was so damaged and fragile that the airship inspector ruled that the ship was no longer airworthy. Only after patching and redoping was she certified to fly again.[51]

After the R38 crash, most of the attention of designers and engineers became focused on strength of structure. That was what mattered. The Air Ministry had formed an Airworthiness of Airships panel in 1924 with the stated purpose of vetting the strength of the metal structures, and with ultimate authority to grant the crucial Certificate of Airworthiness.[52] And strength they had achieved, to several factors of safety. The design of covers and gasbags had never been seen as the main engineering problem to be solved. But what if the most dangerous parts of their airships were these thin and flimsy pieces of fabric that either held the gas or protected the gas?[53] What if the real problem was something they had not quite counted on?

CHAPTER TEN

FRANCE, AND THE MIDNIGHT HOUR

A 11:00 p.m. the watch changed.

Grabby Atherstone, on duty for nearly eighteen hours, yielded his shift as officer of the watch to Bird Irwin, who had been up just as long. In the control car—the small, windowed gondola slung beneath 777 feet of airship and 160 tons of matter, human and otherwise—elevator coxswain Leonard Oughton yielded to Walter Potter, one of the five survivors of the R38 crash. Potter was hoping for better luck this time. On the rudder helm Christopher Mason took over from Ernest Rudd. All were experienced airshipmen. They peered out into the oceanic darkness from the bridge, encircled by the tools of their peculiar trade: airspeed indicator, altimeter, manometer (showing gas pressure), inclinometer (showing tilt), variometer (showing rate of drop or rise), telegraphs to send messages to the engine cars, ballast and gas controls, compass binnacle, thermometer, and speaking tubes. Their work had been difficult. They had never flown in weather like this. Rudder man Mason had to keep the ship on its compass course, flying crabwise while being blown sideways. At 11:00 p.m., in spite of efforts by Rudd and navigator Ernest Johnston, the ship was still twenty miles off its track.

The far more difficult and consuming job, requiring ceaseless concentration, was that of the man on the elevator wheel. Because R101's bow would "hunt" up and down through an arc of four hundred feet or more, porpoising through the air as she always did, height coxswain Oughton had to constantly turn the spoked brass wheel that moved the ship's giant elevator planes, which were mounted on the horizontal fins four hundred feet aft. The planes pointed the nose up or down. This required unflagging attention and hard physical effort. Atherstone's sharp mid-Channel reprimand of Oughton showed how unforgiving the job could be. Unlike the rudder man, who fronted forward like a steamship captain, the elevator cox faced the side of the car. Standing thus, he could feel the pitching of the airship in his legs. Many hours of flying were required to learn how to "feel" the movement of something that large and cumbersome, stretching 400 feet behind you, 300 feet in front of you, and 140 feet above you. Veteran elevator men agreed that, when a shift changed, they needed at least ten minutes to understand what the ship was doing and how to counteract its movements, especially if the ship was flying heavy or light.

At 11:36 p.m., some five hours after casting off in Cardington, R101 crossed the French coast, half an hour later than expected. She made landfall at Pointe de Saint-Quentin, where the lights of Le Crotoy and Saint-Valery were visible below. She flew up the mouth of the Somme River. The passengers, who had been eating, drinking, smoking, and socializing since 7:30 p.m.—four hours earlier—were on the promenade decks on the port and starboard sides, enjoying their last brandies and ports, gazing through the ultralight Cellon windows at the lights of French civilization, which must have been a welcome sight after the featureless blackness of the Channel.[1] The passengers on board from the Royal Airship Works—Reggie Colmore, Vincent Richmond, Bert Scott, Michael Rope, Harry Leech, and Alexander Bushfield (a safety inspector)—would have been intensely interested in the performance of the airship and had to be pleased that she had made France without incident, however slowly. Who knows what Lord Thomson of Cardington was thinking? He had bragged in public about how his airship was "safe as a house . . . except for the millionth chance" and how it could fly "in any weather." Here was heavy weather indeed. Here was the proof. His airship had made the French coast, accompanied by port and fine cigars.

Still, her ground speed had continued to drop. Although her five engines were finally all up and running, she was making no more than 27 mph over land. Thomson and the others got a long, leisurely look at the watery sparkle of lights on the French coastline before heading to bed. Around that time chief wireless operator Spencer Keeley asked the passengers if they had any personal messages they would like to send. The evidence shows that two of them did: William O'Neill, the deputy director for civil aviation in India, and Sefton Brancker, the director of civil aviation for the United Kingdom. O'Neill's was an all's-well note to his wife. Brancker sent his goodnight to his girlfriend, the famous British actress Auriol Lee, at the Hotel Elysée in New York. "Off at last," he wrote. "Love and blessings from R101—B." Lee had starred in many British stage productions and would later appear in Alfred Hitchcock's *Suspicion*, with Cary Grant and Joan Fontaine. Brancker and Lee had been fixtures in London's glittering social scene, sometimes double-dating with Thomson and Marthe Bibesco, to the delight of the London tabloids. On October 3, the night before R101 departed for India, Thomson and Brancker had gone together to see the Noël Coward three-act operetta *Bitter Sweet*. They had seen it together before, in the company of Bibesco and Lee.[2]

Thomson had, before leaving, thoughtfully sent Marthe a note for later delivery. She was very much with him that night, and perhaps he dreamed of her in his curtained berth on the starboard side of the ship with a rush mat on the floor.[3]

Just after midnight R101 sent a wireless message to Cardington reporting her speed, location, and heading, as well as the weather conditions. To which was appended a bit of commentary:

> After an excellent supper our distinguished passengers smoked a final cigar and having sighted the French coast have now gone to bed to rest after the excitement of their leave takings. All essential services are functioning satisfactorily. The crew have settled down to watch keeping routine.[4]

The message, which went out to the world via wireless radio relays— Cardington, RAF Malta, Ismailia, Cairo, Karachi, and Shimla—left no room for doubt. The flight was a signal success. The guests were nestled snugly in their berths. The great airship was weathering the storm and pushing on toward the Mediterranean, and to Egypt beyond.

SHORTLY AFTER 11:00 P.M., engineer Alfred John Gale Cook emerged from the No. 4 engine car, port midships, and climbed the treacherous exposed ladder to the ship in a 50-plus mph wind. If he lost his footing, the gale could straighten him out like a wind pennant. His three-hour shift, working in the hot, cramped, and deafeningly loud nacelle with its inline eight-cylinder, 650-horsepower Beardmore Tornado diesel engine, had ended. He headed immediately to his bunk in the crew quarters. But he was unable to sleep. He lay on his back watching the gasbag, visible directly above him, surge and move in ways he had never before seen. Gasbags moved about because the ship was rolling and pitching, tugging on the parachute wiring. But they could also move because of airflow inside the huge envelope of the ship's outer cover. The ship had been designed with air vents in the bow and gills in the aft outer cover to let air in and out. The idea was both to equalize the interior pressure on the cover with that outside and to provide a way for leaking hydrogen to be vented. Either way, the movement of something that big was unsettling. Cook's sleeping compartment was directly under bag 8-A, the largest of all the gas cells, more than ten stories tall. The idea of that much hydrogen gas, contained within membrane-thin, cotton-backed goldbeater's skins and sitting virtually on top of the berths, might have distressed most people. Not Alfred Cook. He had been working on R101 since 1928. What he noticed was simply how much movement there was, not whether he could have been turned to smoldering carbon in seconds.

His lack of concern would have been shared by most of the airship community. While all of them would have conceded that hydrogen was flammable, so was the gasoline in their cars, they pointed out, and they did not worry about their cars exploding. Nor did they touch matches to their gas tanks to try to find out what might happen. Said R100's First Officer George Meager, a longtime airshipman, "The thought of potential danger [from hydrogen] never entered my head. Nor, I think, that of any other airship pilots or crews."[5] Hydrogen was unparalleled as a lifting gas. Helium was inferior in that regard, brutally expensive, and controlled by a handful of American politicians sitting on committees in Washington. So hydrogen wasn't really a choice. Hydrogen was the premise of European airship travel, not some dangerous add-on.

Testimonials abounded that the danger from hydrogen was overrated. One argument, pushed by R101 engine specialist Thomas R. Cave-Browne-Cave, was that the gasoline fuel on board an airship was far more dangerous than hydrogen. "To the uninstructed mind," he wrote, "the danger of fire in airships is generally thought to be due to the presence of hydrogen. If the fate of an airship carrying from twenty to fifty tons of briskly burning petrol [gasoline], whether inflated with hydrogen or helium, is contemplated, it will be readily realized that the advantages in the use of helium are not so obvious as would at first sight appear."[6] To the instructed mind, therefore, the thing to be afraid of on R101 was not the extremely explosive 5.5 million cubic feet of hydrogen gas, occupying a greater volume than that of the *Titanic* and held in flimsy balloons, but the extremely explosive gasoline sitting in tanks underneath it. This was woolly logic, at best.

Others were more pointed in their dismissals. "The risk of using hydrogen for commercial vessels has now been proved to be extraordinarily small," wrote R101 chief designer Vincent Richmond. "On the other hand, the use of petrol as a fuel, introducing no more than a justifiable risk in a military vessel, is hardly to be contemplated in a commercial vessel, especially for operation in tropical temperatures."[7] Here, too, petrol is the danger, so much so that Richmond used enormously heavy diesel engines—with predictable consequences—instead of the far lighter and more practical gasoline burners. Gasoline was the danger, not hydrogen. Richmond was terrified of fire, but not fire related to millions of cubic feet of hydrogen gas. This, too, seems a convoluted piece of reasoning. And of course Richmond later changed his mind about it. Airship fuel was held in steel tanks. There was no record of fuel tanks or airship engines catching fire and igniting the hydrogen. That was a theoretical worry, based on what might happen in the tropics. R100, the sister ship, was fitted with gasoline engines and performed well and safely with them.

Perhaps the greatest proponent of the hydrogen-is-not-dangerous school of thought was Zeppelin company president Hugo Eckener. He explained that hydrogen was only potentially dangerous, and only when it was allowed to leak out into an airship's internal space and accumulate. Hydrogen, Eckener insisted, only became extremely volatile when mixed with at least 15 percent air. One could even, he insisted, light a candle three inches from a hydrogen gasbag and nothing would happen![8] At a state dinner for Eckener in Piccadilly on April 25, 1930, thrown by Lord Thomson and attended by the leading figures in the British airship establishment, Eckener argued that, though he preferred the idea of helium, with an experienced crew there was no danger at all from the use of hydrogen as a lifting gas.[9]

This was gold-plated nonsense. Hydrogen was violently explosive and prodigiously dangerous, particularly in the way it was used in airships—held in the flimsiest containers in proximity to many tons of metal, electrical wiring, and conduits. It might have been possible to dismiss most of the combat-related hydrogen fireballs in World War I as the result of incendiary ammunition. But undeniably, *at least fifteen* giant rigid airships had gone up in immense and horrific hydrogen explosions *that had nothing to do with fighting or combat missions.* They were LZ-4, LZ-6, LZ-10, LZ-12, LZ-18, LZ-87, LZ-94, LZ-97, LZ-102, LZ-104, LZ-105, LZ-117, R27, R38, and *Dixmude.* The presence of a good deal of gasoline on all of these airships just made the fires worse. Hydrogen had no problem igniting gasoline.

One of the greatest dangers posed by hydrogen had nothing to do with flying itself: the threat came when an airship crashed to the ground, even at a low speed. "The chief danger, I thought, was of fire after hitting the ground," wrote Nevil Shute Norway, R100's chief stress calculator, "when broken electrical cables could make sparks in the presence of large masses of escaping hydrogen or petrol. In that case the fire would spread instantly. . . . It seemed to me that in such a case the only chance for survival would be to jump on the inside of the outer cover and cut one's way out, and drop onto the ground, and one would have not more than five seconds to do it. For this reason before the first flight of R100 I bought a very large clasp knife and sharpened it to a fine point and razor edge, and I carried this knife unostentatiously in my pocket throughout the flights that the ship made."[10] (Count von Zeppelin's LZ-4 had caught fire on the ground at Echterdingen, to take one example.)

The truth is that hydrogen burns readily in open air and, when contained, is potentially explosive. When it burns in a controlled way in, say, a Bunsen burner, the gas produces a colorless flame. But when hydrogen in a sealed container encounters flame, a very different reaction occurs. An experiment conducted by the University of Nottingham shows just how reactive the gas can be. A balloon filled with pure hydrogen is suspended by a string. A match is applied to it and the reaction filmed with a high-speed camera. In real time, the balloon explodes instantly with a loud bang and a brilliant flash of red-orange flame several times the size of the balloon. Watching the film, which shows the reaction at ultraslow speed, you see first the balloon itself shredding and flying away, unburned. For a microsecond hydrogen burns clear, then a hot flame erupts as hydrogen mixes with air. When the contents of the balloon are filled with a two-to-one mixture of hydrogen and oxygen, there is no moment of clear flame. The contents light up much brighter, the reaction proceeds much faster, and the bang is much louder. The latter would most likely approximate what happened when an airship exploded, having been ignited by spark or flame touching the ultrathin bags in an envelope where hydrogen and air were likely mixing. Some of the most famous explosions of the twentieth century—the Space Shuttle *Challenger* and the Chernobyl reactor, to take two—were produced by the combination of hydrogen, oxygen, and a spark.[11]

AT 1:00 A.M. Foreman Engineer Harry Leech and R101's chief engineer, William Gent, were conversing in the smoking lounge when Captain Bird Irwin walked in. The lounge was a great boon to the crew, as well as to the passengers, in an era when most men smoked. A long voyage without cigarettes, cigars, or pipes was a great hardship for inveterate smokers. Irwin was pleased that they finally had all five engines running smoothly and told them so. Irwin told them he was confident that the airship would reach Ismailia, in Egypt, the stopover before they continued on to Karachi, India.

Then he made an interesting comment. He said that he only wished that R101 could fly higher into steadier air conditions, away from the usual ground turbulence. But he said he could not do this without discharging fuel, which he was anxious to conserve. What did he mean by that? He meant that if the airship rose above her pressure height of fifteen hundred feet, she would release gas through Michael Rope's automatic valves, thus reducing lift. To counteract the loss of lift, Irwin would have to discharge ballast in the form of water or fuel. He explained to them that all of the water ballast forward had been dumped when leaving the mast, which meant that fuel would have to be dropped.[12] And R101 needed all the fuel she was carrying. Irwin, in other words, felt obliged to fly low, even though he did not want to.

This was quite a remarkable statement when its implications were considered.

When they had finished talking, Gent went off to bed, and Leech, who was not a member of the crew but felt great responsibility for the airship, went down to check each engine car once more, climbing down those perilous ten-foot ladders to speak with the engineers. Irwin, as officer of the watch, would have returned to either the control car or the control room just above it.[13]

So R101 thundered on into the great, dark, wet, and mostly featureless night, crossing over the opaque wooded valleys of the Somme and Bresle Rivers. Most of the fifty-four men on board were asleep. A dozen remained on duty. At 1:00 a.m. the ship sent a wire updating the Journey Log. R101 was a mile from the small twelfth-century town of Poix-de-Picardie and roughly ninety miles north-northwest of Paris. She was traveling at an airspeed of 54 mph and an altitude of fifteen hundred feet. The wind was at 49 mph. In the eighty-four minutes since crossing the French coast, R101's ground speed had averaged only 27 mph. She had made a slight turn in a southerly direction and was now heading more directly into the southwest wind than ever before (steering 209 degrees into a 226-degree blow), which meant that she would be lucky to make Paris by 4:00 a.m.[14]

THE PERFECTLY SAFE EXPERIMENTAL PROTOTYPE

In the spring of 1930, Christopher Birdwood Thomson's most embarrassing and least tractable problem had nothing to do with the heaviness of his airships, their leaky, glued-intestine gasbags, or their cracked cotton/linen covers. It existed in the form of a 775-foot-long German airship called the *Graf Zeppelin*, one of two rigid airships in the world that were then fully operational. The *Graf* flew long distances and flew often and apparently effortlessly and made a mockery of faltering British attempts to fulfill the promise of the grandly conceived Imperial Airship Scheme. That year the *Graf*—the German word for "count"—was the airborne symbol of everything the British aspired to and had failed to achieve, a nagging reminder that the idea of filling the skies with the huge weightless fish was not some impossible dream. The Germans were showing it could be done, to applause and adulation. The *Graf* was a reproach especially to men such as Barnes Wallis, Reggie Colmore, Vincent Richmond, Michael Rope, Bert Scott, and Tom Cave-Browne-Cave, whose job was to bring the old vision to life, and who were beginning to run out of excuses.

The Treaty of Versailles, at the end of World War I, effectively killed the German airship program, including Hugo Eckener's attempt to beat the treaty's draconian restrictions with his small passenger zeppelins, *Bodensee* and *Nordstern*. Still, the remarkably persistent Eckener, who controlled the Zeppelin company, found a loophole: he received authorization to build a 656-foot-long zeppelin for the Americans, nominally as a war reparation. He flew it across the Atlantic in 1924 with a battle-tested crew and delivered it to the U.S. Navy, which filled it with helium and renamed it *Los Angeles.* After making only the second Atlantic crossing by air from east to west, the *Los Angeles* became the Americans' most successful rigid airship. She was used mainly for naval training.

Eckener had kept his company alive and his zeppelin factories working. In 1925, the Treaty of Locarno allowed the Germans once again to build big rigids as long as they were not used for military purposes. Eckener, unable to raise funds from his own government—the impoverished Weimar Republic—went back to Count von Zeppelin's old formula, public subscription, appealing to ordinary Germans who still believed in the myth and glory of big airships. And he succeeded, just as the count had. Eckener raised enough money to build a single ship, the *Graf Zeppelin,* which made her maiden flight in 1928. She was at the time the largest airship ever built, with a gas volume of 3.7 million cubic feet. (R101 would later depart for India with roughly 5.5 million cubic feet of gas.)

While R101 and R100 languished in their sheds, years late on their contracts, the *Graf* astounded the world with her swashbuckling exploits. In 1928, she crossed and recrossed the Atlantic, nonstop, becoming only the second aircraft to do so.* Her crew was given a full-scale ticker-tape parade in New York City. Eckener was invited to the White House. In 1929 the *Graf* became the first airship and the second aircraft of any type to circumnavigate the earth. The first were a pair of U.S. Army airplanes, which in 1924 took 175 days to fly the route, with sixty-nine stops. Eckener, in command of *Graf Zeppelin,* made his 20,651-mile journey in an astonishing twenty-one days, five hours, and thirty-one minutes,

---

* The first to make a round-trip nonstop crossing of the Atlantic was R34. Alcock and Brown were the first to cross the Atlantic nonstop, traveling west to east—with the prevailing breeze. R34 was the second to cross, going both west to east, and east to west. In 1924, LZ-126 (*Los Angeles*) crossed east to west, and in 1927 Charles Lindbergh became the first to cross in an airplane, flying west to east.

with only three stops. Along the way the *Graf* became the first aircraft of any type to cross the Pacific nonstop. In March and April 1930, she made two separate Mediterranean cruises, one to Palestine and another to France, Spain, Portugal, and Morocco. All seemingly with ease. All without accident. She was acclaimed everywhere she went. The portly, avuncular Hugo Eckener was hailed as a new Magellan. By 1929 he was one of the most famous men in the world.

Members of Parliament were running out of patience with the British airship program as a whole, and the *Graf*'s exploits only exacerbated this. "It is well-known to anyone who has been following the construction and development of R100 and R101 that these two airships are failures," stated Cecil L'Estrange Malone, member of Parliament for Northampton, on the floor of the House of Commons on March 18, 1930.

> They can never be run on regular services. They can never be used for commercial purposes. All the press photographs about lunches on board the airships at the mooring mast at Cardington carry no weight. It is easy to tie a football up to a mast and get it to remain there for twelve months. That is not the test. The real test is whether the airship can fly regularly and efficiently during a large proportion of the weeks of the year. Neither of these airships can do that. They are too slow to fight against the average wind that they will have to meet, and they cannot carry a load which will make them commercial propositions. . . . There is nowhere they can land.[1]

Other members of Parliament were openly jealous of the *Graf*'s achievements. "I should like to call attention to what has happened in Germany, where the *Graf Zeppelin* flew round the world last August," said Sir Richard Wells, member of Parliament for Bedford, the town next door to Cardington, in a speech on the floor of the House of Commons on March 18, 1930. ". . . That was a very remarkable achievement, and it shows the interest taken because in the United States the utmost enthusiasm was shown for those on board and for the ship itself. [The *Graf*] has made fifty flights averaging 1,462 miles and totaling 73,000 miles."[2]

How could the *Graf* do this? At a time when Great Britain's best minds were struggling to build a ship they could take to India, how did this zeppelin fly over Europe and Russia, cross a high mountain range on the Russia-China border, land in Tokyo, then blithely sail five thousand miles across the Pacific to California? Lord Thomson, who was to his annoyance often asked this question, answered it this way in the House of Lords:

> You may well ask why it is that the *Graf Zeppelin* can go round the world and make enormous flights while our two ships spend their time mainly in their sheds. That is a very easy question to answer. The Germans have thirty years' experience of building airships. They ran commercial airships from Lake Constance before the war. I do not wish to decry the virtues of our own people, but in view of that experience, it is only natural that we should accept the fact that there are very few Dr. Eckeners in this world. We have not yet had time to produce our Dr. Eckener.[3]

He was right. The *Graf*'s crew was the lighter-than-air equivalent of the 1927 New York Yankees. From captains and pilots to rudder men and elevator coxswains, riggers, navigators, and engine mechanics, the Germans were without peer in their ability to fly airships. They had had thousands of hours of practice. The German captains, who had vast experience before, during, and after the war, made virtually any British airshipman look like a rank novice. They made airship travel look easy when it was not. Eckener was indeed, as Lord Thomson suggested, the greatest airship captain in the world.

Thomson then offered another reason for R101's lagging development: her many innovations. He was right about that, too. From her diesel engines to her gas valves, umbrella gasbag wiring, unbraced transverse frames, pre-doped linen cover, power-assisted steering, extensive passenger and crew quarters and amenities located *inside* the hull, and a host of other new ideas, R101 had departed from time-tested zeppelin practice. Eckener had meanwhile largely stuck to his old formulas, making only incremental changes over many years of building and flying rigid airships.

In March 1930, the *Graf Zeppelin* stopped at Cardington, long enough for Eckener to be feted by Lord Thomson at a state dinner and to pick up Vincent Richmond and Michael Rope, who were flown to Friedrichshafen and given full tours of the airship and factory. They were generally unimpressed with the *Graf*'s technology. Considering the *Graf*'s achievements, their report on the findings from their trip was oddly dismissive: "The general arrangement of the structure of the *Graf Zeppelin* does not exhibit any noticeable departures from previous zeppelin practice. Very little novelty was observed in the structural detail. . . . The fins were noticed to be remarkably wide for their depth, so much so that we suspect from our own experiments in this country that they are not particularly efficient."[4] So the Germans had no magical technology that the rest of the world did not know about.

Richmond and Rope did note one large difference, however, between the *Graf* and every other zeppelin or airship that had ever flown. Her twelve-cylinder Maybach engines were made to run on either gasoline or on a gaseous fuel similar to propane known as Blau gas, and the preference was for the latter.* The *Graf* carried enough of it, in gas cells slung under her seventeen hydrogen gasbags, for one hundred hours of flying. Because Blau gas was only a bit denser than air, when it was consumed the airship became only slightly lighter, thus obviating the release of precious hydrogen gas. In airships powered by gasoline or diesel the fuel load was constantly changing, meaning constant worry and adjustments, both to the amount of hydrogen and to the angle of the ship's flight.

---

* Named after its inventor, Dr. Hermann Blau, not because it was blue.

Still, Richmond and Rope seemed unimpressed. While they devoted part of their report to the technical aspects of the Blau gas system, they also noted, critically, that the presence of fuel gasbags meant less space for hydrogen, and also that, because the slightly heavier gas when it leaked tended to fall and accumulate along the keel, "where the most likely sources of ignition will lie," Blau gas presented a safety hazard. They were not impressed.[5]

Despite her triumphs, and the glory that trailed behind her wherever she went, the *Graf Zeppelin* and her smaller, Eckener-built sister ship, *Los Angeles*, were not the flawless paradigms of airship travel their supporters cracked them up to be. They were, rather, the exceptions that proved the rule, and the rule was that, after thirty years of earnest experimentation in five countries, they were *the only two airships in the world fit to fly in the spring of* 1930. The *Graf*, held up to the British Parliament as immutable validation of the Imperial Airship Scheme, was more aptly a symbol of the failure of Ferdinand von Zeppelin's technology to catch on. The rarity of big rigids proved the point. Airships were expensive, flawed. Eckener himself admitted in 1928 that the twenty-four-passenger *Graf* was too small and too slow for regular North Atlantic service—his own version of the conclusion that Richmond and Colmore came to about R101 in the fall of 1929.[6] *Graf* was just a showpiece to secure new business, just as Eckener's fair-weather DELAG airline had been.

The explosion of airplane travel in the 1920s showed how badly airships had lost the competition. The number of miles of air routes across the British Empire had increased from 4,860 in 1926 to 22,901 in 1930, a 371 percent rise. In the United States, passenger traffic had risen 6,550 percent in four years, from 5,782 in 1926 to 384,506 in 1930.[7] The British Royal Air Force alone had 778 planes; the French and Italian air forces had 1,350 and 900, respectively.[8] The Lindbergh Effect, as it was known, was prodigious and permanent. Thousands of airplanes were flying everywhere in the world.

Meanwhile airship promoters, and Hugo Eckener in particular, continued to cling to the outdated notion that to compete against airships, with their great lifting abilities, airplanes would have to have wings so large they could not take off. In his view, planes were severely limited by the square footage of their wings. But new technology had changed all that. Airplanes, using new "wing-loading" design techniques, were obliterating the old standards. To take just one example, three years after the launch of the Sikorsky twin-engined S-38 passenger plane in 1928, its successor, the S-40, had more than *triple* the S-38's takeoff weight.[9] Airplanes were evolving with stunning speed, carrying heavier and heavier loads for lower and lower costs.

Finally, the notion that the *Graf Zeppelin* was a model of safety was simply not accurate. Though no passengers or crew had been killed, the German airship had a long history of accidents, close calls, and near misses. On her maiden round trip across the Atlantic, she had sustained serious damage when a squall tore off the cover on her port fin. A surface ship had to be summoned in case the *Graf* had to ditch in the sea. Another storm near Bermuda tore the covering of her upper port fin. On the way home the ship was blown backward and two hundred miles off course and went into a steep dive that ripped hundreds of square feet of outer fabric. Again, a surface ship was summoned for a possible rescue at sea.[10] In August 1929, on her way to Tokyo, she cleared the six-thousand-foot Stanovoy Mountains on the Russian-Chinese border by a mere 150 feet, narrowly avoiding catastrophe.[11] In May 1930, near Lyon, France, an ice storm caused her to plummet from 1,000 feet to 160 feet—ten minutes of stark terror accompanied by the crashing of plates and glasses. Eleven days later, a hailstorm caused the *Graf* to fall again, this time to a height of two hundred feet, where Eckener saved her by applying full power and full up elevator. In summer 1930 overheating caused her to do a vertical nose-stand near Hamburg, and overheated by the desert sun over Mexico and Arizona, he took her crew and passengers on a white-knuckle, roller-coaster ride, rising and dropping a thousand feet, making passengers and even Captain Eckener sick.[12]

In the most perilous of her mishaps, she was flying near Pernambuco, Brazil, when a heavy tropical rain added seven tons to her weight in seconds. In spite of dropping all available ballast—five tons—the *Graf* hit the ground, lost her lower rudder, and dragged for three hundred feet. When she came to rest, the chimney of one of the local huts was sticking up into the belly of the ship. A fire was burning in the stove inside the hut. One of the engine mechanics jumped from the car, grabbed the pot of coffee that was heating on the stove, and doused the fire. Several palm trees were also sticking up into the ship.[13] A single spark might have ignited the Blau gas and the hydrogen, blowing everyone on board to kingdom come. There were more such incidents. Collectively they suggested that the *Graf Zeppelin* was, while certainly the world's most successful airship, also one of the luckiest.

ON JUNE 3, 1930, Thomson rose in the House of Lords to deliver a speech on airships. He was by now a commanding presence in the chamber. At six feet five inches he seemed to be a head taller than everyone else. His slight stoop seemed only to accentuate his great height. He was a clever and precise speaker, relaxed and casually glib when answering questions. He could be funny or cutting. He delivered his words with sweeping movements of his thin, expressive hands. On this day he told the assembled peers that after six years and many delays, the expenditure of 2.3 million pounds sterling, and much impugning of his ministry's competence in Parliament and in British newspapers, his prize airships were finally going to make their long-distance flights.* R100 would cross the Atlantic in June. She would land in Montreal, at a 200-foot

---

* By contrast, the total cost of research and development on the Supermarine Spitfire fighter plane, from 1931 to 1936, was £20,765. The Spitfire was obviously a much smaller aircraft. But it did change the balance of airpower in World War II.

mast, like the one at Cardington, built at great expense by the Canadian government. R101 would fly to Karachi in September, stopping at Ismailia, then flying over Baghdad, the Arabian Desert, and the Persian Gulf. Ismailia and Karachi, too, had their own masts.

Thomson reminded his listeners that these airships were as much about geopolitics as engineering, as much about the destiny of English-speaking peoples as global commerce: "It is unnecessary for me to point out what the airship may mean to our race and our empire. It is essentially a vehicle for going over wide-open spaces—the oceans. It will link up our empire in a way which, so far as I can see, no other means of transport can approach."[14]

FOR ALL OF HIS socialist ideas, Thomson remained a creature of empire. He was true to his heritage. Though British overseas holdings were already embattled in ways unimagined when he had launched the Imperial Airship Scheme in 1924, the ideology had not changed.

What occupied the body of Thomson's speech, however, were two ideas he had repeated so many times that they had taken on the light of deep conviction: (1) that these aircraft were experimental and (2) that they were completely safe. "The airship programme, which I had the honour to introduce in this House in 1924, was described by me not once but several times as experimental and tentative," he said. "It was never once claimed that we were going to build two commercial airships which would at once take the air as their native element and fly to all parts of the globe." He hit the theme again and again. "These ships are still scientific experiments. They will not cease to be experimental until their overseas tests have been completed." They were "test" ships. In the parallel world of heavier-than-air flight, everyone knew what a test pilot was: someone willing to take risks far beyond what normal people or normal pilots would do. The test pilot was *expected* to be injured or to die. He was lucky if he did not.

But while such arguments amounted to a defense against criticism of delays and design and manufacturing problems, Thomson also continued to insist on the almost complete absence of danger to crew or passengers. He even edged up on the bizarre suggestion that there was no risk at all. "This is one of the most scientific experiments that man has ever attempted, and there is going to be no risk while I am in charge of the thing being rushed or of any lives being sacrificed through lack of foresight. It is a far too scientific and important matter for that."

He manifestly could not have it both ways.

His rationalizations became even harder to follow when, in the same speech, he walked back his old insistence that taking half of Parliament up in R101 in November 1929 had been a good idea. He seemed genuinely contrite: "Sometimes undue publicity is a little inconvenient as when people get the impression that we were building an airship which will take one hundred MPs all over the country. To suggest that was the greatest error of my life. I was punished by the weather, which made the flight impossible." (He was *saved* by the weather from the sort of infamy he could never have lived down.) But he apparently only regretted the parachute-less hundred-MP flight that never happened, not *actual* joyrides with all sorts of politicians, mayors, and local celebrities, whose lives he had placed in danger.

Somehow these circular arguments made sense to Lord Thomson. But as any RAF test pilot could have told him, he had a profound misunderstanding of the concept of risk.

R101 WAS BEING ALTERED, profoundly. She was losing weight, gaining hydrogen capacity. This was the theme of summer in the Cardington shed. That and the enormous pressure to finish by the end of September. The work would be done in two phases. In the first, which would be finished before the RAF's Hendon air show at the end of June, the gasbag harnesses would be let out, and equipment and matériel would be jettisoned. In the second, in August and September, the ship would be split in two and a new bay added with a five-hundred-thousand-cubic-foot-capacity gasbag.

Phase one was a success: the loosened harnesses added more than 3 tons of lift. The jettisoning of equipment and features—including passenger quarters and lavatories, steering motors, reefing girders, and a long list of smaller objects that weren't nailed down—removed 2.3 tons of weight. Everyone was pleased.

They were about to become much less happy. With the staff's attention focused on disposable lift, it was easy to miss the disaster that was unfolding in another part of the ship: the six acres of cotton and linen that were draped over and lashed to the ship's longitudinal girders. Tests run by Michael Rope revealed that the ship's outer cover was rapidly decaying because of one of R101's touted innovations: the use of pre-doped linen on most of the airship. The linen had cracked when "tautened," which let water in, and the water had turned the linen to mush. The crew had another term for the process: *rotting*. The cover, in Rope's assessment, would not hold up at high speeds or in bad weather. A cover breach could cause the ship to lose its streamlined form, lose speed, and pitch wildly. Rain and wind could tear holes in the unprotected gasbags. The ship could lose lift and hit the ground.[15] The cover had another function, too. Through openings in the nose, air flowed into the envelope, both equalizing pressure on the cover and sweeping away any leaked hydrogen gas through innovative "gills" farther down the hull.

The cover was so badly rotted that Rope, the diffident, self-effacing engineer's engineer who was the quietest man in the room, sent an extraordinary memo to his bosses, Vincent Richmond and Reginald Colmore. Rope told them bluntly that the cover's condition meant that "there is no margin of safety for flight in a rough atmosphere." Then he added what was, in the context of the R101 project, nothing less than shocking: "It is for consideration as to whether the risk involved in sending either ship on an overseas flight is . . . greater than is justified by the need to fulfill public expectation. Is it not conceivable that a public statement could be made which would satisfy the people who matter—to the effect that overseas flights have been postponed for, say, six months?"[16] Thus the number two designer in Cardington and the acknowledged engineering genius of the program was recommending that the India flight be canceled.

He must have summoned all of his courage to write the note.

Colmore and Richmond ignored his request. With Thomson bearing down on them, canceling or rescheduling would never be an option. Colmore made sure Rope's note went no further than the councils at the Royal Airship Works. Its contents were kept from Thomson, the Air Council, John Higgins, and Thomson's powerful secretary, Louis Reynolds. Then Colmore and Richmond had the pre-doped portions of the cover replaced with fabric doped in place, a time-consuming and labor-intensive task. Because R101 was scheduled to fly in the Royal Air Force's annual display on June 28, this work could not be done right away. Instead, fabric patches were glued on top of the worst and most decayed parts of the cover.

Thus bolstered, on June 23, R101 was taken out of its shed for the first time in seven months and moored to her mast. Trouble started immediately. In a freshening wind, ripples and waves soon appeared in the cover, running from bow to stern and back again. Then the cover split, opening a ninety-foot gash. No sooner had patches and glue been applied than a new, forty-foot section ripped open. That, too, was quickly repaired. A few days later, First Officer Noel Atherstone wrote that a piece of fabric taken from the cover could be "torn without using any force at all, just like paper." He thought that the airship should never have flown.[17]

R101 kept flying anyway, under Colmore's orders, but now a new and even more distressing problem appeared. During a June 27 rehearsal flight for the Hendon air pageant, Captain Irwin and First Officer Ralph Booth, the captain of R100, who was filling in for Atherstone, found themselves flying what seemed to be an enormously heavy ship,

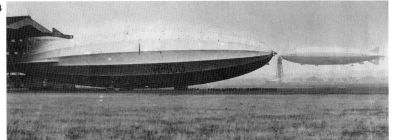

24

SISTER SHIPS R100 AND R101 IN CARDINGTON: They were the glittering flagships of the Imperial Airship Scheme, meant to stitch the far-flung British Empire together through the medium of air. Their builders couldn't stand each other.

25

THE MEN IN CHARGE OF FLYING R101 FROM ENGLAND TO INDIA: (left to right) navigator Ernest Johnston, Captain Carmichael "Bird" Irwin, Herbert Scott, Noel "Grabby" Atherstone, and Maurice Steff. The gondola behind them—a 20-foot-long piece of a 777-foot airship— housed the airship's main handling and engine controls and instrumentation.

26

A MASSIVE PRESENCE IN BEDFORDSHIRE: In the month before R101's takeoff for India, more than one million people came to see her, including the Prince of Wales. There was something strange and wonderful about an object bigger in volume than the *Titanic* that bobbed weightlessly at her mast. The gargantuan sheds at Cardington were also tourist attractions—they were among the largest man-made objects on earth.

27

DINING IN LUXURY, OR THE ILLUSION OF LUXURY: R101 featured a sixty-seat art deco dining room trimmed in white, gold, and Cambridge blue, presided over by a chief steward. But the opulence was all surface. The pillars were not pillars; they were illusions of ultralight aluminum alloy, balsa wood, linen, and paint. Walls and ceilings were paper thin.

THE SHIP'S LOUNGE AND PROMENADE DECK AWAIT MEMBERS OF PARLIAMENT: Lord Thomson invited more than a hundred members of Parliament to take a ride on R101, a move that R101's first officer called an "unjustifiable risk." For the occasion the lounge had been spruced up with curtains, tablecloths, ferns, and flowers. Foul weather prevented a likely tragedy.

THEY COULD SEE FOR MILES: One of the airship's great amenities was a promenade deck, just off the lounge, fitted out with thirty-two feet of cellulose-based windows. From here the passengers watched the spires of London pass below them and the sparkling lights of France loom into view. Another superb amenity was the flame-proof smoking room, a floor below, where smokers could puff away with enormous quantities of hydrogen a few feet above them.

30

LASHING R101'S CLOTH COVER INTO PLACE: Her outer cover was her greatest weakness. It failed continuously over a year of test flights and was virtually untested before R101 left for India. The tearing of the cover at the top of the bow, which led to the rupture of a gasbag, was likely a primary cause of the crash.

31

CARDINGTON WOMEN REVIEWING THEIR WORK: Some five hundred thousand ultrathin pieces of cattle intestines, known as goldbeaters' skins, were glued together to make the gasbags. The process was long, smelly, labor-intensive, and done exclusively by women.

32

GASBAGS THE SIZE OF TEN-STORY BUILDINGS: R101 got her 160-ton lifting capacity from seventeen enormous gasbags. The bags, which contained 5.5 million cubic feet of hydrogen gas, were leaky, easily punctured, and vulnerable to flame of any kind.

33

LORD THOMSON AND ASSOCIATES, MOMENTS BEFORE EMBARKING FOR INDIA: (left to right) navigator Ernest Johnston; Director of Civil Aviation Sefton Brancker; Thomson's powerful secretary Louis Reynolds; Thomson; and chief designer Vincent Richmond. They are standing at the foot of the mast, waiting for the lift, happily unaware of what was about to happen to them.

THE AIRSHIP'S LOUNGE UNDER CONSTRUCTION: Behind the ultralight balsa-wood pillars was the metal frame that held R 101 together. The ship contained more than five miles of girders and tubing and miles more of electrical and bracing wire.

R 101'S TAIL SECTION, WITH GIRDERS LARGELY INTACT: Since the airship hit the ground bow-down, and burned from front to back, the duralumin frame in the stern survived. It provided the clues that enabled an investigator to solve the mystery of the crash ninety-seven years after it happened.

AFTERMATH OF THE CRASH: Splayed across the Bois de Coutumes like the skeleton of a long-dead animal, R101 posed a problem familiar to crash investigators since the dawn of manned flight. Most of the evidence had been destroyed. Fire had swept the vessel in seconds, burning away with ruthless efficiency almost everything that was not made of steel, duralumin, or alloy, carbonizing human flesh, vaporizing the vast organic expanses of her cover and gas cells.

ANOTHER LEVEL OF HORROR: Many of the corpses were frozen in the postures of their final agonies. Some had their arms raised, as though to block the fire. Others had arms outstretched, as though reaching for help. Still others showed spine arched and head thrown back, as though burning to death on their beds.

GREAT AIRSHIP DISASTER: PAGES OF PICTURES

32 PAGES — DailyMirror
THE DAILY PICTURE PAPER WITH THE LARGEST NET SALE

R101 MEMORIAL NUMBER

No. 8,257 ... MONDAY, OCTOBER 6, 1930 One Penny

THE TRAGIC END OF R101
AIR MINISTER AND AIRSHIP EXPERTS LOST—46 VICTIMS

Looking along the wreckage of R 101, which ran into a storm, crashed and burst into flames soon after 2 o'clock yesterday morning at Allonne, near Beauvais, while on an attempted flight to India. Only seven of the crew and an official of the Royal Airship Works at Cardington were saved. Forty-six of those on board, including Lord Thomson, the Air Minister, Sir Sefton Brancker, and famous pioneers of airship development, perished in the flames which consumed the giant airship. It is thought that the airship struck the side of a hill. The explosion following the crash shook Beauvais, four miles away. See also pages 3, 7, 16, 17, 19, 28 and 32.—("Daily Mirror" photographs.)

BANNER HEADLINES: The R101 tragedy dominated British newspapers, and indeed newspapers all over the world. They were filled with speculation. R101 had been too heavy, the storm too strong, the hull too weak, the crew too inexperienced. No one really knew what had happened. The papers were flush with criticism of the government policies that had put R101 in the air.

39

CLAMORING FOR NEWS OF THE CRASH: Back home in Cardington, a panicked crowd gathered in front of the office of the *Bedfordshire Times*. Desperate for information, people clawed their way forward to see the names of the dead and living. There were so few living, so many dead. So many dreams and designs, so many lives touched—a whole world, really—had vaporized with R101.

40

SURVIVORS OF THE R101 CRASH: When R101 exploded into a giant hydrogen-and-gasoline-fueled fireball, which swept the length of the airship in a matter of seconds, these men somehow emerged alive. Their survival was seen as a miracle. (Left to right) Arthur Bell, Arthur Disley, Alfred Cook, Joseph Binks, Victor Savory, and Harry Leech.

THE FUNERAL CORTÈGE: After a memorial service at St Paul's Cathedral, coffins containing R101's dead were taken by horse-drawn artillery carriages through Whitehall in London to Euston Station. The pomp, circumstance, grandeur, and sheer scale of the events were equivalent to a royal funeral. The last such outpouring of national grief had taken place after the sinking of the *Titanic* in 1911.

becoming heavier as each hour went by. She was unstable in flight.[18] Ballast had to be dropped just to keep her above a thousand feet.[19] While practicing a "bow" before the royals, the ship went into a sudden steep dive. She was so heavy that *nine tons of ballast* had to be dropped to keep her from grounding and to enable her to land at the mast. What was happening?

None of the Royal Airship Works people knew the answer. Not yet, and since the Hendon RAF display was the next day, there was no time to find out. Ballast, fuel, and gas were topped up, and off R101 went. The voyage to Hendon (in the northwest part of London) from Cardington went smoothly, as did R101's dip and salute over the aerodrome. But all was not well. The patched and jury-rigged cover was back to its old ways. In the words of AMSR Hugh Dowding, "It was like wind blowing over a field of corn, the ripples going down the cover."[20] But the more serious problem was the unexplained heaviness, this time making R101 almost impossible to control. "The airship would go into short, sharp dives," wrote George Meager, "and then the cox'n would get her nose up and we made a long, slow climb back to our flying height. Directly the cox'n leveled his elevators in order to maintain height, down would go the nose and the procedure would be repeated."[21] Meager recalled that the profusely sweating height coxswain Leonard Oughton told him, "It's as much as I can do to hold her up, sir." The ship simply wanted to go down, and it was all they could do to prevent it. She had to drop a staggering ten tons of ballast to come to equilibrium in Cardington before landing. Until that moment she had been carrying all that heaviness by means of dynamic lift. As soon as she stopped flying, she would have fallen hard to the ground. After burning more than two tons of fuel, the ship ought to have been light.

A close examination of the airship revealed that, as Michael Rope had predicted seven months before, letting out the harnesses had brought the bags in contact with sharp projections: nuts and bolts on the girders and struts. This had resulted in "a large number of holes." The airship was leaking significant quantities of gas. Richmond wrote in a note to Scott on July 2, "I find that the rate of [gas] loss is about 1 ton per square inch of opening in 12 hours. . . . In my opinion this result is somewhat startling."

The ship had spilled gas the previous fall at a catastrophic rate (51,070 cubic feet per day) for the same reasons—building-size bags bumping against small, sharp projections—and this had led to the installation of more than four thousand fabric "pads" to stop the chafing. Now that the bags had been let out, the chafing was worse than ever. Fixing one problem had made another problem worse.

On July 3, Frederick M. McWade, the chief inspector at Cardington for the Air Ministry's Aeronautical Inspection Department (AID), wrote the most explosive memo in the history of the Imperial Airship Scheme. The forty-eight-year-old McWade, who had worked on British airships since 1903, was the most capable and experienced airship inspector in Great Britain.[22] His work was notable for its thoroughness and for his deep knowledge of his subject. R101's lead inspector's opinion carried enormous weight, and his London-based department had the power to prevent R101 from flying. The confidential letter, addressed to Director of Aeronautical Inspection Harold Outram, was so sweeping and categorical in its condemnation of R101's condition that it is worth quoting at length:

> Owing to the modifications which have recently been carried out on the wiring system, the gasbags are now hard up against the main longitudinals and rubbing very hard on the nuts and bolts. . . . Further the gasbags foul very badly the heads of the taper pins at the joints of the main and intermediate struts at the inner ridge girder ends. . . . The points of fouling occur throughout the ship and amount to thousands. . . .
>
> Padding to the extent now necessary is, in my opinion, very unsatisfactory because the bags move when the ship is in flight and the

padding becomes loose and the projection complained of is again exposed.

Although the gasbags have recently been reconditioned and were in good order when placed in the ship a few weeks ago, there are now many holes in them.

I am fully aware that to remedy the faults complained of is in the nature of a large undertaking and it may be necessary to remove the bags from the ship. Until this matter is seriously taken in hand and remedied I cannot recommend to you the extension of the present "Permit to Fly" or the issue of any further Permit or Certificate.[23]

McWade had inspected the airship in mid-June, had found everything in order, and on June 26 had issued a Permit to Fly, an approval that was valid for a month and without which R101 could not take off. Now he was withdrawing it. Now he was saying that putting on thousands more pads was not a sufficient remedy. He was saying he fully understood the implications of his demand: R101 would have to go back in her shed for many months. The gasbags would have to be pulled in. Anyone could see what that meant: *R101 was not going to India in September.* In another world, McWade's demand might have been seen as simple prudence, the sort of guidance the Air Ministry might hope to get from its inspectors. But in the context of Lord Thomson's all-or-nothing deadline, this was the worst thing anyone at Cardington could possibly say.

Outram was alarmed by the letter. He believed it his duty to forward it to Sir John Higgins, the member of the Air Council responsible for airships, the position just under Thomson's. That is what Outram should have done. But before he did, he asked Reggie Colmore for his opinion. This was an interesting move, considering that the Colmore-led Royal Airship Works was the very thing being criticized by McWade.

Colmore pushed back hard. He replied to Outram on July 8:

I feel sure you will agree that we cannot accept, as a matter of principle, that the gasbags in an airship should be clear of all girders.
Also I expect you will agree that we can accept padding as being a
satisfactory method of preventing holes from forming in gasbags
from this cause. . . . We have little doubt that the padding will be a
permanent remedy and, if this is accepted, then it is certainly not a
large undertaking to put the matter right.[24]

Colmore was bullying Outram, who knew little about airships. The
bullying continued in a subsequent telephone conversation, after which
Outram became convinced that "the situation was not as serious as he
had first supposed."[25] Outram wrote an oddly fatalistic note to McWade
on July 11, which at once slapped him down and seemed to suggest
that fixing the holes was now *his* problem.

Of course I fully realise the necessity of avoiding the contact of these
damaging points to the gas-bags. I have taken the matter up with
D.A.D. [Director of Airship Development Reginald Colmore] who
is in agreement but, as you yourself realise, it is impossible to alter
the hull structure of the ship at this stage. The only expedient at the
moment is to pad and it is your duty to see that every point which
may lead to damage is padded in the proper manner.[26]

AND THAT WAS THAT. The workers at the Royal Airship Works
set about padding the steel and replacing the cover. Rope and McWade
would be ignored. With Outram's acquiescence, Colmore and Richmond
became, in effect, judges and juries in their own case. They could not
be expected to rule in favor of their own incompetence. Since McWade
was not the sort of man to go over the heads of two powerful department
chiefs, his memo would never be read by anyone else. He put his head
down and went back to work, running a few more tests just to see how

bad the problem really was. He reported, "R101 had suffered a loss of gas equivalent to about a ton of lift an hour," which was three times Richmond's earlier estimate. On a flight to India such leakage could result in a reduction of a staggering forty-eight tons of lift, resulting in a forced landing after only twenty-three hours in the air.[27] And no one at the Air Ministry had a clue about what was going on. As Air Member for Supply and Research John Higgins said later, "I never got any written report of the flights in June 1930."[28]

ON JULY 29, 1930, at 2:48 a.m., R100 slipped her mast at Cardington, headed for Montreal in the British Dominion of Canada, a city and country that were wildly enthusiastic about airships in general and in particular about the idea of regular transatlantic flights. Lord Thomson was not on board. In spite of constant contractual disputes with the ever-rambunctious Dennistoun Burney and his private Airship Guarantee Company, which irritated Air Ministry people to no end, Thomson had never paid much attention to R100. It was in his mind the lesser ship, the ship with smaller ambitions, the more conventional, less interesting, and less innovative airship. He had visited Cardington many times during R101's construction. He had never once visited Howden. Perhaps he saw R100 as the sop he had to throw to Parliament to allow him to build his marvelous India-bound socialist airship. Still, while R101 languished in her shed undergoing major fixes, R100 would go first. R100 would attempt to become only the fourth airship to cross the Atlantic and the first critical piece in Thomson's empire scheme. She carried a crew of thirty-seven, with seven passengers. Among the latter were Reggie Colmore (who hated to fly), Dennistoun Burney, Nevil Shute Norway, Frederick McWade, Archie Wann (a former captain of R38), and Scott, in an ill-defined command role that had been the subject of many memos. (The crew included four key members of R101's India flying team: meteorologist Maurice

Giblett, Second Officer Maurice Steff, Navigator Ernest Johnston, and wireless man Arthur Disley.)

While professing confidence and optimism, many of the men, including Colmore, Captain Ralph Booth, First Officer George Meager, and chief calculator Nevil Shute Norway, were worried about the cover.[29] It had been patched and repatched, doped and redoped, sewn up again and again with needles and thread, and bolstered with more fabric. It had never ceased to be a problem. Something was always wrong with it. It was not watertight. Which meant that gasbags got soaked, and R100's wet bags had already split. The cover was subject to ripples and waves, like R101's. It frayed and tore. The R100 team had decided in March not to replace the entire cover, but the piecework fixes did not inspire confidence. "As usual with compromises," wrote Meager, "this one was only partially successful. . . . The cover still leaked very badly, especially at the main frames, so much so that whenever we flew through a heavy rain a perfect cascade of water would fall between the bags."[30]

In spite of this, R100's Atlantic crossing was mostly uneventful. The weather was good. The crew played cards. Some of them even became a bit bored. Many caught up on sleep. At midday on the second day two foot-long rips appeared in the cover on the ship's underside. They were quickly repaired from the inside with needle and thread. R100 made landfall over the coast of Belle Isle, between Labrador and Newfoundland, at 1:15 a.m. on July 31, forty-six hours and twenty-seven minutes after leaving. She was running full power to make Montreal by nightfall. All was well.

At around 3:00 p.m. that day, over the St. Lawrence River about 125 miles northeast of Quebec City, with the sun shining and mostly clear blue sky above them, R100 was struck broadside by a gust of wind. The result was, in Meager's words, "the most terrific roll I have ever experienced in an airship." The ship rotated in a stomach-churning ten-degree arc, yawed violently, then whooshed upward from one thousand to eighteen hundred feet. The crew had no idea what had hit them, though locals could have told them that it was a katabatic wind off the northern mountains that they all knew well as the Cannon.[31] A crew sent out to inspect the damage found that the fabric on the bottom of the port horizontal fin was in complete tatters over an area twelve by fifteen feet. As Meager put it, "There was an enormous gaping hole large enough to drive a double-decker bus through."[32] In addition, two three-foot tears had opened in the cover along the bottom fin, along with a twelve-foot split on the starboard horizontal fin. Armed with needles, thread, and dope, the airship's eight riggers made emergency repairs, often clinging to lacing wires a thousand feet above the earth.

Crippled, R100 now limped toward Montreal at 25 mph, hoping to arrive by midnight. But she was about to get another lesson in North American atmospheric currents. At around 7:30 p.m. the airship ran dead into a fifteen-mile-long squall line—basically a set of thunderstorms in a line. The squall was clearly visible ahead of R100, and the storm clouds also clearly did not extend far south. The line could easily be skirted. But Scott, standing in the control car next to Booth, ordered him to fly into the center of it. "We had ample fuel," wrote Shute, "and there was no occasion to take the ship, already damaged, through this storm. . . . Scott should have known better."[33] Scott did this in spite of a clear ruling from the Air Ministry's John Higgins before the flight that the captain was to have complete authority over the ship.[34] Booth did not challenge Scott. The order stood.[35]

For some odd reason, at this moment Burney, Booth, Scott, and Shute all went off to drink sherry in the lounge.[36]

Flying at twelve hundred feet just below the bottom of the thunderheads, R100 entered the storm. She was immediately hit by a violent updraft that tilted her nose up twenty-five degrees. Then the storm caught up with the rest of the giant airship, flipped her to a nose-down angle of thirty degrees, then sent her careening up to three thousand feet in less than a minute. The ship was out of control. Crew and passengers were hanging on to anything they could grab. Crockery and glassware

smashed, equipment went airborne, and anything that wasn't secured
went cascading toward the bow, stopping only when it hit something
solid. Some of the debris just kept on flying through the hull. Nevil
Shute recalled, "Supper laid on the centre table of the saloon shot off,
downstairs, up the corridor, til some of it reached Frame 2 [near the
bow]. I think the ship must have been at least 35 degrees nose down
for a bit of cold meat or a slice of bread to get as far up as the nose
curvature of the ship."[37] She had just begun to level out when another
burst of turbulence sent her soaring even higher, into a nose-stand at five
thousand feet. In the middle of all this, a crew member knocked over a
bucket of bloodred fabric dope, which flowed downward through the
ship, threatening an electrical short and requiring the electrical master
switch to be turned off. That meant much of this violent movement
took place in the dark. Repairs were made by flashlight, and the ship
crept to Montreal and reached her mast at 4:37 a.m.

The Canadians loved her anyway. Enormous crowds thronged the
mast to see her and cheer her. R100 was tethered for nine days while
repairs were completed, then went off on a tour of Canadian cities that
covered 926 miles and lasted twenty-six hours. There was more trouble:
this time an engine broke up and smashed a gear housing, causing
pieces of engine to destroy the propeller and damage a main girder. The
engine was useless for the rest of the trip. On the way back across the
Atlantic, water from a rainstorm poured through the outer cover into
the crew compartment. The water short-circuited the electrical heating
and cooking systems, dropping the interior temperature to forty-five
degrees and ending any hot food or drink. As the ship neared landfall
in Ireland, an inexperienced height coxswain put the ship into a dive
from two thousand feet to five hundred feet. Captain Booth grabbed
the wheel at the last moment, commenting, "The silly young mutt
almost had us in the drink."

She landed in Cardington at 11:06 a.m. on August 16, welcomed by a
small crowd that Noel Atherstone called "really rather disappointing . . .

mostly composed of crew's relatives and some of the locals."[38] But Lord Thomson was there, and he praised the crew for "having accomplished the first and successful step in the development of our new generation of British airships. This contribution to our imperial communications will be of incalculable significance." R100's problems were not quite over. While the airship was being refueled at the mooring, three fuel tanks broke free of their mountings and fell through the ship's cover, where they hung in space until they were drained of fuel. Such an event, en route, would have been a disaster.[39]

Colmore said that he was delighted with the flight. In a letter to his friend Air Chief Marshal Geoffrey Salmond, he said, "With the exception of the lift of the ships, both have exceeded my expectations. They handle in the air perfectly."[40] The latter statement was manifestly untrue. He also conceded that the overland portion of the trip in Canada was too dangerous for an airship to fly. In this he concurred with Hugo Eckener, whose experiences with American thunderstorms and air currents over the western desert had scared him. Scared as well were the surviving crew of the USS *Shenandoah*, the giant helium-filled, American-built airship that was struck by violent updrafts and crashed in an Ohio thunderstorm in 1925, killing fourteen. Such was Colmore's concern that he wanted to build a new mast on the Atlantic coast, so future ships would not have to fly over land.

The number two structural designer under Barnes Wallis at Howden, Nevil Shute, who was otherwise quite proud of his creation, wrote later, "Our outer cover was just good enough for the service demanded of it, but only just."[41] In his view, they got lucky.

CHAPTER TWELVE

THE VIOLENT, UNSEEN WORLD

At just after 2:00 a.m. on October 5, 1930, engine mechanic John Henry "Joe" Binks is awakened in his berth by George Short, the engineer of the watch. Short has just left the nacelle where Binks works and knows that Binks is late. Binks jumps from his bunk. Short hands him a cup of hot cocoa and tells him that R101's five engines, including the one Binks is responsible for, are in good working order. Binks's graveyard shift is about to begin. Binks, a cheerful, square-jawed Yorkshireman who was a member of the heroic crew of R33 on its wild North Sea ride, gulps down the cocoa, then heads aft, traveling about 150 feet along the narrow walkway that runs nearly the length of the ship. He heads for his engine car, where he climbs ten feet down a rope ladder to where his thrumming nine-foot-long, two-and-a-half-ton, 650-horsepower diesel engine with its enormous propeller awaits him.[1] On his way to the ladder, he passes Michael Rope going the other way.

He sees Rope hoist himself up into the tangle of girders, wires, gigantic harnesses, and dark, surging gasbags.

What is Rope doing at this late hour? That is a good question. He is the man most responsible for the physical form of R101. But he is not part of the crew for the Egypt-India voyage and has no role in flying the ship. He is a passenger with no official duties. Yet there he is at two in the morning, ascending into the dim, cavernous spaces inside R101's 777-foot by 130-foot interior. Rope, the strict Catholic who moved his family away from Cardington to avoid the alcohol-fueled culture there, has almost certainly not been drinking and socializing with the others. Most likely, he is up in the rigging at that hour because he is worried. Rope wrote the letter four months before raising an alarm about the outer cover, making the heretical suggestion that R101's flight be delayed. In the fall of 1929 he protested the letting out of his ingenious wire harnesses. He was ignored then, too. Rope knows that a failed cover means soaked gasbags, and waterlogged goldbeater's skins tend to split along their seams. He is perhaps just acting rationally, checking on the cover and bags after seven and a half hours of rain and high winds.

At the same moment, engineer foreman Harry Leech is in the smoking lounge, which is located on the center line of the airship, aft of the chart room and wireless room, and below the deck where passengers and off-duty crew sleep peacefully. Like Rope, Leech is a passenger and not an official member of the crew. Like Rope, he feels responsible for the ship he helped build. Leech is a handsome forty-year-old who, in his trademark heavy, round-rimmed glasses, looks a bit like the comedian Harold Lloyd. He worked on nonrigid airships during the war, earning the Air Force Medal for gallantry in 1919. He is a brilliant automobile mechanic, too, part of legendary British racer Malcolm Campbell's engine team from 1921 to 1924.

After visiting the lounge earlier for a smoke with Irwin and Gent, Leech made a tour of the ship's five engine cars. He returns at around 1:45 a.m. for another smoke and a drink. He sits alone now on a cushioned wicker settee against the wall in the sixteen-by-twelve-foot space with asbestos walls and ceiling, with his glass, ashtray, decanter, and soda siphon in front of him. The image is arresting. A man alone in a small white room, engines droning and clacking somewhere beneath him, above him so many sleepers, in berths he cannot see. Though he doesn't know the particulars, the airship that looms invisibly above him is coming up on the ancient town of Beauvais, France. She is running hard against a 50 mph wind at an elevation of twelve hundred feet. According to later statements from one witness on the ground, "The wind was very violent and the rain was rather strong. The wind was coming in gusts, a tempest from the southwest, very strong, but not lasting. The wind was in heavy gusts and changing in direction." Another witness said, "The wind was blowing in squall."[2] The air temperature is fifty degrees Fahrenheit. R101 continues to labor forward, going so slowly—20 mph over ground—that a witness on the ground thinks that she seems "in difficulty."[3] She has averaged a mere 33 mph over the 248 miles they have traveled since leaving Cardington. She is two and one-half hours behind schedule. Her crew will have to do much better if they are to make Lord Thomson's state dinner in Ismailia.

Nor does Leech witness the change of watch, which happens on schedule at 2:00 a.m. Captain Irwin retires. Second Officer Maurice Steff takes command of the ship. He is the least experienced of R101's officers.[4] The chief coxswain is the handsome veteran George "Sky" Hunt, who supervises the rudder and elevator coxswains.

In the lounge, Leech, sitting peacefully, feels a massive shift in the unseen world around him. The movement is violent and sudden. In an instant everything in the lounge is moving, including Leech. He is thrown forward. He slides along the settee and comes up hard against the forward bulkhead along with his table, ashtray, glass, and other glasses and the soda siphon. Because he is in a sealed chamber with no view on the outside world, he has no horizon lines, no landmarks, to tell him what is happening to the ship. But he can *feel* the world drop away. The airship is in a dive. He tries several times to get to his feet. He has the strong sense that, as he says later, "we must have dived a considerable distance.[5] He finally manages to stand and realizes that the sealed container he is in has leveled out. The crashing sounds have stopped. He drags the table back into position, picks up the glasses and soda siphon, and places them back on the table.[6] For a moment—it will not last long—everything again seems right in the world.

CHAPTER THIRTEEN

FOOLS RUSH IN

By the late summer of 1930, when the final preparations were being made for R101's departure, Christopher Birdwood Thomson had become a force to be reckoned with in British politics. He was a leading light in the British Labour Party. His remit as air minister took him deep into areas of defense and economic policy. His speeches, always witty and thoughtful and occasionally barbed, seemed to rise from a man who had spent decades, instead of less than two years, on the national political stage. His friendship with Prime Minister Ramsay MacDonald gave him access and influence at No. 10 Downing Street that few politicians in the United Kingdom could match. MacDonald, in fact, tended to overload his friend with assignments. Thomson was a member of seven different cabinet committees and chairman of three of them.[1] He worked long hours, traveled about in the ministry motorcar, and lunched at the best clubs in town with the most powerful people in the kingdom. He loved good food and good wine. "At one famous restaurant, where he was a familiar figure when his means allowed it," wrote his friend Basil Liddell Hart, "he used to indulge in his foible of discussing the menu in French with a fellow connoisseur, the head waiter."[2] That summer he moved into a bigger and more comfortable flat at 122 Ashley Gardens, in Westminster, half a mile from Westminster Palace and Parliament.[3]

He was still infatuated with his married Romanian princess, Marthe Bibesco, though his workload had begun to get in the way of their meetings. He was no longer the swoony forty-year-old military attaché who wrote her adolescent love poems in wartime Bucharest ("How may

she catch the sunlight, / and wear it in her hair?") or the struggling
politician of the early 1920s who complained that she had no time for
him. Their roles had reversed. In the summer of 1930 she found herself
in the role of supplicant.

They did manage what Marthe called "a happy, intimate weekend."[4]
On July 18 she arrived at the Ritz Hotel in London, where she was
welcomed by a bouquet of red roses from Thomson. The next day Kit
and Marthe were conveyed by an Air Ministry car forty miles northwest to Chequers, the splendid sixteenth-century country house of
British prime ministers. Except for one other guest—the niece of the
Marquis de Breteuil—they had the prime minister to themselves. "He
is the most amiable—and teasing—of hosts," Marthe wrote. She and
MacDonald became fast friends—a friendship that would last many
years and eventually include a bit of romance. She was amazed at how
close Thomson and MacDonald were. "They understand each other
without words," she wrote.[5]

Back in London, Thomson looked after state affairs while Marthe
made social rounds: a garden party at Buckingham Palace; visits with
her usual sparkling array of political and literary celebrities, including
Countess Margot Asquith, widow of former prime minister Herbert
Asquith, and Lytton Strachey, a founding member of the Bloomsbury
Group. Marthe saw Thomson a few more times before she left London.
They watched cricket at Lord's, dined with friends, and took in Noël
Coward's *Bitter Sweet* with Sefton Brancker and Auriol Lee. They met
each other for tea on the terrace of the House of Lords and walked in
St James's Park. "We sat on a bench in the park for a long time," Marthe
recalled later, "talking about his possible nomination as Viceroy. 'I think
I can have it if I want it,' he said." (Thomson wrote to a friend that
he believed MacDonald's Labour government would be lucky to last
another year, meaning Thomson would soon be needing a new job.[6])
"He told me the airship was making good progress and would surely
be ready on time," Marthe wrote. "We parted at the door of the Ritz."[7]

Their contentment would not last. On August 20 Thomson wrote her a letter apologizing for three unanswered letters she had sent him and telling her that, in addition to having ignored her, he was too busy to see her that month. She did not take this well. She protested that he had not accepted her invitation to come to Paris "when all the world was on holiday . . . all but CB." He countered by suggesting they might meet there in September. She answered that she had to be back in Romania to attend a reception for a delegation of legal professors— hardly a pressing cause. They were having a spat. Now it was his turn to protest. He answered on August 25, saying, "You write, dearest, as though I did not understand—and had hurt your feelings. This is unjust. There is nothing in the world I should less like to do than cause you any pain. But not only is my work absorbing . . . it never ends." In September, the month that led up to R101's departure for India, the two exchanged no letters at all.

THE RACE TO INDIA—the final push—was on. It had not started out as a race and as a matter of policy made no sense as a race, and it wasn't a race against anyone in particular, certainly not the Germans, who were merrily circling the globe in the *Graf Zeppelin*. But there it was: all of Cardington working furiously to finish R101, fix her problems, gas her up, test her, and get her up in the air and pointed toward the distant East by the end of September. So, a race against *time*, on terms set entirely by the Right Honourable Christopher Birdwood Thomson, First Baron Thomson of Cardington. He had decided—and his decision seemed quite irrevocable, no matter how polite his demurrals—that R101 *must* complete her London–Karachi–London round trip in time for him to address the delegates to the Imperial Conference at Westminster Palace on October 20. Everyone could do that math. Departure would have to take place no later than October 4, preferably sooner. Among other subjects, Thomson would talk at the conference about the future of airships, which was not an academic question. The British Treasury had approved his plans to expand his program with two larger, 7.5-million-cubic-foot airships, but had made the approval subject to endorsement by the Imperial Conference. The people in Cardington knew perfectly well what that meant: if R101 failed, then so did the British airship program. The future of British airships, and the future of all jobs at Cardington, depended on R101 not only completing the ten-thousand-mile voyage but doing it in fifteen or sixteen days, including a five- or six-day stopover.[8] Hence the race, which sometimes looked more like panic.

Nestled inside that two-week-plus trip, unknown to almost everyone, was Thomson's planned pilgrimage to Shimla, India, to visit Lord Irwin, the reigning viceroy, at his magnificent viceregal lodge in the foothills of the Himalayas. In a letter to a friend, Thomson confided that he would spend two days there.[9] This seemed reasonable enough until one noted the distance between Karachi and Shimla: 750 miles. How Thomson figured to make that trip and return in four days to Karachi is not known. But his reasoning was clear enough: if the future of airships was on the line, so was his own future as ruler of a nation of 300 million people.

Much work remained to be done on the airship before she was ready to fly. She had to be split in two and a new bay added that would accommodate the single, gigantic new gas cell containing 510,300 cubic feet of hydrogen. A new cover had to be lashed to most of the ship, gasbags rehabbed and padded, and two new engines with reversing propellers installed in the gondolas. This colossal volume of work would involve 162,000 man-hours of design and 437,000 of manual labor.[10] The Cardington crew labored furiously, and by mid-September almost all of it was finished. The crews waited only on the last reversing Tornado diesel. Engines—including the problem of reversing propellers—had bedeviled the work crews for years. Now those problems had been solved. The stunning innovation of placing diesel engines in a flying machine had worked. The builders were sprinting toward their deadlines, and it seemed, finally, as though they might make it, as though Lord Thomson might really get to India, and back, on time.

Which was why Chief Inspector Frederick McWade's discovery on September 23—in Imperial Airship Scheme terms the very last minute—was so disturbing. He had been examining the cover, most of which was brand-new. The original plan to use pre-doped fabric had failed miserably, so the airship had been refitted with linen that was then laboriously doped in place. This work, which covered three-quarters of the airship—more than four acres of cloth—had been completed in August.

What had not been replaced—because it had originally been doped after being set in place—were three large sections of the cover: eighty-six feet near the bow, fifty-three feet in the aft section, and sixty-three feet behind the tail. Thirty-three thousand square feet in all. McWade found that in these sections a rubber solution that had been used to apply patches to weak spots had interacted with the dope and caused severe deterioration. He found the fabric so weak in many places that he could put his finger through it. R100 team members George Meager, Ralph Booth, and Nevil Shute Norway handled pieces of the same rotten R101 cover around the same time. They found that "in parts it was friable, like scorched brown paper, so that if you crumpled it in your hand it broke up into flakes."[11] Vincent Richmond, called Dope because of his wartime expertise in these matters, gave immediate orders "for additional reinforcing strips to be stuck all over places where the rubber solution had been used."[12]

Thus a cover that had already been shored up by glued-on patches was now subject to even more glued-on patches—patches on patches. Many of these were in the forward part of the ship, just behind the bow curvature, where enormous amounts of stress would occur when flying nose up. The jury-rigged cover had been jury-rigged again. The most prudent solution would have been to replace all of the fabric. But

McWade's discovery had come less than two weeks before the scheduled flight. Time had run out. The RAW team had no choice but to patch the patches and hope for the best.[13]

On September 27, R101 was ready for her final trial, which was supposed to last twenty-four hours. That only a single trial was scheduled for a radically modified airship seems strange now and seemed strange then. She was a very different ship from the one that had flown in the Hendon air show in June, where she had handled badly. This was really her first trial. She was longer and heavier, with new engines and an untried cover. Her control systems had been modified. The gasbag padding had never been tested. Nor had the older parts of the outer cover ever been flown at full speed—the critical test of the fabric exterior. In her ten trials and 103 hours aloft R101 had not flown faster than 55 mph and at that speed for only a few minutes. She had never flown in bad weather. None of this was incidental. The stress on the cover increased as the square of the speed, meaning, twice the speed, four times the stress. This was precisely the time to give the chronically weak cover a challenging trial.

With all systems set to go for the trial, the great silver airship, hope of the empire . . . waited in her shed. The northeasterly wind was too strong.[14] For four days R101 languished, offering a live demonstration of one of the greatest weaknesses of airships: the difficulty of getting them in and out of their sheds without damaging or destroying them. The handling crews of three-hundred-plus men, recruited from Cardington and nearby Henlow Air Force Base, were summoned repeatedly, then called back when the weather did not improve.

The clock ticked down. In an effort to buy himself time, the ever-resourceful Reggie Colmore sprang into action. From his desk in the three-story, colonnaded, brick-and-stone administration building in Cardington, the director of airship development evolved the idea that there was *no particular reason* the airship had to fly twenty-four hours. What was important was not the *time* in the air, or even the *flying conditions*, he reasoned, but whether, as he put it, "Major Scott was sat-isfied with the behavior of the ship." Suddenly, after years of research, development, and flying trials, the final assessment of her flying ability was being loaded onto an alcoholic former captain with a reputation for pressing on regardless of risk.

Colmore took his idea to the brand-new Air Ministry official in charge of airships, Air Vice Marshal Hugh Dowding, who had exten-sive experience of military aircraft but knew nothing about airships. Dowding had been on the job for less than a month following the oddly timed retirement of John Higgins, who departed the project for a corporate job just at the moment when his four years of work on airships would have been most valuable.[15] Dowding, whose deference to Colmore and ignorance of airship principles could sometimes make him seem both foolish and incompetent, was anything but. He was simply too new to the job to know better. He would later be in charge of the RAF Fighter Command during the Battle of Britain and play a critical role in Britain's heroic defense. He was known for his sincerity and humorlessness and was so outspoken that it would ultimately cost him his job.

But today he deferred. He bought Colmore's pitch. On the morning of October 1, R101 emerged from her shed and was walked to her mast. At 4:30 p.m. she finally departed on a flight that lasted only sixteen hours and fifty-one minutes and took place entirely in fair weather and light wind. Richmond noted in his diary that "the conditions were very perfect" and that except for the failure of an oil cooler on one of the engines, "all other items on the ship behaved perfectly." The pugna-cious Atherstone, who could often be biting in his commentary, seemed pleased, too. He wrote in his diary that the flight was "very successful." The cover didn't flap. The gasbag padding seemed to work.

Amid all of this perfection, it was easy to forget that such a trial flight in good weather was virtually meaningless as a predictor of the airship's behavior on a ten-thousand-mile trip. She had never flown longer than twenty-nine hours, but would be making forty-eight-hour flights en route to India through unpredictable weather. Worse still, mechanical problems had prevented R101 from flying faster than 51 mph—not even close to full speed. Which meant once again that the cover—the greatest threat to the ship's safety—had been only minimally tested.

R101's Certificate of Airworthiness was rushed forward, too. Consultants Leonard Bairstow and John Sutton Pippard, university professors who had since 1924 constituted the Airworthiness of Airships panel under the Air Ministry's Aeronautical Research Council, had always been considered the last word on the viability of both R100 and R101.[16] They were meant to be a guarantee against the sort of practices that had doomed R38, which included the inspection of the airship by the same people who had built her. Their very presence on the panel was the result of investigations into the crash of R38. After complaining, on October 1, that "we have not had time since essential information from the RAW [was provided] to prepare a sufficiently considered final report," they issued an oral approval on October 2 after a single limited test flight with no full-speed run and without any written report to back it up.[17] If this seems overly casual and undemanding for such a large national project, and with so much at risk, at the time R101 took off Bairstow and Pippard had *still* not produced a written Certificate of Airworthiness. Frederick McWade said later that if the decision had been up to him, he would never have granted R101 the certificate.

Though Dowding did not yet know how an airship flew, he was still perceptive enough to understand that skipping a full-speed trial was a bad idea. In an evening meeting on October 2 with Thomson, Colmore, and Louis Reynolds, Dowding put forward an unusual idea: R101 could perform her full-speed trial on the way to Egypt. He proposed to order Colmore to carry out the full-power trials en route. "If anything was not satisfactory over the full-power trials, there would still be time to turn back and abandon the flight to India," he said.[18] Though Dowding's idea was at odds with the theory and practice of aircraft trials, it was no odder, in its own way, than flying a virtually untried ship over the forbidding terrain of the Middle Eastern deserts to Karachi. There is no record of how the others in the meeting reacted; perhaps it was simply thoughtful silence. Dowding came away thinking that he had received tacit approval for his idea. He was, in fact, ignored, commenting later that the airship crew "was not complying. . . . I don't know what the reasons were."[19]

At the same meeting, Thomson pushed again for an early departure, first for Friday evening, October 3, and then for Saturday morning, October 4. For once Colmore dug in, insisting that the men were exhausted and that leaving earlier would mean arriving at Ismailia in daylight, when the sun might create havoc by heating R101's gas and making it difficult to land. Thomson yielded and even apologized. "You mustn't allow my natural impatience or anxiety to start to influence you in any way," said the man who had for nearly a year relentlessly pushed to leave for India on time. "You must use your considered judgment."[20]

Thomson, in any case, was well pleased. As the 8:00 p.m. meeting ended, he pronounced, with some satisfaction, "Well, that is all settled. I can make certain of being back on the twentieth."

Or perhaps not quite settled. The following morning, October 3, he paid a call on Ramsay MacDonald at No. 10 Downing Street. MacDonald had never understood his friend's urgency and now asked again if he had to go. MacDonald mentioned the potential risk. Why couldn't Thomson stay and help the prime minister with the Imperial Conference? Thomson was steadfast. "CB brushed aside any risk," MacDonald wrote later. "He had his heart set on the flight, he said. It was the right thing for him to do. He believed in the ship. It was his child. . . . Later, as he descended the stairs, and I leant over the balustrade at the top to see the last of him, he stopped and called up in lightsome words that if the worst came it would soon be over and that the fate of all of us was written."[21]

That same afternoon Thomson's old friend Sefton Brancker, the pint-size, monocle-wearing bundle of energy who was Great Britain's director of civil aviation, also pleaded to cancel the flight. What Brancker thought of the flight's prospects is not clear. But he did believe, according to one of his senior staff officers, Major Oliver Villiers, that "the whole policy of the trip was nonsense." Brancker did not try to persuade Thomson that the voyage was too risky. (Brancker's Directorate of Civil Aviation was the agency charged with issuing R101's Certificate of Airworthiness.) Instead, he told Thomson—as Brancker had done before—that it would be a far better idea if the airship stayed in England for the duration of the conference. That would give the delegates to the Imperial Conference the chance to fly, eat, and even sleep on board. Brancker said, according to Villiers, that "he had told Lord Thomson that if he did go to India, it would not convince any of the dominion premiers." Though Lord Thomson could say he had had a marvelous journey, "it was not going to be the same thing as though they had gone up in the ship themselves," Brancker had said.[22]

Thomson brushed off Brancker, who told Villiers later, "I got rapped over the knuckles and I got no change. He [Thomson] repeated all his old arguments again."

Thomson received a final challenge from an unexpected quarter: his brother Colonel Roger Gordon Thomson, with whom he was quite close. Roger told Kit that he felt, as Roger put it later, "desperately anxious" about the flight, and that his brother was taking a large risk. Roger believed that the remedial work done on R101 "would upset all of the mechanical strains in the ship and would be highly dangerous." Thomson reacted angrily. "He flared up and lost his temper with me for the first time in my life," Roger later recalled. But Roger went on, pleading on behalf of the other people on board R101: "Don't put everyone you know in that ship."[23] Thomson was, again, unmoved.

Though Roger was likely unaware of it, one of the last tasks Lord Thomson performed before leaving was to write out his will. "In the event of my death during the flight of R101 to and from India, or as a result thereof," he wrote, sitting in his office at Gwydyr House, "I bequeath everything of which I die possessed (cash, shares, chattels, and papers) to my brother, Colonel Roger Gordon Thomson, CMG, DSO, of Springhill, Widdington, near Newport, Essex."[24]

CHAPTER FOURTEEN

A VERY VIOLENT END

Minutes matter now. Seconds matter. In the wind-torn, rain-swollen night over Northern France, we can see only flashes. We can see only pieces of light and darkness. We can see only what the men see, the precious and lucky few.

Joe Binks, late for work and fortified by hot chocolate, hustles along the gangway toward the stern of the ship, traveling about 150 feet.[1] He climbs through the hatch, then down the rope ladder, a perilous space between the dark hulk of the airship and the suspended engine nacelle where the wind exceeds 60 mph. A lost step or missed handhold and he is gone into the night, or perhaps into the propeller. Though airships are known for being quiet and tranquil, the world inside R101's cramped engine cars is anything but. The air is piston-pounding loud, hot, and smoky. Between the engine block and the wall of the car there is barely room to turn around.

Inside, Binks is kidded for his lateness by his fellow engine mechanic Arthur Bell, the man he is relieving, a veteran who has been in the airship service since 1919 and served on the ill-fated R33. Bell points to the engine chronometer, which reads 02:03 hours. Bell could be in bed by now. Minutes matter. Seconds matter. Though conversing is hard, the two men manage it anyway: they discuss engine temperature and pressure.[2]

Binks has no idea that his late arrival has saved Arthur Bell's life.

A minute or so later the ship pitches precipitously forward. The men can feel it. They know that R101 is in a steep dive. Thirty harrowing seconds later she levels. Inside the cramped, dim, noisy nacelle, Binks and Bell understand nothing. An order comes across the ship's telegraph to slow the engines, for what possible reason is impossible to say. Bell barely has time to do this before he is thrown forward again, this time in a dive that lasts probably fifteen seconds. But it is an excruciatingly long fifteen seconds. Time slows. Binks, who in his own description is looking out the door of the nacelle, begins to understand what is going to happen. The ship drops, and he sees nothing, nothing, as she continues to drop, nose at a terrifying downward angle of twenty degrees, plunging into the darkness of the unimaginable French countryside below. He sees the ground come up and feels the airship crash into the earth. She hits nose down, an oddly nonviolent action—more of a massive crunch—followed by an explosion in the forward part of the ship so powerful that a pedestrian more than eight hundred feet away is blown off his feet and the sky is filled with burning debris, some of which lands two miles away.

The time is 2:09.[3]

The aft engine car bumps along the ground for a short distance and lands in a world of fire. Flames rise through its collapsed floor, through the doorway; they encircle the engine and the fifteen-gallon gas tank for the starter engine—a point of weakness on the otherwise all-diesel airship. Fire is everywhere. Smoke fills the car, which has been jammed upward into the ship's hull. Binks and Bell are trapped. As they conclude simultaneously that they are going to be burned to death—"We gave ourselves up for lost," according to Bell—somewhere above them in the inferno that used to be an airship a two-hundred-gallon water tank ruptures, sending a cascade of water over the engine car and drenching Binks and Bell. The waterfall has given them a way out. With wet rags over their faces, they jump clear, landing in rough grass on the edge of a wood. The world around them glows incandescent red. From later photos of their engine car, smashed and burned and collapsed beyond recognition, its duralumin sheet metal sagging like wet paper, it is a miracle they escape at all.⁴ The sight of their burning, skeletal airship astounds and saddens them. Her cover is burned away, her gasbags gone, her entire "accommodation" section collapsed and burning furiously, girders glowing and collapsing, flames shooting up from fuel tanks and burning puddles of oil on the ground, minor explosions still taking place. They circle the ship, shouting, trying to find other survivors.

IN THE SMOKING LOUNGE Harry Leech hears the bell of the engine telegraph, feels the ship dive a second time and then the surprisingly mild shock of impact. Two seconds later the explosion produces, in his words, "a blinding flash of fire" and then sends a "mass of flame" sweeping aft from the region of the control room, a massive *whoosh* as though a large pool of gasoline has been ignited. Leech watches this through the doorway, which has been sprung open. He is miraculously unharmed. "Ironically," he would say later, "the smoke room was the one place in the airship which gave a certain protection against fire. But I knew I was safe only for a time." In the next second the upper passenger deck—the smoking lounge is on the first level, with the crew quarters, control room, and dining room—collapses on top of him, crashing down and settling on the backs of the settees, trapping Leech in a space three feet high that is filled with choking fumes and smoke. The flaming airship, its hydrogen/air combination burning at 3,713 degrees Fahrenheit, is collapsing around him.⁵

He is aware of human sounds.

He hears "people screaming and moaning in the crew quarters and also from the upper passenger deck, which was then blazing."

Only seconds have passed. Red fire is tearing through the airship, which has not yet fully settled to earth.

Leech tears a settee from the bulkhead, punches through the ultra-light faux-mahogany wall, and escapes the room. R101's famous trompe l'oeil architecture and asbestos linings have saved him. He forces his way through the burning Cellon windows of the promenade and jumps, landing in a tree. He scrambles to the ground, walks away from the burning ship, and only then realizes that he is on fire. His clothes are burning, scorching his neck. His hands are badly burned. Still, his first instincts are to search and rescue. He soon finds Binks, Bell, Victor Savory, an engineer from the port midships engine car, and Arthur Disley, the electrical manager and wireless operator. Disley is pinned and must be rescued. Leech crawls back into the burning ship, under red-hot girders and across pools of flaming oil, to drag him out. He saves Disley's life.

Disley has his own tale to tell. He was dozing on his bed in the switch room when he became, as he says later, "conscious of the ship dipping a little, not more than it had done before, and this change of attitude seems to be corrected immediately." He is drowsy, half-awake. He is wrong. In his half-dream state he has mistaken the airship's thirty-second dive for routine pitching. One imagines the same thing happening in the crew and passenger quarters: forty men nestled comfortably in their berths, fast asleep, opening their eyes and coming to consciousness for a moment. What was that? Nothing, the ship is level. Back to sleep. In seconds they will all die screaming in a fire fueled by 5.5 million cubic feet of hydrogen.

But Disley is lucky. He wakes himself up, and then a curious thing happens. George "Sky" Hunt, the chief coxswain, who is in charge of not only the elevator and rudder men and watch-keeping riggers but has general responsibility for the hull, cover, gasbags, gasbag wiring, ballast, and flight controls, walks into the switch room and announces in an oddly matter-of-fact way, "We are down, lads." He then heads off in the direction of the crew quarters. The statement is curious because the airship is emphatically *not* down. She is airborne. She has leveled off.

Some unseen catastrophic event has happened, but there is no one to explain what it might be.

Disley stands—or rather tries to stand because R101 has just dropped into her second dive. He is thrown back onto his bed. He has the presence of mind to trip one of the electric field switches, shutting off some of the airship's power. He is worried, correctly, about what sparks might do to all that hydrogen. He, too, experiences the crash as "more of a crunch than a violent impact." But it is followed, in his words, by a "first explosion immediately after the crash that was very violent." The airship's lights go out. Just how Arthur Disley went from the quiet comfort of the switch room to being pinned under a burning airship and suffering severe burns is not known. He does not know it himself.

In all only eight men emerge alive from the fiery destruction of His Majesty's Airship R101. Four of them are engine mechanics, all working in cars outside the airship's envelope: Binks and Bell from the aft nacelle, Victor Savory and Alfred Cook from the midships nacelles. Leech and Disley have different jobs but at the time of the crash are just a few feet from each other. The other two are riggers, men who patrol the inside of the ship's envelope: Walter Radcliffe and Samuel Church. Both are grievously burned: Church dies on October 6, Radcliffe on October 8.[6]

Which leaves six men alive from the fifty-four passengers and crew of R101.

ONLY ONE PERSON witnessed the crash: Alfred Rabouille, a rabbit poacher, who was 250 meters (820 feet) from where R101 hit the ground on the edge of the Bois de Coutumes, in the commune of Allonne, just south of Beauvais, about sixty miles north of Paris. He saw her forward running lights dip, then saw her hit the ground nose down with engines running. He watched as three violent explosions ripped through the hull—"one terrible one and two lesser ones," he recalled, starting with "a sheaf of red flames" in the forward section and sweeping almost instantly toward the stern. The first explosion blew him off his feet. "After she settled on the ground the middle part collapsed as if she had broken her back."[7] The middle part was where most of the people were.

The fields filled with people. The explosions, the fireball, and the pieces of burning airship that illuminated the skies had awakened everyone in Beauvais and Allonne. The locals gawked and tried to get close to the colossal wreckage and helped get the survivors medical help—though Arthur Disley refused treatment until he had telephoned the British Air Ministry to report the accident. Soon French soldiers, gendarmes, and members of fire brigades appeared, forming a cordon around R101 and working to extract the bodies. R101's blackened skeleton smoldered on the edge of the wood, looking less like an airship and more like a collapsed wire cage, an impossible tangle of naked girders and struts and wires. Almost all of the outer cover and gasbags were burned away. The only fabric left was in the region of the elevators. At considerable personal risk, a local man climbed up and retrieved the ship's ensign, scorched and ripped but intact, which had flown from the tail.[8] (For his action he was given one hundred francs by the British vice-consul general from Paris, who for some reason thought it appropriate.[9])

The first representatives of the British government arrived at 9:30 a.m. from the embassy in Paris. They learned quickly about this peculiar and horrifying tragedy. The dead, without exception, were burned beyond recognition. Early rumors were that Lord Thomson and Sefton Brancker had been found.* But they were soon put to rest. "In no instance were features recognizable," wrote Group Captain R. J. Bone, who led the British deputation that examined the bodies. All of them, he said, "were terribly incinerated." Many, too, were frozen in the postures of their final agonies, an alarming and horrifying sight that the searchers found deeply disturbing. Photos showed charred and blackened bodies with arms raised and crossed in front of their faces, as though trying to block the fire; others had arms outstretched, as though reaching for help. Others showed spine arched and head thrown back, as though burning to death on their beds. The cause was later

---

* Brancker's body would later be identified when it was brought back to England.

determined to be a rare form of muscular stiffening known as cadaveric spasm, which occurs at the moment of death and persists into rigor mortis—often freezing the body in its last movement before death. The condition of the bodies caused one press photographer, sent over from Great Britain, to be violently sick and to return home.[10]

Bodies, too, were found in pieces, and which fragments went with other fragments was not always clear. "In one instance," wrote Bone in his report, "some parts of a body (without head or trunk) had been placed in a box with some belongings we found nearby. We did not consider that these parts constituted a body. . . . The parts were put into a coffin with a body which was deficient of limbs." Some of the heads were shrunken nearly to the size of a fist, according to one of the workers who searched the crash site. Some of the bodies were the size of children.[11] The searchers did their best to make identifications, but that day they could only manage five. Eventually only twenty-four would be identified, from whatever personal articles or dental work had not been consumed by the fire. Vincent Richmond, for example, was identified by his cigarette box, flask, and camera; Sefton Brancker by his gold fillings and crowns; Noel Atherstone and Ernest Johnston by their cigarette cases; and Maurice Giblett by his wristwatch.[12] The bodies without names included those of Lord Thomson, Herbert Scott, and Sky Hunt.

One of the items recovered was a lady's shoe—with toe and heel portions intact—which immediately led to a wave of speculation and rumors in Allonne and Beauvais that a woman had somehow been secreted on board. The notion was so provocative that the shoe was subjected to X-ray examination by pathologists from the Home Office. They concluded that, while the black patent leather shoe indeed belonged to a female, "there are no human remains in the shoe. . . . There was no foot in the shoe at the time it was burnt."[13] No female remains were ever found. The story has been repeated over the years that the shoe belonged to Marthe Bibesco, and that the sentimental Thomson had carried it with him in his luggage. This would fit perfectly with Thomson's sentimentality, and that it was patent leather and probably foreign made argued in favor of its being Marthe's. But the fire obliterated the proof.

Thomson had brought another Bibesco-related good-luck charm with him: the ten-foot Sulaimaniya carpet that he had brought back, strapped to the outside of a de Havilland 9A, from Kurdistan in 1924, which bore an astonishing resemblance to a carpet that Marthe had brought back from Isfahan, Persia, in 1906. Marthe's rug, which lay at her Posada Palace, had been burned in a 1915 fire with everything else.[14] But the Kurdistan carpet remained, and it held fond memories for both of them. "I look on this carpet from Sulaimaniya as a talisman," Thomson had told Ramsay MacDonald. "So long as I have it, I can be sure that Marthe will always come to me."[15]

Marthe had spent the night of the R101's crash at her Mogoşoaia Palace, near Bucharest, more than a thousand miles from Allonne. She had awakened at 2:00 a.m. with a feeling of desperate malaise. "I knew something dreadful was happening," she said later. "I experienced a frightening tightening in my chest; afraid I might be having a heart attack, I woke up the servants. George [her husband] appeared and tried to calm me." He drove to the city that morning and returned with the news of the crash. Marthe was devastated. She wept for hours.

She was comforted by a note she received from her new friend Ramsay MacDonald: "You and I know what each other feels. Life will be more weary without him, but we must go on. This is the day of the memorial service and tomorrow is the funeral. I go to both and shall take you with me. He would like that. I met him at 2 o'clock at Victoria Station. I could not let him come back without being there to greet him."[16] At Marthe's request, MacDonald dropped a single red rose for her into the mass grave.[17]

In Cardington the reaction was a sort of bewildered horror. The crushing sadness was made worse by the sheer weight of human endeavor that had gone into R101. So many dreams and designs, so many lives touched—a whole world had vaporized with her. For many, the sadness of R101's destruction was crushing. Families and loved ones had said goodbye at the ship's mast only hours before. A panicked crowd gathered in front of the office of the *Bedfordshire Times*. Desperate for information, people clawed their way forward to see a board where the names of the dead and the living were being chalked. There were so few living, so many dead. Cries of anguish came up from the crowd as new names were added.[18] Meanwhile, the news rocketed around the world through the relatively new medium of radio. Like Charles Lindbergh's flight, R101's crash was one of the first mass media events.

Events moved quickly. On October 7, two days after the crash, the bodies were brought back in coffins, recrossing the Narrow Sea from Boulogne to Dover on board the British destroyer *Tempest*. On October 10 they lay in state, in flag-draped coffins, in Westminster Hall, built in 1097 and once described by Thomson as "the most beautiful gothic room in the world." The "silent, endless crowd," as the *Daily Express* called it, waited outside in queues that stretched all the way past Big Ben to the RAF Memorial. They filed through from 8:00 a.m. until after midnight and were evidence of how deeply the nation felt this tragedy.[19] At noon the same day, St Paul's Cathedral was packed to capacity for a memorial service.[20] In the congregation were His Royal Highness the Prince of Wales, the prime minister, the Lord Mayor of London, and all members of the cabinet. (Also present were the three survivors well enough to travel: Binks, Bell, and Leech.) R101's scorched and torn ensign was draped over the cathedral's altar. The same day a requiem mass was offered at Westminster Cathedral, conducted by Harry Rope, the brother of the deceased Michael Rope.[21]

On October 11, the dead were carried by horse-drawn artillery wagons across London, through city streets packed with silent crowds. The two-mile-long procession included detachments from the Royal Air Force and the Royal Navy, and the crew of R100. Next came cars with relatives of the dead, and cars with the prime minister, cabinet members, and representatives of the dominions. The bodies were taken by special train to Bedford, thence on gun carriages to a fifty-foot-square mass grave in a churchyard in Cardington, in sight of the Royal Airship Works. Thousands of people, from all parts of the country, lined the three-mile route.[22] Hugo Eckener, president of the Zeppelin company, was there. The pomp, circumstance, grandeur, and sheer scale of the events were equivalent to a royal funeral. The last such outpouring of national grief in Great Britain had taken place in 1912, after the sinking of the *Titanic.* That only forty-eight died on R101 a decade after a war in which over eight hundred thousand British and empire soldiers died did not seem to lessen the sadness. Something about the airship tugged at national heartstrings, something about its colossal size and ambition, something bigger and harder to grasp than her linen-wrapped girders.

The R101 tragedy dominated British newspapers—and indeed newspapers all over the world. They were filled with speculation. R101 had been too heavy, the storm too strong, the hull too weak, the crew too inexperienced. Articles appeared about the gas leaks during R101's trials, and the problems with the outer cover. No one knew what had happened. The papers were also flush with criticism of the government policies that had put R101 in the air. Some of it was surprisingly virulent, considering the rawness of the national wounds. "The best defence of the dirigible cannot convince the man in the street that it is not an unwieldy and expensive engine," wrote one paper in an article entitled "Stop Building the Gasbags!" "He looks skeptically at its huge bulk and fragile framework. He knows that the envelope is filled with a deadly, dangerous gas. Can it be wondered that the lay critic of these gas bags can see no future for a machine that is, after all, founded upon the most helpless of all aircraft, the primitive balloon?" Another paper found the crash unsurprising "in view of the history of airships. On the contrary, it was to be expected, and was predicted by many people who have studied the subject and whose writings are on record." Airships, the article said, could only be "navigated in fair weather to lift a small load."[23]

Of the passengers and crew who were celebrated in print for their bravery and their accomplishments, none was more prominent than Lord Thomson, the visionary whom many viewed as a national hero. Typical of many of the tributes that appeared in print was this sentimental poem:

> We mourn his loss with national, heartfelt grief,
> A golden harp and immortal laurel wreaths,
> Heaven and earth with Angels' tears bequeath.
> We lov'd him dear. And sometimes fain would weep
> Whilst memory fond, her loving vigil keeps.[24]

The city council of Bucharest announced that it was naming a street after Thomson as a "token of gratitude for the highly appreciated services he rendered to Roumania."[25]

He would have been pleased. He had loved the country as much as he had loved his Romanian princess.

Not a few people in Cardington, including the families of the dead, shared a different view of Lord Thomson. "Whatever the technical or operational causes of the disaster," wrote Ernest A. Johnston, son of R101's navigator, Ernest L. Johnston, who perished in the crash,

> . . . Colmore, Richmond, Scott, Irwin, Atherstone, Johnston, Rope and all their colleagues died in the same instant as Thomson because, in the end, they had not been strong enough to stand up against the ruthless determination of that ambitious politician who had hitched his political reputation to the performance of "his" ship. Thomson too had courage, for he must have had an inkling that the dice were loaded against the successful accomplishment of the Indian voyage; yet, having laid his timetable on the line, he was too proud and obstinate to listen to those who counselled caution.[26]

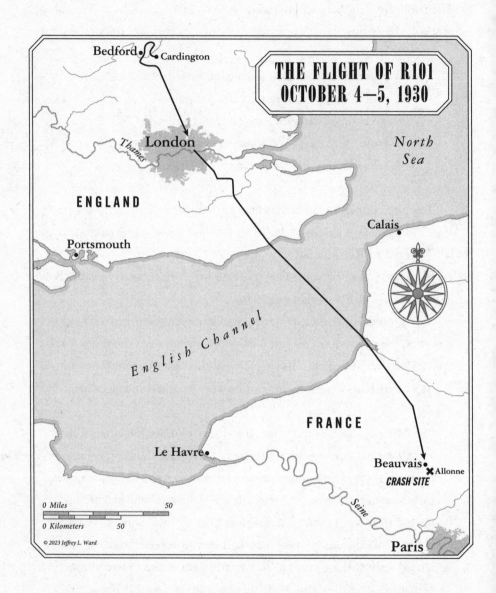

THE FLIGHT OF R101
OCTOBER 4–5, 1930

Bedford • • Cardington

London

Thames

ENGLAND

Portsmouth •

North Sea

Calais •

Le Havre •

FRANCE

English Channel

Beauvais • ✕ Allonne
CRASH SITE

Seine

Paris

0 Miles   50
0 Kilometers   50

© 2023 Jeffrey L. Ward

CHAPTER FIFTEEN

SOLVING THE MYSTERY: WHAT CAUSED THE CRASH?

R101, splayed across the Bois de Coutumes like the skeleton of a long-dead animal, posed a problem familiar to crash investigators since the dawn of manned flight. Most of the evidence had been destroyed. One hundred percent of the gasbags and all but a few strips of the cover had been burned away. All the officers and key crew members were dead. None of the survivors had been in command positions. None had been flying the ship. They had experienced the crash but were in no position to understand why it had happened. Fire had swept the vessel in seconds, burning away with ruthless efficiency almost everything that was not made of steel, duralumin, or alloy, carbonizing human flesh, vaporizing the vast organic expanses of her cover and gas cells.

A team of British officials, dispatched by the Air Ministry and commanded by the brisk Major J. C. Cooper, inspector of accidents, arrived in Allonne eleven hours after the crash. They probed the wreckage, interviewed survivors and witnesses. They were horrified, as everyone else was, by the condition of the bodies. They did not yet understand what had gone wrong, but they discovered certain truths. The time of the crash, for example. Minute and hour hands on wristwatches belonging to crew members had been fused in place the moment they died: close to 2:09 a.m. When the ship hit the ground, she was moving slowly and bumped ahead sixty to seventy feet before coming to rest, her forward section in a wood of small trees and her aft section in a meadow. The crash was followed by a single shatteringly loud explosion and then two lesser ones. One piece of cold comfort: 101's steel structure had not failed. The loss of R38 had caused designers to give R101 a strong, heavy frame—excessively so—and it had held fast, as it had not on R38 or the American airship *Shenandoah.*[1]

Major Cooper's investigators reported their findings to a newly established Court of Inquiry, based in London and chaired by Sir John Simon, a former attorney general and home secretary and a key investigator in the RMS *Titanic* inquiry eighteen years before. From October 28 to December 5, Simon's court sat in four sessions and interviewed forty-two witnesses. They gathered an immense volume of data. They hired Britain's National Physical Laboratory to run tests on a four-foot-long model of R101. They probed deeply into R101's history. For the first time the public would hear about the airship's many problems, dating from her emergence from the construction shed in October 1929. These included design and engineering errors that led to torn, chafed, and leaking gasbags, and fragile outer covers that developed 90- and 140-foot tears. They included misguided fixes to existing problems—such as letting the wire harnesses out, or patching the cover with a rubber solution, which caused severe deterioration—that led to new and even more serious problems. Investigators looked into R101's flying problems and her unexplained dives around the time of the Hendon display. The lengthy hearings—the published *Minutes of Proceedings* of the Court of Inquiry would run to seven-hundred-plus small-print pages—also dug into the politics of R101. Why was she rushed into flight? Why were so few trials made with a ship that was obviously experimental? Why had she never been tested in high winds or bad weather? How had she managed to get a Certificate of Airworthiness when her chief inspector opposed it? Had Lord Thomson pushed too hard?

At the heart of R101's mysterious death was a sequence of events that, from start to finish, took no more than five minutes. Despite the foul weather, nothing in the airship's condition at 2:00 a.m. had suggested trouble. She was in stable, level flight. Evidence of this was the uneventful change of watch. When Joe Binks arrived late for work in the aft nacelle, the engine chronometer read 2:03. Between then and 2:09 an apparently sound 777-foot airship with all engines running became a hellish, flaming wreck. What catastrophe, or series of catastrophes, as yet unseen and unknown, could account for that?

All the expert witnesses—who included Professor Leonard Bairstow, scientists from the National Physical Laboratory, Hugo Eckener, Cardington inspector Frederick McWade, R100 captain Ralph Booth, and R100 first officer George Meager—agreed that the principal cause of the disaster, and the catalyst for the events that followed, was a loss of hydrogen gas in the forward part of the ship. Such a consensus was possible in part because massive gas loss was the only way—short of structural failure or a violent thunderstorm—that a giant airship could fall a thousand feet out of the sky in a few minutes, and in part because no one believed that the R101 team had ever tested, let alone fully resolved, her problems with her cover and gasbags.[2]

Two main gas-loss theories emerged. In the first, gradual loss from holes in the gasbags or malfunctioning valves led to a critical condition in which the airship became 13.5 tons heavy—the point at which her aerodynamic lift could no longer carry her weight. In this theory, gas that was loose inside the ship's envelope made the problem worse by moving rearward as the ship pointed down, increasing the buoyancy in the stern and accentuating the dive. The problem with this conjecture was that it seemed inconceivable that an experienced airship crew would not have noticed how heavy the ship was becoming, or how much they were having to compensate for the loss of lift by flying nose up.

The second and far more plausible explanation, which the Court of Inquiry accepted, was that the wind tore the fragile cover open, exposing the huge intestine-lined gas cells to gale-force wind and rain, leading to their rupture and to a sudden and severe loss of lift.[3] The court did not dismiss the idea that some gradual loss of gas might also have occurred, but believed that this was a secondary effect. The cover had most likely failed in the section where the original linen had not been replaced but instead patched and doped.

The investigators saw the accident in three phases. In the first, R101 plunged abruptly from an altitude of "at least 1,000 feet above the ground," dropping at a steep angle for about thirty seconds and sending Harry Leech, along with his whiskey, siphon, and glasses, tumbling hard up against the bulkhead.[4] The crew may or may not have understood that an enormous, hydrogen-spewing hole had opened in the airship's forward section. But when the dive started, the height coxswain reacted properly by spinning his wheel, using the ship's powerful elevators to try to bring her nose back up. As evidence for this, the steel drums that controlled the elevators were found after the crash to be wound with cable nearly to their full "up" position.

In the second phase, the dive ended and the ship was restored to a horizontal position.

In phase three, which began fifteen seconds later, R101 dived again, this time fatally.

Explaining the second plunge was a far more difficult problem. Various solutions were proposed. Cutting the engines had caused a loss of dynamic lift. The release of ballast had—counterintuitively— prompted a further dropping of the airship's nose. Additional leakage of gas from ruptured cells had the same effect. A "sudden gust of wind" drove the airship down. None of these seemed satisfactory. Nor could the National Physical Laboratory, working with its scale model and wind tunnels, account for the fifteen- to twenty-five-degree angle of impact. The scientists were not satisfied by their results.[5]

In the 1980s, half a century after the demise of R101, an attempt was made to deconstruct the crash using computers. The analysis was done by Alan Simpson, a professor of aeronautical engineering at Bristol University and later Glasgow University, using the raw data from the National Physical Laboratory from 1930.[6] Though Simpson's work did not significantly challenge the NPL's basic conclusions, it offered a provocative, second-by-second look at how the crew might have reacted to the crisis—a model of *plausibility*, the story as it might have happened.[7] In Simpson's study, a "substantial split" in the fabric of the outer cover occurred at 2:04 a.m. By 2:05 R101 had lost 26 percent of her speed, and her nose was pointing up—sure signs that buoyancy was being lost. The captain was almost certainly summoned to the control car. At 2:06:30 water ballast was let go to lighten the ship, which caused the nose to drop, which in turn exposed the gasbags to the gusting wind, which further tore into the bags.

At 2:07 the ship entered her first dive, dropping at a rate of eleven hundred feet per minute with her nose down eighteen degrees. She was in mortal danger. In desperation the captain ordered fuel released, which in combination with the up elevator brought the airship to a fully horizontal position. But she was still falling through the sky. By 2:08:25 all of the forward ballast had been released, the nose was again dropping, and the captain knew he could not avoid hitting ground, Simpson said, so he dumped whatever ballast was left and slowed the engines, aiming for a soft landing, as the final dive began.[8] Simpson found no "catastrophic event" to explain the second dive, just a version of the same problem—gas loss—that caused the first. He believed that a strong gust of wind played a part in bringing the aircraft to ground. He did conclude, in opposition to the Court of Inquiry, that the crew erred in slowing the engines. They should have *increased* speed, he said, which, combined with the use of up elevator, could have saved the ship.

But that didn't really solve the problem of the second dive, either.

The fire and the explosions, not the crash, caused most of the mayhem. But the investigators offered no clear proof of what caused them, either. Other airships, notably the *Graf Zeppelin*, had hit the ground without going up in flames.[9] Hydrogen being hydrogen, the spark could be accounted for in any number of ways. One intriguing possibility was that the ship's calcium-phosphide flares, which were normally dropped

from the control room into the sea to measure drift, had ignited the
fire. They were contained in perforated cardboard cylinders to allow
salt water to penetrate, which would trigger an intense white blaze that
would last for thirty seconds. Later analysis determined that a large
supply of water flowed through pipes in the control car near the place
where Harry Leech had seen an open box of flares.[10] The impact with
the ground could easily have caused water to be dumped onto the flares.
The possibility was tantalizing but could not be proved. Other potential causes were (1) the forcing of the starboard forward engine up into
the hull; (2) the ignition of the starter gasoline for the diesels, which
was carried in four engine compartments; (3) the snapping of the main
electrical cable between the forward generator and the switchboard; and
(4) sparks caused by the breakup of the nose structure.[11] All of these
were possibilities. When an object that large hits the ground—full of
steel and electricity and throbbing 650-horsepower diesels—there are
bound to be sparks somewhere.

Any attempt to explain the second dive had to account for two
extraordinary pieces of evidence from the testimony of survivors. The
first was Chief Coxswain Sky Hunt's comment—overheard by electrician Arthur Disley—just before the ship went into its second dive
and as the engine telegraphs were ringing: "We are down, lads." On
its face, Hunt's statement made no sense. Hunt was an airship veteran
of immense experience. Yet he had said something that was manifestly
untrue. The ship was at that moment horizontal, apparently recovered
from her steep, thirty-second nosedive.

The only possible interpretation of Hunt's remark was that something so final and calamitous had happened that the men in command
knew immediately that there was no way to save the ship. Duty would
normally have dictated that Hunt stay in the control car, supervising the
coxswains. But the officer of the watch—Maurice Steff, unless Captain
Irwin had taken over—had evidently given Hunt an order to tell crew
and passengers that R101 was about to hit the ground.[12] Hunt was

merely carrying it out. Hunt had, moreover, made his remark *before* the second dive started, which meant that the crew *already knew* she was going down. They had given orders to the engine crews, via telegraph, to slow the engines, received just as the second dive started—a move that would have taken away whatever remained of R101's ability to lift herself up. As the men in the control car saw it, there was no point in doing anything else. With no other options, the crew were trying for a soft landing.

But what did Hunt and the others suddenly know that they had not known a few minutes before? One theory was that Michael Rope, whom Joe Binks had encountered traveling forward in the ship and then observed climbing into the girders, had reported severe damage there. This was a sound enough idea in principle—Rope wouldn't have been up late at night unless he was worried about his airship—except that when Binks encountered Rope, he was amidships, several hundred feet from where the cover-and-gas-cell catastrophe was unfolding. He was moving forward, too, at 2:02 or 2:03 a.m., which meant that, wherever he had come from, he had been even farther from the problem. Another theory was that the crew had finally become aware of just how large the hole in the cover was. But the rip by itself would not have been a reason to abandon all hope. Sky Hunt had been one of the heroes of R33, flying the ship across the North Sea in 1925 with her nose crumpled and a gasbag deflated.

The second curious bit of evidence came from the rigger Samuel Church, who was rescued from the ship but died soon after. When Major Cooper interviewed him, he was barely coherent but gave a brief account of what had happened. Church had probably gone on duty as rigger of the watch in the forward part of the airship at 2:00 a.m. He would have made his way to the bows, reaching them at 2:05 or so and reporting to Sky Hunt in the control room by means of a voice pipe.[13] That would have been the normal routine. Church had started to walk back toward the control car, he told Cooper, when, he said, "the ship took a steep diving attitude. At this moment I received an order to release half a ton of emergency forward ballast. But before I could get to it, the crash came."[14]

What did Church's orders mean? They were evidence of intent to lighten the ship—evidence, beyond the wound-up elevator cable, of the crew's response to the crisis. Evidence, too, that the crew still believed they might save the ship. The purpose of ballast was to help keep the hull level, make it possible to take off and land, but also, most critically, *to stop a vertical descent.*

But the orders seemed odd. Two ballast bags were located in the nose of the ship, each containing half a ton of water. Why had Church been instructed to drop only one of them? One explanation, put forward by airship historian Ernest A. Johnston, was that Church, while walking aft, encountered another rigger heading forward with orders from the captain to drop the full ton of ballast. The order he gave to Church might have been intended to speed up the release of the two half-ton bags.[15]

Such explanations still left unaddressed the central mystery of the R101 disaster. What had happened to make Hunt so certain that the crash was coming?

Another odd bit of evidence seemed to bear on that question. In the wreckage Major Cooper had found two broken control cables and one damaged control cable. (Control cables connected the control car beneath the middle of the ship with the rudder and the flaps in the stern.) One of the broken cables and the damaged cable were products of the crash, caused by contact with parts of the steel frame when the giant bottom fin was jammed upward into the hull. Those two damaged cables could not have caused the crash. Their condition was an *effect* of the crash.

The other broken cable presented a different problem. It had not been smashed, crushed, or nipped by pieces of broken steel. Why it had broken was not immediately clear. This cable, used to raise the elevators, was critical to the control of the airship. It ran from a drum, or spool, in the control car more than three hundred feet to an auxiliary control drum in the tail, thence a short distance to the elevator. The break had occurred in this final section of the cable. A fractured elevator cable in flight was a calamity.

To solve the problem the Court of Inquiry hired W. E. Woodward, a professor of metallurgy at Cambridge University. The fracture was "short" and "brittle"—think of a wooden match snapping cleanly in two—rather than the messier sort of "ductile" fracture that would normally be caused by pulling too hard on the cable. What could have caused it to break like that? Woodward had the solution. Heating comparable pieces of wire with a hydrogen flame, he created, with relatively low tension, a short fracture. He concluded that the cable had broken in the fire, not while in flight. This was surprising since one might have expected steel wire to become more ductile and less brittle when subjected to heat. But Woodward insisted that "dissociated" hydrogen, which caused "embrittlement," was the culprit: hydrogen atoms had diffused into the hot cable, causing the cable to weaken and break.[16]

The members of the Court of Inquiry accepted his conclusion without reservation. The elevator cable could not have been responsible for the crash, they decided, because it had broken during the fire. Woodward's study was cited only briefly in the court's report. After that, the subject appears to have been dropped entirely and was not revisited by subsequent researchers.

THEY SHOULD HAVE paid closer attention.

In 2014, Dr. Bryan Lawton, a retired reader in thermal power at Cranfield University, where he had published widely on subjects ranging from engine dynamics to erosion and heat transfer in gun barrels, began to look into the unsolved, eighty-four-year-old mystery. Though aerospace had never been his field, his curiosity about airships had grown out of his interest in hometown hero Reginald Warneford, the first aviator to bring down a zeppelin in World War I. Lawton read the report of the Court of Inquiry and crash-related documents in the National Archives. Though he possessed formidable mathematical and analytical skills, his investigation began with a simple thought experiment with information that was readily available from the old Court of Inquiry and the NPL.[17]

When Major Cooper's team examined the wreckage, they found the ship's two huge elevator flaps, port and starboard, structurally intact and in the full "down" position, to which they had fallen under their own weight after impact. This was to be expected. But Lawton spotted a glaring inconsistency that had somehow escaped everyone's notice in 1930. If the elevator cable broke after the crash, he reasoned, the fall of the elevators from full up to full down should have *unwound* cable from both the control car drum, three-hundred-plus feet away in midships, and the auxiliary drum, nearby in the tail. But the reverse was true: both drums were wound to full up. How to reconcile this with Woodward's study?

Lawton found a reasonable explanation for the state of the control car drum. When the ship hit the ground, her front section telescoped, causing a loss of eighty-eight feet in overall length. This compression moved the control car some forty-five feet closer to the tail, which left considerable slack in the elevator cable. The slack explained why the control car drum did not unwind.

Now came Lawton's breakthrough. The only logical explanation for the fully wound auxiliary drum in the relatively undamaged rear of the ship, where no telescoping had occurred, Lawton concluded, was that *the cable must have broken before the ship hit the ground.* Because it was already broken, the wire remained on the spool when the elevators fell. No other interpretation was possible. Viewed in this light, Sky Hunt's cryptic comment made perfect sense. The crew in the control car would have felt the cable break and would have known immediately that it meant that the ship had lost her dynamic lift and was going to crash. *That* was the catastrophe that had been missing from all the other studies. Contrary to the Simpson analysis, the crew had done exactly the right thing in slowing the engines. The best they could hope for was a soft landing.

Woodward's conclusions had prevented the Court of Inquiry from thinking hard enough about the consequences of their assumptions.

Lawton now had to pull off what the National Physical Laboratory, in fourteen tries with all sorts of inputs, had failed to do: mathematically calculate R101's path through the air to a nose-down crash. Fortunately he had a full array of twenty-first-century computer technology to analyze the raw data from 1930, now assuming that a cable broke before the crash.* To his surprise this was relatively easy. With little modification, the calculations lined up. Lawton's model, with broken cable, accurately predicted R101's impact at a twenty-degree angle.[18] Unlike in the NPL's analysis, Lawton's model did not have to assume a gust of wind to bring the ship to earth.[19] His analysis agreed with Simpson's study on one important point: if R101's elevators had not failed, she would have survived if all ballast had been dropped and the engines had remained at speed.[20]

In Lawton's revised scenario the crisis began with a tear in one of the forward gasbags, slowing the airship and causing the loss of seven tons of lift. Thirty seconds later it was clear to R101's crew that she was in trouble. The coxswain spun the elevator wheel, which took another thirty seconds to hit the full up position, by which time the ship was in a dive. At that point the cable broke, the elevator helm turned freely, and, though the ship had come back to horizontal, the crew realized that she was lost. All available ballast was thus immediately dropped, which caused a nose-down moment—accounting for the angle of impact—and four of five engines were stopped.[21]

Lawton's last challenge was to find what had caused the cable, which

---

* Lawton took the same equations of motion, lift, drag, and moments that the NPL used in 1931, then prepared a program using Mathcad Professional to analyze them, using a fifth-order Runge-Kutta method to integrate the equations. He published these results in the paper "Control, Response, and Crash of HMA R.101," in the *Journal of Aeronautical History* in 2018.

was supposed to be several times stronger than necessary, to break. He had an answer for this, too. During the original investigation of the crash, two different sets of scientists discovered to their surprise that the zinc-coated steel cable was in places significantly weaker than it was supposed to be.[22] The manufacturer said that the defects were caused by corrosion of the cable during storage at Cardington. Galvanic corrosion creates hydrogen, which diffuses into the steel, reducing its tensile strength and causing the common phenomenon of "hydrogen embrittlement." Such corrosion doesn't happen overnight; it takes months or years. But R101 was delayed for years while its components, including the steel wire, languished in humid warehouses. Lawton pointed out that the cable could also have weakened from diffused hydrogen from the many and voluminous gasbag leaks—literally millions of cubic feet of gas—in R101 throughout late 1929 and 1930. In both cases, hydrogen embrittlement was the cause of the break, as it was in Woodward's analysis. The difference was that Woodward theorized hydrogen flame as the agent.

In 2017 and 2018 Dr. Lawton published the results of his work—the solution of the mystery—in two scholarly articles that forever changed our understanding of the R101 crash: "R.101 Airship Disaster and the Broken Elevator Cable" in the *International Journal for the History of Engineering and Technology*, and "Control, Response, and Crash of HMA R.101" in the *Journal of Aeronautical History*.

THE CRASH HAD another feature, too, that had nothing to do with engineering or manufacturing incompetence or Whitehall politics or Scotty's recklessness or the crew's decision-making or a failure to put the airship through adequate trials. Following the wreck of R101 considerable effort was expended proving that the crew were not guilty of flying the airship into the ground. They clearly were not. As noted earlier, they flew R101 at the altitude at which she was expected to fly. They were following the big rigid rule book.

And that was the problem.

No one knows exactly how high R101 was at 2:00 a.m., but most of the educated guesses put her elevation above sea level at around 1,200 feet. This would have been perfectly normal. Since 1,500 feet was her pressure height—where gas would start to be automatically valved—the slightly lower altitude would have been a good choice. Perhaps flying below the cloud base was a good idea, too—it would have improved visibility. The elevation of the wreckage of R101 was 270 feet. Subtract that from 1,200 feet to get the airship's actual distance aboveground: 930 feet. (No wonder some of the residents of Beauvais thought she was trying to land. One of them, a decorated former artillery spotter who knew something about distances, estimated her height at 200 to 300 meters—656 to 984 feet.[23])

But other considerations applied, too, when determining height above ground. Airship "hunting"—the rising and dropping of the vessel's nose—was an accepted feature of big rigids. Some hunted more than others. "Normally you should keep within two hundred and fifty to three hundred feet on either side of your flying height," R100 captain Ralph Booth told the Court of Inquiry. "That is under normal bumpy conditions. That might be extended possibly to four hundred to five hundred feet under bad conditions."[24] Thus 930 feet above ground was only a median height, a benchmark around which R101 rose and fell. No one knows how much she was hunting that night. Based on Booth's testimony—he had just flown across the Atlantic and back in a ship very much like R101—we might guess three hundred feet. Now we are down, theoretically, to 630 feet.

But even that number—147 feet shorter than the airship—was only true if R101's altimeter was to be trusted. And, as we have noted, it wasn't. R101 did not carry an Echolot or any other independent means of verifying barometric height, though navigator Ernest Johnston had recently been shopping for one, claiming dissatisfaction with R101's current instrumentation.[25] The case is not being made here that an altimeter was responsible for the crash. No one made that argument in 1930 and no one would make it today. (As Dr. Eckener later pointed out, barometric readings in Cardington and Beauvais on the night of the accident were roughly similar, meaning that R101's altimeter should not have needed significant recalibration.[26]) But the possibility that it was wrong, even marginally, was yet another reason flying low was a bad idea, especially in foul weather.

Whether R101 fell from eleven hundred feet or nine hundred feet or seven hundred feet above the ground, her flying altitude meant she had no room for error, no space for recovery. Would the crash have taken place if she had been flying at thirty-five hundred feet? Likely not. With airships, one could always drop all ballast, trim the ship, and free-balloon, a tactic Dr. Eckener had used on several occasions. The crew did not need an elevator to accomplish that. Such a scenario is absurdly hypothetical. However the accident is viewed, R101 went down because, after a disastrous cover rupture, loss of gas, and a snapped control cable, she did not have room in space to save herself.

CHAPTER SIXTEEN

BLOODY END OF A BLOODY ERA

The British public was greatly relieved, in March 1931, to learn that no one was to blame for the crash of R101. Oh, there had been problems, to be sure. R101 was not perfect. Perhaps she had been pushed along a bit too fast, but that wasn't anyone's fault, either. Those were the conclusions of the *Report of the R101 Inquiry*, the 130-page document summarizing the Air Ministry's investigation of the accident. There were surprisingly few criticisms. The court's assessors did concede, in remarkably hedged and circumlocutory language:

> It is impossible to avoid the conclusion that R.101 would not have started for India on the evening of Oct. 4 if it had not been that reasons of public policy were considered as making it highly desirable for her to do so if she could.[1]

But the assessors took pains to point out that such political considerations could not possibly have caused the crew, designers, or managers at the Royal Airship Works to make bad or negligent decisions. "This is not to say," the report continued,

> ... that the authorities, political and technical, who were responsible for, and acquiesced in, this decision would ever have done so if they had considered that the risk that was being taken was unjustified. The Secretary of State expressly stated that he had relied on his experts. ... We do not for a moment believe that Colmore or Scott would have

accepted, without the strongest protest, the carrying out of a course
which would in their judgment expose the whole enterprise to ruin,
and risk the lives of men under their orders as well as those of distinguished passengers, to say nothing of threatening to make havoc
of future airship policy.[2]

The managers and crew did not, in other words, deliberately commit
suicide. What caused the rushed departure of an airship that had been
minimally tested and for which no operational proof of airworthiness
existed was instead what the court called an "atmosphere" made up of
several "elements." These were, the court said: (1) the conviction that,
yes, the job was risky and experimental but some "resolute men" had
to do it; (2) the feeling of impatience, caused by the endless delays and
difficulties; (3) the fear that, if the ship did not perform, there would
be no more development money; (4) the need to emulate the success of
R100; (5) the reassuring knowledge that R101 had been the product
of more research and development than any other airship in history;
and, finally, (6) the zealousness of the secretary of state himself, whose
"enthusiastic backing" of the project "provided a most comforting
support" to the staff at Cardington.[3]

All of which sounded, collectively, like an elaborate and uncon-
vincing excuse.

The driving force behind the report was less the court's desire to find
the truth than its need *to avoid blaming the dead*. The nation was still
awash in grief. A popular cabinet minister had died horribly, by fire,
as had most of the skill, experience, and dreams of the British airship
service. To critically examine the crash and the practices that led to it
meant assigning responsibility. No one had the heart to do that. The
final report had to be exculpatory—of crew, engineers, managers, and
politicians—and it was, and no one complained about it. There was no
outcry in the press or even among the eternally carping critics in the
House of Commons. Reggie Colmore's horribly mutilated corpse was

lying in the mass grave at Cardington. What could, conceivably, be the point in hauling him up on charges? Or subjecting Lord Thomson, disfigured beyond identification, to public scorn for his pile-driving obsession with the trip to India? Instead came the rather flat conclusion that the crash was the result of loss of gas in the forward part of the ship. The crew had done its job as well as it could, the ship had been well designed. The ship probably shouldn't have started for India in bad weather. Accidents happened.

Ironically the hearings themselves were remarkably pointed, thorough, and sometimes adversarial. Sir John Simon and his assessors were tough, informed, and determined interrogators. The record of those hearings, the *Minutes of Proceedings at Public Inquiry into the Loss of the Airship R.101*, is the best and most complete documentation of the tragedy.[4]

Plenty of truth was on display here. From the testimony of witnesses it was possible and indeed easy to conclude that Thomson's imperious demands led directly to the death of R101; that Colmore's toadying kept critical information from the Air Ministry and inflicted Thomson's amateurish enthusiasms on the professionals at Cardington, while Colmore's squashing of Frederick McWade, with the connivance of Director of Aeronautical Inspection Harold Outram, was catastrophically stupid and placed the airship in needless danger; that the designs of Richmond and Rope were often flawed, especially with regard to the gasbags, harnesses, and outer cover; that both the Aeronautical Inspection Department and the Airworthiness of Airships panel did not adequately do their jobs; that Professor Leonard Bairstow, in spite of his bizarre claim before the court that his job as airworthiness inspector only covered the airship's metal structure, should never have allowed R101 to fly; that the decision to conduct greatly shortened trials in fair weather violated every principle of aircraft testing; and that the decision to leave the original patched cover in place and then neglect to properly test it may have been the main cause of the crash.

But the court chose not to draw any of those conclusions.

Having aggressively pursued information, the assessors proceeded, equally aggressively, to ignore it. Having concluded that "loss of gas forward" caused the crash, they did not seek to blame anyone, or any policy, for the implicit failure of both the outer cover and the gasbags, which had been the airship's most persistent and insoluble problems since 1929. Perhaps this was what the country wanted. (For reasons noted earlier, the court determined on scientific grounds that the elevator cable was not to blame.) Because few people in the press or the public followed the hearings, and even fewer read the seven-hundred-plus pages of small print, the whitewashed verdict of the Court of Inquiry stood as the final word on R101.

Soon it did not matter what the court thought. The crash of R101 killed the British airship program. The end did not come immediately. In the weeks after the crash, Royal Airship Works employees traveled to Allonne to retrieve various bits of wreckage and strategic components, including the diesel engines, which were taken back to Cardington for analysis. The employees performed routine maintenance on R100, which was sitting alone and forlorn and deflated in her shed, her cover badly deteriorated. But mostly the hundreds of Cardington staff had nothing to do except hope their contracts might be extended. They weren't. After a brief shimmer of hope that R100 might be revived, and even that plans for the long-dreamed-of R102 might be advanced, in May 1931 the government decided to shut down most of the Royal Airship Works.[5] Six months later contractors arrived to take R100 apart. She was dismantled, flattened by a steamroller, and sold off as scrap.[6] In 1936 the works were renamed Royal Air Force Station, and in the ensuing years Cardington became a center for the manufacture of unmanned barrage balloons (used against dive-bomber attack) and the training of their operators. At the peak of its production, the factory turned out twenty-six "kite" balloons a week. The hydrogen-filled balloons and their ground crews did brilliant work in World War II.[7]

*   *   *

THE GREAT ERA of airships was not over. Not yet. Airships, as we
have seen, were hard to kill. While R100 was being deconstructed, the
Americans launched the biggest, most expensive, and most technologically sophisticated airship ever built, the USS *Akron*. Built in Ohio
for the U.S. Navy by a joint venture of Goodyear Tire and Rubber and
the German Zeppelin company, she was 785 feet long and had a gas
capacity of 6.5 million cubic feet. She had the advantages of German
engineering, German engineers, and German patents. She was the
world's first purpose-built aircraft carrier, carrying up to five "parasite"
fighter planes, which were deployed from a hangar inside the hull.*
She was, moreover, filled with *helium*, a guarantee that she could never
succumb to the hydrogen fires that had destroyed R101 and so many
other airships.

   In the eighteen months that followed, *Akron* flew seventeen hundred
hours and had a spotty safety record. She suffered three significant accidents. Twice her tail hit the ground, and once while landing she became
uncontrollably light and caused the deaths of two crew members. A trip
from California to New Jersey in 1932 was marred by often-harrowing
moments due to bad weather and mountainous terrain. But she had
survived.

   At 7:28 p.m. on the foggy evening of April 4, 1933, she slipped her
mast at Lakehurst, New Jersey, for a routine coastal training mission.
She did so in spite of a weather forecast that showed thunderstorms
approaching from the southwest.[8] Her crew saw the first lightning
at 8:30 p.m. They spent the next four hours in panicky flight from
thunderstorms that seemed to close in from all sides. *Akron* turned
west, saw lightning ahead, turned southeast, but had to spin around

---

* The fighter planes were Curtiss F9C Sparrowhawks, light biplanes. The British had experi-
mented with airship-launched fighters, both with R23 and R33, but had never built an airship
for that express purpose. Robin Higham, *The British Rigid Airship, 1908–1931*, 168, 266.

again to the northeast in the direction of Lakehurst. There was seemingly no escape. She was fleeing blindly, desperately. One of the signal weaknesses of the big rigids was that they had nowhere to land in a storm. Ships could find harbors or safe havens, airplanes could land on the many airstrips that dotted the countryside, or on a road or even in a field. But in wind and storm an airship could land neither at a mast nor on the ground. Even attempting such landings was to invite destruction. Her massive surface area, acting as a gigantic sail, was a guarantee that she would be hammered to pieces.

So *Akron* continued to flee in wild panic. At 10:00 p.m. she steered a course out over the ocean, where, according to a later government report, "the lightning became general."[9] By 10:45 p.m. captain and crew knew they were in deep trouble. They reversed course three more times, always to escape the lightning. But they could find no way out. Just after midnight the already rough air became extremely turbulent, filled with violent vertical air currents. This was characteristic of thunderstorms and was a lethal enemy of airships. *Akron* now experienced the storm-driven effect of her huge surface area: wild rises and drops as she rode the unstable air, the same conditions that had destroyed the *Shenandoah* and the *Dixmude* and had nearly wrecked R100 over the St. Lawrence River in Canada. *Akron* plunged from sixteen hundred feet to seven hundred feet, rose back to sixteen hundred, then went into a second dive. The crew dropped ballast, to no avail.

Sometime around 12:30 a.m., about twenty miles east of Barnegat Light off the southern coast of New Jersey, the *Akron*'s lower fin hit the ocean and was torn off. The rest of the ship subsided into the water and quickly sank. In the frigid water and large waves the crew—who had no life jackets—didn't stand a chance. Seventy-three of the seventy-six crew died—the worst airship disaster in history. The three who survived were rescued after they clung to an empty fuel tank. A subsequent government inquiry blamed poor navigation. "It really seems that any other course than the one taken would have compassed her salvation," wrote the report's authors, who granted that it was easier to say this than to actually navigate through darkness, fog, rain, wind, and thunderbolts. They concluded that safety lay in the west if the captain had only steered in that direction.[10] The investigators also felt strongly that the ship had been flying too low, and that her altimeter may have contributed to the crash. "It was probable," they wrote in their report, "that the ship was flying at an altitude of 300 feet more or less lower than the reading of the barometric altimeter."[11] The suggestion was that the altimeter had not been recalibrated to match the low pressure in the storm. At such an altitude, Commander Frank McCord had not fully accounted for his ship's length—785 feet—when trying to climb out of a downdraft, and his ship's tail had hit the water. As with R101, flying low meant that there was no room for error.

The agony of the Americans—who had lost, successively, R38, the *Roma*, *Shenandoah*, and *Akron*—was not over. Less than two years later, *Akron*'s sister ship, the 785-foot USS *Macon*, was lost in the Pacific Ocean off the California coast. On February 12, 1935, she ran into a storm off Point Sur that ripped her upper tail fin away and punctured a gasbag. The ship started to lose altitude. The crew overreacted, dropped too much ballast, and the *Macon*, propelled upward by 6.8 million cubic feet of helium, shot to 4,850 feet, venting gas all the way. Now all control was lost. The crippled airship sank earthward for twenty minutes, settling gently on the ocean, then sinking a few miles from Monterey Bay. Only two members of her crew of sixty-six were lost. That was the good news. The bad news was that helium, the miracle element that was going to revolutionize airship travel, had not saved either the *Akron* or the *Macon*.

Now the American airship experiment ended, too. President Roosevelt announced that he would not spend "a penny more" on airships. The chairman of the House Naval Affairs Committee said he knew a "death knell" when he heard one. The *New York Post* wrote, "No more funds of American taxpayers [should] be squandered on these useless gasbags."[12] The once promising Goodyear-Zeppelin partnership lay in ruins. Its employment dropped quickly from eight hundred to ten. The company was finally dissolved in 1940. America's only airship success story—the German-built *Los Angeles*—had been decommissioned in 1932 and would never fly again. That once glorious and pioneering airship, which had crossed the Atlantic in 1924 and whose crew had been given a parade in New York, was sold for scrap in 1939.

AT THIS POINT in our narrative, it might be assumed that, with the demise of the costly and technologically advanced airships R101 (1930), *Akron* (1933), and *Macon* (1935), no new rigids would be launched. The best German, American, and British technologies had failed, with lethal consequences. If helium could not be made to work—even the Germans now conceded that the nonflammable gas was the only way to make airships safe—then what conceivable future did the big airships have?

Perhaps it was no surprise that the dauntless Hugo Eckener and his colleagues at the Zeppelin company had an answer for that.* The *Graf Zeppelin* was still flying, still trying to prove to an increasingly skeptical world how practical and safe airship travel was. Her 1931 destinations included Egypt, Libya, Palestine, and the north pole. From 1931 to 1937 she flew regularly to South America. But the *Graf*, with her twenty-four-passenger capacity, was too small ever to be economically viable or to be a model for future commercial air travel. She was a showpiece, a demonstration model, a loss leader. In 1935, the year that *Macon* sank into the Pacific Ocean, Luftschiffbau Zeppelin was building the ship that they believed would finally make regular transatlantic airship service possible. At 804 feet, with a massive gas capacity of 7.4 million cubic

---

* It is noteworthy that in 1935 Hugo Eckener lost a power struggle, and while he had nominally been promoted and remained the public face of the Zeppelin company, he lost considerable influence. This was part of a de facto Nazi takeover of the company. Alexander Rose, *Empires of the Sky*, 385.

feet, the new prototype was largest aircraft ever built. When she made her first test flight in March 1936, German troops had just occupied the Rhineland in violation of the Treaty of Versailles, and refugees were already entering the United States from Germany with stories of atrocities and persecution. The airship was to be named the *Adolf Hitler*, but Hugo Eckener persuaded Dr. Joseph Goebbels, *Reichsminister* of propaganda, to name her instead after the recently deceased former German president, the *Hindenburg*.

She was filled with hydrogen.

Hugo Eckener had not wanted it that way. He had always seen the *Hindenburg* as a helium ship, a view deeply influenced by the fate of R101. He was now convinced that helium was the future of airships, and he had gone to great trouble to try to secure a helium contract from the American government. But by 1936, with the rise of Nazi power, the Americans were in no mood to share. They were right not to: the *Hindenburg* was soon working to advance the Nazi cause.

Eckener meanwhile had no choice but to use hydrogen.

That did not stop the *Hindenburg* from flying or from filling her berths with paying passengers. Over the summer of 1936, after her debut flight from Frankfurt to New York, she carried twelve hundred passengers and stayed remarkably close to schedule. Her average westbound transatlantic time was sixty-four hours, beating the new British ocean liners by more than thirty hours.[13] By airship standards, she was an aesthetic marvel. Gone was the old Pullman-car look of R101 and the styling of the *Graf Zeppelin* with its Edwardian lacquered wood, brass, and chintz. *Hindenburg* was modern, streamlined, and handsome. She vastly outdid the *Graf* and R101 in her food offerings, which included Bavarian fattened duckling, strong broth Theodor, roasted potatoes with Madeira gravy, smothered venison cutlets, and grilled sole with parsley butter, washed down with chilled bottles of Rhine and Moselle wine.[14] Still, she couldn't compete with the sort of luxury that was increasingly found on ocean liners. The dining room alone on the French ship *Normandie* was longer than the Hall of Mirrors in Versailles.[15] On the British *Queen Mary*, first-class passengers stayed in cabins with large bedrooms, separate living rooms, and private baths. The more luxurious liners boasted squash courts, pools, barbershops, and children's playrooms.[16] The *Hindenburg* offered nothing like that.

But she did have a number of features that came directly from R101. They included diesel engines, which had been pioneered for use in the air by Vincent Richmond and Thomas Cave-Browne-Cave; two long promenade decks with windows; crew and passenger quarters, dining room, and lounge all located *inside* the ship's envelope—a feature on no airships other than R100 and R101; a smoking room; and a passenger lounge with piano. Unlike R101, the *Hindenburg*'s gas cells were not lined with goldbeater's skins. They were made instead by a new method, pioneered by Goodyear, using multiple layers of gelatinized latex lined with cotton fabric.[17] Three decades after the first rigid airships, the technology had finally moved beyond cattle intestines.

Above all else, the *Hindenburg* was a Nazi airship and was seen that way by the American public, which turned out in ever smaller numbers to see her land at the mast in Lakehurst, New Jersey, at the end of her transatlantic flights. With giant swastikas on her tail fins, she was, by definition, controversial. She was banned from flying over France and Spain, restricted in her overflights of England. Hugo Eckener, who was no Nazi and resented the party's interference with his dreams of global commerce, could not prevent the airship's use as a gigantic flying public relations machine for Dr. Goebbels. The *Hindenburg* and the *Graf Zeppelin* (also sporting swastikas) together toured Germany in the spring of 1936 to rally support for Hitler before the national elections. They spent four days dropping propaganda leaflets and swastika flags and blasting pro-Hitler news and patriotic songs from special loudspeakers. The *Hindenburg* also played a starring role at the opening of the 1936 Summer Olympics.

On the early evening of May 6, 1937, the *Hindenburg* was completing an unremarkable Atlantic crossing and preparing to land at Lakehurst, just inland from the New Jersey coast, about seventy miles south of New York City. She made several sharp turns, slowed, and dropped ballast in preparation for landing. At 7:21 p.m. she hovered at an elevation of around two hundred feet and lowered mooring lines, which would help the ground crew winch her into the mast. Nothing seemed out of place. Most of the passengers were on the promenade decks, watching the landing from the ship's Plexiglas windows. About a minute after the crew dropped the bowlines, witnesses saw several small blue flames flicker along the backbone of the ship in her aft section. At 7:25 these bloomed into a ten-foot-wide column of fire, and suddenly the entire rear part of the giant airship was in flames, and almost instantly the entire ship became a giant mushrooming billow of fire, as her gigantic gasbags ruptured and she sank two hundred feet to earth, collapsing upon herself.

The most striking aspect of the fire was the staggering speed with which it consumed the airship. It took thirty-two seconds for her to hit the ground. In less than a minute she was utterly destroyed, leaving, as R101's fire had, the blackened skeleton of a ship that looked as if it had been picked clean by scavengers. Amazingly only thirty-five of the ninety-seven people on board died in the crash—thirteen passengers and twenty-two crew members—though a number of the survivors had been severely burned or wounded. Many passengers who had survived had been on the promenades. They had saved themselves by jumping out of the zeppelin's windows and running clear of the burning ship.

To watch films of the *Hindenburg* crash was to understand, in horrifying, existential detail, what an airship looked like when it was being destroyed by a hydrogen fire. Residents of London and other European cities had seen zeppelins falling from great heights during the war, engulfed in bright flames. But these events were often seen at a distance and occurred late at night when few were awake to witness them. The few photographs that have survived are blurry, indistinct, and imprecise. No films or photos were taken of R101's fiery death. Nor was there any photographic evidence of the end of *Roma*, R38, or *Dixmude*. By contrast the *Hindenburg*'s final minutes were seen by millions. They were also listened to by millions of radio listeners. When the radio broadcast and films were edited together years later—the reporter's horror-struck voice saying, "Oh, the humanity," married to the spectacular images—the *Hindenburg* became the global media phenomenon she is today. The *New York Times* film critic called the film "the most dramatic spectacle ever seen on screen." He might have said the same thing about R101 if her destruction had been filmed. In this way the *Hindenburg* brought home the dangers of hydrogen airships in a way that no amount of newspaper coverage ever could.

What caused the accident has never been clear. Conspiracy theories about sabotage were soon dismissed. They were embarrassing for the Germans anyway. They suggested that someone or some people might not like Adolf Hitler or the Nazi Party. A likely cause was a gas leak that was ignited by an electrostatic charge. In one theory, a bracing cable for a tail fin had snapped during one of the sharp turns, causing a tear in a gasbag. The leaking hydrogen mixed with air. The freak buildup of static electricity caused by thunderstorms in the area created a spark, which lit up the gas. But no one would ever know. The more the Germans insisted at the later Board of Inquiry that everything had been "absolutely, perfectly normal" on the approach, the more the very concept of the hydrogen-filled airship seemed unsafe. If that was what 100 percent normal looked like, then who would ever want to fly again?

The answer was *the Germans*. The nation and its ruling party reacted to the crash in ways strikingly similar to earlier reactions to the crash of LZ-4 at Echterdingen in 1908. They saw victory in defeat. The ship's crew were treated as heroes and martyrs. The German government, spurred on by Dr. Goebbels, promoted the idea that Germany had only emerged stronger from this experience. "Whoever thinks that the crash would mean the end of the Zeppelin idea doesn't know the Germans!" wrote *Das Schwarze Korps*, the newspaper of the German Schutzstaffel (SS). The official line was, if helium had been used, the crash would never have happened.

Since Goebbels and his propaganda department were busy promoting "forward, despite everything," it was fortunate that Germany had another airship, just as big and impressive as the *Hindenburg*, nearly ready to fly. Eckener, who was by then publicly on record stating that airships were dangerous unless filled with helium, made one last desperate attempt to secure the gas from the Americans. He failed. Germany proceeded anyway with LZ-130, a ship that was virtually identical to the *Hindenburg*. She was christened *Graf Zeppelin 2*. She was launched in September 1938. Her namesake, the famous *Graf Zeppelin*, had been withdrawn from service in 1937 after the *Hindenburg* crash. If the *Graf* had been able to use helium, she would not have been able to carry even twenty-four passengers more than a short distance. Her options therefore were either to keep flying passengers with hydrogen or be grounded.[18] She had flown 1.1 million miles, made 144 oceanic crossings, and flown for 17,177 hours (716 days) without injury to crew or passengers. She was the spectacular and precocious exception that proved the rule.

The *Graf 2* had a brief and undistinguished career. In 1938 and 1939, as Europe tipped into war, she flew thirty times, mostly for purposes of Nazi propaganda and publicity. She never carried passengers. She conducted several spy missions. She performed radio surveillance over Czechoslovakia in 1938, escorted by four Messerschmitt fighters.[19] In August 1939, a month before war was declared, she flew along the British coast to try to determine if the seventeen large towers Great Britain had built on her southern and eastern coasts were to be used for radar installations. The conclusion of the German scientists on board was that British radar was not "operational." They were disastrously wrong. Not only was the British radar working, it had successfully detected and tracked the *Graf Zeppelin 2* on her surveillance mission. The scientists had failed to detect what would become known to history as Chain Home, the first early-warning radar network in the world and the first military radar system to reach operational status. Chain Home became one of Great Britain's most powerful and successful weapons and was a crucial piece of that country's success in the Battle of Britain, in part because the Germans did not expect it to be there.

Since there was no conceivable use for a large hydrogen-filled airship in World War II, LZ-130 / *Graf Zeppelin 2* was the last of the big rigids to fly. She and the original *Graf* were both scrapped in 1940.

Their duralumin frames were used to build warplanes for the Luftwaffe.

IN A STONE CHURCH called St Mary's in a pretty grove of trees in Cardington, Bedfordshire, is a small shrine to the memory of R101 that contains the airship's ensign, which flew from the "crow's nest" in the tip of the airship's conical tail. It was one of the few pieces of organic matter to survive the hydrogen fire intact. Or almost intact. The flag is tattered and torn in places. But Union Jack and RAF roundel are well-preserved. Below the flag is a photograph of R101's smiling, uniformed crew, happily unaware of what was about to happen to them, and another photo of the airship levitating serenely at her mast. There is something at once touchingly innocent, brave, and lonely about this little shrine in a small country church in the gently rolling pasturelands of Bedfordshire.[20]

The dead are nearby. Across the street, in Cardington Cemetery, is the mass grave where forty-eight men were laid out in flag-draped coffins on October 11, 1930. The grave is marked by no large, imposing monument, just a raised white stone sarcophagus with the names of the dead inscribed on its sides. Among them is Lord Thomson, the gifted politician whose most famous legacy was the destruction of the British airship program and the loss of the valiant men who now surround him in death. The man who had always managed to be at the center of things now suffered a sort of double anonymity—of the body that was never identified and the mass grave where it lay. If he had committed, as his predecessor at the Air Ministry, Samuel Hoare, suggested, "the sin of impatience," there is every other evidence that he was a decent man with often unselfish intentions. He left shockingly little material wealth behind. His financial estate, left to his brother, was worth a mere 1,737 pounds sterling—about $40,000 today. Where did the money go? The answer in part is that, as an army lifer with no family wealth behind him, he never had much. When he was struggling to establish himself in politics in the early 1920s, he had little more than his paltry £174 annual army pension to live on. He was then in his forties. Being a lord did not pay. Though the House of Lords was liberal with its travel and expense accounts, no salaries were paid. But when Thomson did have money from his speaking engagements or his government job, he spent freely. He employed a personal valet, James Buck (who died in the crash), who could not have come cheap. Thomson was known for his epicurean lifestyle. He loved food and wine and travel and good company and throwing elaborate dinner parties, which he admitted strained his budget. His lifestyle made him such an expert on wine that, as he wrote in *Smaranda*, he once made a good impression on a senior officer "by knowing the brand and vintage of his champagne without having seen the label."[21]

He was also remarkably generous. According to those who knew him, he simply gave a good deal of his money away. "He had indeed an abounding generosity," wrote his friend Ramsay MacDonald. "Money, time, and trouble he would gladly lavish on anyone who had the smallest claim on him. The generosity came from his own hand and was not formal. . . . Of the many who on one pretext or another appealed to him in the days of his prosperity, none were sent away empty-handed."[22] Thomson's brother Roger wrote, after his death, "For all his mental attributes and gaiety of heart, I loved him for his abounding generosity and for his warm-hearted desire that, while there was money in his pocket, others should get the benefit from it."[23] His penury at death was at least part proof of that.

Thomson left no wife or children behind. His great love and pre-occupation had been his fairy-tale princess, Marthe Bibesco, who mourned his death and later wrote a book about him. In the days and weeks following the crash, she remained in seclusion in her Posada Palace in Romania, heartbroken, bereft, and sleepless. Two months later, in early December, she traveled to Allonne to see R101's remains. Dressed in black, she was accompanied by the Abbé Mugnier, a close friend to both her and Thomson, and famous as confessor to literary celebrities.

"Here is the denouement," he told her, gazing at the site of the crash. "Here is the end of a long, long journey."[24]

Or perhaps not quite. Later that month, on Christmas Eve, a basket of red roses arrived at Marthe's residence in Paris. They were from Lord Thomson, who had arranged for the delivery before he left for India on R101. The note that accompanied them read, "Here, with all my love now and forever, some more of our roses of yesterday and for tomorrow. They come for one who has brightened fifteen long years since 1915—so long ago and now so far away. They come from one who cheerfully then began to suffer that incurable malady, which some call love; and I call Marthe. A very Happy Christmas, dearest, From my heart and mind, with my devotion eternally. Ever yours." The note was signed, "Kit."[25]

ACKNOWLEDGMENTS

This book would not have been possible without the cheerful and unselfish help of several of the world's leading authorities on airships. Peter Davison, whose 2015 study of R101 in the *Journal of Aeronautical History* is one of the best pieces of R101 research, was unfailingly generous with his time and advice. When COVID slapped draconian restrictions on archival access, he sent me several thousand pages of materials he himself had gleaned from archives. He became my tour guide and adviser during my research trip to England. We spent a wonderful day touring Cardington, where Peter arranged a look inside one of the two enormous sheds where R101 and other airships were built. Gazing up into those century-old rafters was one of the thrills of my book research. Peter also took me to Brooklands Museum, in Weybridge, where he is the founder/curator of Sir Peter Masefield's private archive, one of the best sources for R101 research in the world. Stepping into the Vickers engine-testing vault—the location of the archive—and reading documents fed to me by Peter in the shadow of a Concorde flight simulator (literally) were unique experiences, to say the least. Visiting Brooklands, one of Great Britain's most interesting museums, was like journeying backward in time.

Dr. Giles Camplin, who dwells at the center of the British airship community, was helpful to me throughout my research as a source of information and advice. I queried him many times on technical aspects of airships, and he was always patient and informative. As a council member of the Airship Heritage Trust and editor of *Dirigible* magazine, he is the broker and focus point for much of the current research and information on airships. The magazine, now some thirty-three years old, was invaluable to me as a resource for all manner of information about airships and R101 in particular. Its many articles on the personalities of R101's builders and crew were particularly valuable. I also found the Airship Heritage Trust's online materials helpful. They are often cited in this book. Researching the life and death of R101 would have been so much more difficult without them.

My journey to visit Nigel Caley at his residence near Blackpool, England, was one of my favorite parts of my R101 odyssey. In his home he has amassed an astounding private archive on airships, materials he has been collecting since the age of eleven. It is difficult to find a corner of airship history he does not know in detail. Though his voluminous collection is not yet indexed, he knows the location of every piece of it. Sitting in his living room while he summoned forth some of the crown jewels of R101 research was a great experience.

It took eighty-seven years for someone to solve the mystery of R101's crash. In 2017, Dr. Bryan Lawton published a paper in the *International Journal for the History of Engineering & Technology* entitled "R.101 Airship Disaster and the Broken Elevator Cable," which finally answered the question of why R101 hit the ground. He supported his conclusion later with a more technical piece in the *Journal of Aeronautical History* entitled "Control, Response, and Crash of HMA R.101." I have chronicled his groundbreaking results in detail in this book. Dr. Lawton was a reader in thermal power at Cranfield University for more than thirty years, where he focused on work for the Ministry of Defence and developed sophisticated and computer-driven mathematical models to tackle subjects such as erosion and heat transfer in gun barrels. We are lucky that in retirement he turned his attention and considerable mathematical and analytical talents to one of the oldest mysteries in aviation. Dr. Lawton was patient and generous in answering my queries.

I would like to thank the helpful archive managers at the National

Archives of the United Kingdom in Kew, at the Royal Air Force Museum in Hendon, and at the Harry Ransom Center at the University of Texas. With their diligence and attention to detail, they make the sort of work I do possible.

The photo research for this book was done by Drury Wellford, a former colleague of mine at *Time* magazine. This is the third book we have worked on together. She is nothing short of brilliant, and her resourceful approach to research has always yielded wonderful results.

Finally I would like to thank my editor at Scribner, Colin Harrison— who is also editor in chief of the company—and my agent, Amy Hughes. The three of us have been riding together now for fifteen years and five books, so someone must be doing something right. I count myself exceedingly fortunate to have the privilege of working with them.

NOTES

Chapter One: Dreams, Pipe Dreams, and Imperial Visions

1 Karachi became part of Pakistan in 1947.
2 The account of the drive from Westminster to Cardington comes from Major L. G. S. Reynolds, Thomson's private secretary. Reynolds was interviewed in 1943 by Sir Peter Masefield at Gwydyr House.
3 Thomson, *Air Facts and Problems*, 123.
4 Maitland, *Log of H.M.A. R34*.
5 Hoare, *Empire of the Air*, 127.
6 Thomson, *Air Facts and Problems*, 136.
7 Chamberlain, *Airships—Cardington*, 149. Chamberlain was an eyewitness to the departure of R101.
8 Masefield, *To Ride the Storm*, 110.
9 Thomson speech before House of Lords, June 3, 1930, *Hansard*, cc1359/1363.
10 Thomson address to the Imperial Press Conference, June 27, 1930, AIR 5/904.
11 Chamberlain, *Airships—Cardington*, 148–49.
12 Masefield interview with L. G. S. Reynolds.
13 Inventory of weight on board calculated per passenger, compiled by R. A. W. Cardington on October 30, 1930, AIR 11/23.
14 6:36 p.m. Greenwich Mean Time; or 7:36 p.m. British Summer Time.
15 *Report of the R101 Inquiry*, 69; Chamberlain, *Airships—Cardington*, 147–48.
16 Masefield, *To Ride the Storm*, 43; Chamberlain, *Airships—Cardington*, 147.
17 Letter from Thomson to Marthe Bibesco, August 20, 1930.

Chapter Two: Brief History of a Bad Idea

1 Rose, *Empires of the Sky*, 107; Botting, *Dr. Eckener's Dream Machine*, 47.
2 From Hugo's account of his first meeting with Zeppelin in 1906, in Eckener, *Count Zeppelin*, 22.
3 Rose, *Empires of the Sky*, 82.
4 "The Giffard Airship—1852," Science Museum website.
5 Botting, *Dr. Eckener's Dream Machine*, 35; Rose, *Empires of the Sky*, 98.
6 Rose, *Empires of the Sky*, 105.
7 Fritzsche, *Nation of Fliers*, 13.

8 One of the most interesting accounts of this moment came from former British prime minister David Lloyd George, who was there and was astonished when the Germans started singing.

9 Rose, *Empires of the Sky*, 114.

10 Salter, "Curiously Underwhelming Reaction."

11 Paris, *Winged Warfare*, 128.

12 In World War II, the term *Wunderwaffen* described a number of different German weapons and technologies, including the V-1 and V-2 rockets.

13 Rose, *Empires of the Sky*, 130.

14 Hedin, *Zeppelin Reader*, 81.

15 Ward, "How the *Deutschland* Was Wrecked."

16 Dick and Robinson, *Golden Age*, 25.

17 Rose, *Empires of the Sky*, 147–48.

18 Rose, 153.

19 Chamberlain, *Airships—Cardington*, 31.

20 Rose, *Empires of the Sky*, 174. The newspaper that wrote the story was *Magdeburgische Zeitung*.

21 Campbell, *Zeppelins*, 27.

22 Harvey, "Against London," 16.

23 Rose, *Empires of the Sky*, 174.

24 Chamberlain, *Airships—Cardington*, 42.

25 Chamberlain, 46.

26 Fegan, *Baby Killers*, 124.

27 Botting, *Dr. Eckener's Dream Machine*, 76.

28 Campbell, *Zeppelins*, 20–21; Hartcup, *Achievement of the Airship*, 104. Historians have repeatedly cited the figure of £1.5 million in damage, a number that is suspect to begin with and also difficult to translate into modern currency, though the modern-day value has been estimated at £102,500,000. In any case, an insignificant number.

29 Rose, *Empires of the Sky*, 174. Rose makes the comparison to the *Lusitania*, which puts the zeppelin damage into its proper perspective.

30 Botting, *Dr. Eckener's Dream Machine*, 76.

31 Rose, *Empires of the Sky*, 172.

32 Mieth, "Shot Down by the British."

33 These figures were cited by Commander O. Locker Lampson in parliamentary debate on airships, May 14, 1931. He had reviewed the German airship logs. In *Hansard*.

34 Masefield, *To Ride the Storm*, 446.

35 Higham, *British Rigid Airship*, 10; Chamberlain, *Airships—Cardington*, 7.

Chapter Three: Night and Storm

1 Thomson's September 9, 1930, paper, "The Progress of Imperial Communications," for the Imperial Conference.

2 Thomson, *Air Facts and Problems*, 135.

3 History does not record exactly what became of the various monocles Brancker swallowed, only the front end of his trick. They were presumably passed through his digestive system.

4 By contrast, the *Graf Zeppelin*'s gondola, including control area, was ninety-eight feet long.

5 Walmsley, *R101*, 35.

6 Masefield, *To Ride the Storm*, 73.

7 Masefield, 107, describes an incident with R101; another incident of an R33 crew member falling through gasbags is found in "R33: Civil Registration G-FAAG," Airship Heritage Trust online.

8 One of Lord Thomson's closest friends, Dick Casey, noted "with misgivings" on a tour of R101 "that every ten yards or so a hand fire extinguisher was installed." Masefield, *To Ride the Storm*, 93.

9 *Report of the R101 Inquiry*, 71; the ship did not turn toward London till 7:19, forty-three minutes into her flight, having covered 29.5 miles. Masefield, *To Ride the Storm*, 366.

10 AIR 5/912; see also Masefield, *To Ride the Storm*, 337.

11 AIR 5/912; this was an old problem, too, dating from 1929.

12 In his diary from December 1, 1929, First Officer Noel Atherstone wrote, "The question of who was in command of the R101 was never properly finalized. Was it Scott? Or Irwin, who had the title of captain? If Irwin was in command, what was Scott's role?"

13 The reference is to R100's Atlantic flight, which will be described later in detail.

14 Crewe, "Met Office Grows."

15 Crewe; also Johnston, *Airship Navigator*, 76; Masefield, *To Ride the Storm*, 376.

16 Crewe, "Meteorology and Navigation"; quote from Enid (Giblett) Holmes in *Dirigible* 76 (Autumn 2015), letters section.

17 This quote is from F. A. de V. Robertson of *Flight* magazine, told to Peter Masefield in conversation in 1938: Masefield, *To Ride the Storm*, 338. Robertson also wrote up the departure in an article in *Flight* in October 1930.

18 *Report of the R101 Inquiry*, 69.

19 Gold quoted from recorded interview in Chapple, *Great Grey Ghost*.

20 These voices were discovered by the audio research of airship archivist Nigel Caley, of Blackpool.

21 Lamond, *First Memory*, 26.

22 Lamond, 73.

23 Meager, *My Airship Flights*, 13.

24 Higham, *British Rigid Airship*, 115.

25 Higham, 115.

26 Meager, *My Airship Flights*, 84.

27 Swinfield, *Airship*, 50ff.; taking an airship into a shed still required hundreds of handlers. This refers only to docking at the mast.

28 Hall, "Two Conflicting Patents," 18.

29 The British airship No. 9 flew for the first time on November 16, 1916.

30 The political and policy background to this flight is astonishingly complex, involving many players, including Americans, as detailed by Higham, *British Rigid Airship*, 175ff. But it was essentially a government project.

31 Dick and Robinson, *Golden Age*, 74–75.

32 Dick and Robinson, 76.

33 Chamberlain, *Airships—Cardington*, 80.

34 "U.S. Navy's Curtiss NC-4."

35 Lamond, *First Memory*, 153.

36 E. A. Johnston, "Scott of the Atlantic," *Dirigible* 2 (July–September 1989); the ship had been under the command of a Colonel Hicks, who asked Scott to take command when the trouble started.

37 *Report of the R101 Inquiry*, 8.

38 Maitland, *Log of H.M.A. R34*, 11.

39 Maitland, 75.

40 Maitland, 78.

41 Higham, *British Rigid Airship*, 183–85.

42 Higham, 185.

43 Swinfield, *Airship*, 71ff.

44 Letter from crewman Granville Watts to his mother, 1921, cited in Swinfield, appendix B, 280–83; *R34, the Record Breaker*.

45 Johnston, "Scott of the Atlantic."

46 Letter from Sir Peter Masefield to Lord Beswick, 1982, based on Masefield's interviews with Scott's Cardington contemporaries. Masefield Archive, Brooklands, cited in Davison, "R.101 Story."

47 Letter from Molly Bloxam Wallis to Turner, March 21, 1929.

48 Masefield correspondence with Eve Waley Cohen (Atherstone).

49 Eve Waley Cohen (Atherstone) to Ernest A. Johnston, letter.

50 Masefield, *To Ride the Storm*, 337. Told to Masefield in conversation, June 1938.

51 *Report of the R101 Inquiry*, 71. Engineer Harry Leech noted that the ship was rolling and pitching more than he had seen her do and spoke to Michael Rope about it.

52 Masefield, *To Ride the Storm*, 370.

53 Johnston, *Airship Navigator*, 150–51.

54 Masefield, *To Ride the Storm*, 380.

55 Johnston, *Airship Navigator*, 151.

56 Memo from secretary general of the Air Ministry (France) to Colonel R. J. Bone, air attaché, British Embassy, September 27, 1930, *Dirigible*, Autumn 2006.

57 Scott and Richmond, "Detailed Consideration."

58 Parliamentary debate on airship policy, May 14, 1931, *Hansard* 252.

59 Thomson, *Air Facts and Problems*, 89–90.

60 Shute, *Slide Rule*, 98.

Chapter Four: Flying Death Trap

1 "ZR.2 (R38): A Visit to the Royal Airship Works," *Flight*, June 9, 1921.

2 "R36, Registration G-FAAF."

3 Masefield, *To Ride the Storm*, 358–59. Masefield offers a similar summary of short-comings of airships; Robin Higham commented that the movement to get rid of airships was happening "in view of the failure to make rigids operational during World War I and the German abandonment of zeppelins by the end of it." Higham, *British Rigid Airship*, 210.

4 "Imperial Air Communications Special Subcommittee Report."

5 "R38/ZR-2: The First."

6 Submarines and airships both could float weightlessly in their mediums and relied on equilibrium and ballast. Both could also use dynamic action to move through their mediums.

7 Masefield, *To Ride the Storm*, 443.

8 The seven British airships were HMA No. 9, R23, R24, R25, R26, R27, R29.

9 "Historical British Airships."

10 Masefield, *To Ride the Storm*, 447.

11 Note that two postwar ships, R31 and R32, which were built in England in 1918 and 1919, had wood frames and were modeled on actual drawings from a former employee of the German Schütte-Lanz Luftschiffbau, the Zeppelin company's major wartime competitor.

12 One of the two "reparations" zeppelins the British received was L-71, a 693-foot superzep that was delivered in June 1920, rather too late to be much help in the design of R38, whose construction was in the final stages.

13 "Hydrogen and Helium in Rigid Airship Operations," airships.net; see also Higham, *British Rigid Airship*, 375.

14 Higham, *British Rigid Airship*, 216.

15 Higham, 219.

16 Chamberlain, *Airships—Cardington*, 98; the term used to describe the rudder's condition was *overbalanced*.

17 "R38/ZR-2: The First."

18 Even though the Royal Naval Air Service and the Royal Flying Corps had officially been merged into the Royal Air Force in 1918, political rivalry and confusion over the design, construction, flying, and management of airships continued. R38 had begun as an Admiralty project and finished, officially, as a Royal Airship Works project under the Air Ministry. The fight between the RAF and the Royal Navy over who was to blame for what happened was bitter and prolonged.

19 Pritchard memo to Air Ministry, dated August 11, 1921, cited in Chamberlain, *Airships—Cardington*, 106.

20 Chamberlain, 100, 106.

21 Robinson and Keller, *Up Ship!*, 41; Higham, *British Rigid Airship*, 222.

22 Pritchard, "Jack Pritchard."

23 Jamison, *Icarus over the Humber*, 54.

24 Shute, *Slide Rule*, 55–57.

25 "R38/ZR-2: The First."

26 The interests of the Short brothers had already been nationalized.

Chapter Five: "The Feeling of Utter Loneliness"

1 A modern approximation of the effect on ground watchers of a large object flying at low altitude would be a 239-foot Airbus A380 superjumbo flying at 450 feet. The jet would loom quite large.

2 Masefield, *To Ride the Storm*, 380.

3 "Incidents on the Flight to India," timeline prepared by Royal Airship Works, AIR 5/906.

4 *Parliamentary debate on airship policy*, Sir William Brass, *Hansard* 252.

5 Maitland, *Log of H.M.A. R34*, 6.

6 R101 had once experienced higher winds, when moored to the mast at Cardington in October 1929.

7 Masefield, *To Ride the Storm*, 357.

8 "R36, Registration G-FAAF," citing Alfred G. Pugsley, *Biological Memoirs of Fellows of the Royal Society* 7:75–84.

9 Camplin, "Old Cover Story."

10 Peake, "Life and Death of Major Scott"; Morpurgo, *Barnes Wallis*, 67.

11 Meager, *My Airship Flights*, 136.

12 Masefield, *To Ride the Storm*, 129, 134.

13 Williams, *Airship Pilot No. 28*, 194–95.

14 Dick and Robinson, *Golden Age*, 65ff.

15 *Parliamentary debate on airship policy*, Brass.

16 Masefield, *To Ride the Storm*, 358.

17 R101 carried 35.5 tons of fuel in forty-nine tanks. Fourteen of those, containing some ten tons of fuel, were "jettison" tanks. Masefield, 113.

18 Maitland, *Log of H.M.A. R34*, 62.

19 It was possible to fly at more of an angle, but at ten degrees nose up or down, for example, the ride became uncomfortable for passengers. Glassware and crockery slid across tables.

20 Meager, "Theory to Explain the Crash."

21 Maitland, *Log of H.M.A. R34*, 167; per the above note, the crew apparently had no choice but to fly ten degrees up by the bow.

Chapter Six: The Idea That Would Not Die

1 "*Roma* Crashed in Virginia"; "Requiem for *Roma*."

2 The American airship *Los Angeles* was built by Germany and was filled with hydrogen when she crossed the Atlantic. The Americans, who commissioned her in November 1924, converted her to helium.

3 "The *Dixmude*: Commander's Body Recovered," *Manchester Guardian*, December 29, 1923.

4 "Du Plessis and *Dixmude*."

5 The U.S.-built rigid airship *Shenandoah* was first launched September 4, 1923. She flew for two years until her crash in September 1925, which happened well after the British Imperial Airship Scheme was underway. The German-built LZ-126, sold to the Americans and later renamed *Los Angeles*, first flew October 12, 1924.

6 The empire lost 908,371 combatants dead, 2,090,212 wounded, and 109,000 civilians dead.

7 In 1922 a new ratio of sea power was determined that effectively ended Britain's longtime role as guarantor of the high seas. The ratio for Great Britain/USA/Japan was 5:5:3, with France and Italy at 1.75. Britain had to scrap 657 ships.

8 Higham, *British Rigid Airship*, 231; as Higham points out, these figures now seem absurd.

9 Higham, 231.

10 "Imperial Air Communications Special Subcommittee Report," testimony by Air Minister Samuel Hoare.

11 Burney, "Air Power," 118.

12 Cornford, *Paravane Adventure*, 77.

13 Proposal from Vickers Ltd. dated November 1918, entitled "Airship Transport Services," Nigel Caley Archive.

14 Hoare, *Empire of the Air*, 220.

15 Masefield, *To Ride the Storm*, 448.

16 The carrier idea was tried out a number of times in the coming years, with some limited success, but would never prove practical.

17 Noted airship designer Barnes Wallis, always a good check on Burney's ideas, thought most of them "wildly optimistic."

18 National Archives, ADM 1/8657/34, Cabinet Paper 4053, June 21, 1922.

19 Morris, *Farewell the Trumpets*, 277.

20 Masefield, "Catch the Sunlight." Masefield conducted extensive interviews with family members for this unpublished work centering on Lord Thomson's relationship with Marthe Bibesco.

21 Tonsing, " 'Earth's Proud Empires.' "

22 Masefield, "Catch the Sunlight."

23 Thomson, *Smaranda*, introduction by Ramsay MacDonald.

24 Lieutenant-Colonel Edward M. Mosely, writing in the *Royal Engineers Journal*, March 1931.

25 Hart, "Lord Thomson."

26 Thomson, *Old Europe's Suicide*, 178.

27 Thomson, *Smaranda*, introduction.

28 Hoare, *Empire of the Air*, 104.

29 Thomson, *Smaranda*, 89.

30 Hoare, *Empire of the Air*, 104.

31 From Thomson's brother Roger Thomson's description of him in November 1930, Sir Peter Masefield Archive, Brooklands Museum.

32 Sutherland, *Enchantress*, 6.

33 Sutherland, 27.

34 Sutherland, 78.

35 Thomson, *Smaranda*, 97.

36 Masefield, "Catch the Sunlight," citing Thomson's diary.

37 Thomson, *Smaranda*, 16.

38 For his work on the Supreme War Council he was made Commander of the British Empire (CBE).

39 Sutherland, *Enchantress*, 162.

40 Thomson, *Smaranda*, 113.

41 Thomson, introduction.

42 Thomson, 120.

43 Sutherland, *Enchantress*, 165.

44 Masefield, "Catch the Sunlight."

45 Thomson, *Smaranda*, introduction.

46 Letter from MacDonald to Bibesco, October 8, 1930, in Masefield, *To Ride the Storm*, 21; David and Jonathan were heroes of the kingdom of Israel, whose unusual friendship is described in the book of Samuel.

47 Sutherland, *Enchantress*, 165.

48 Sutherland, 166.

49 Thomson, *Smaranda*.

50 Thurman, *Secrets of the Flesh*, 320.

51 Introduction to Lord Thomson for his lecture tour in the United States, January/February 1925, Sir Peter Masefield Archive, Brooklands Museum.

52 Debate in House of Lords, March 4, 1924, *Hansard* 56, cc482–555.

53 Chamberlain, *Airships—Cardington*, 115.

54 Thomson to House of Lords, May 21, 1924, *Hansard* 57, cc557–600.

55 Rose, *Empires of the Sky*, 238.

56 Rose, 241.

57 Masefield, *To Ride the Storm*, 33.

58 Masefield, 27.

Chapter Seven: India Seems a Very Long Way

1 *Report of the R101 Inquiry*, Arthur Disley testimony, AIR 5/903-YM 08,109. Disley, in charge of the port mid-engine, "observed that the white spume on the waves seemed awfully close."

2 T. R. Cave-Browne-Cave, comments from 1962, CBC Archive, Imperial War Museum.

3 *Report of the R101 Inquiry*, Disley testimony.

4 Disley narrative from timeline compiled by the Air Ministry, "Incidents of the Flight to India," AIR 5/906; *Report of the R101 Inquiry*, 72.

5 *Report of the R101 Inquiry*, 69.

6 Masefield, *To Ride the Storm*, Leech testimony before the Inquiry; *Report of the R101 Inquiry*, 72.

7 "Ex–Larchfield Pupil Died."

8 Airship Heritage Trust, airshipsonline.

9 Callanan, *"Titanic of the Skies."* Note that the Sea Scout Zero class was a slight improvement on the original Sea Scout class.

10 R29 was also credited with a U-boat kill, though neither Irwin nor Atherstone was aboard at the time. "An Airship Claims Prize," *Flight*, May 20, 1920.

11 "Ex–Larchfield Pupil Died."

12 It must be kept in mind that airworthiness requirements for airships held that 10 percent of the gross lift had to be available as water ballast. So there were certain minimums. The idea of dropping *fuel* ballast would have been nearly unthinkable on such a long trip except in the most dire emergency.

13 As we have seen, rain added weight to the ship by soaking the cover. Fuel burned in flight reduced weight. Both had to be taken into consideration.

14 Masefield, *To Ride the Storm*, 112.

15 Leech interview with Canadian Broadcasting Corporation, "notes on Peter Masefield's discussion with Mr. Leech in August and Sept. 1962 and in March 1966," cited in Davison, "R.101 Story"; see also Masefield, *To Ride the Storm*, 51.

16 Parliamentary debate on airship policy, Major Archibald Church, May 14, 1931, *Hansard* 252.

17 Dick and Robinson, *Golden Age*, 61.

18 "Control Car, Flight Instruments, and Flight Control," Airships.net; Dick and Robinson, *Golden Age*, 61.

19 Dick and Robinson, *Golden Age*, 67.

20 Gratton, "Flight Testing the *Titanic*." See also the excellent coverage of the German suspicion of altimeters and their solutions in Dick and Robinson, *Golden Age*, 65ff.; this important subject is treated at greater length in chapter fifteen.

21 Johnston, *Airship Navigator*, 94.

22 Masefield, *To Ride the Storm*, 62.

23 Masefield, 38.

24 Davison, "R.101 Story," 65.

25 Masefield letter to Douglas Robinson, March 19, 1984, Masefield Archive, Brooklands; Masefield interviewed Pugsley.

Chapter Eight: She Floats Free

1 "Programme for Government Research."

2 Rose, *Empires of the Sky*, 162.

3 Atherstone, diary, October 1, 1929.

4 Thanks to *Dirigible* magazine for compiling a list of R101's innovations. Not included here are the variable-pitch propellers.

5 Masefield, *To Ride the Storm*, 111–12.

6 Nevil Shute observed in his 1954 memoir, *Slide Rule*, "It is curious after over twenty years to recall how afraid everyone was of petrol in those days, because since then aeroplanes with petrol engines have done innumerable hours of flying in the tropics, and they don't burst into flames on every flight" (68).

7 Memo from Colmore and Richmond to AMSR, November 18, 1929, AIR 2.349/522039/29-06130.

8 Masefield, *To Ride the Storm*, 108–9.

9 Richmond, diary, June 26, 1929, B1410.

10 In June 1929 Richmond had told Thomson that the ship might weigh 105 tons, which meant that it could only carry twenty-four passengers to India, not the one hundred the ministry specifications required. But this revelation made even that impossible.

11 The cost of R101 alone as of 1929 was £527,000, 26 percent of the total of £1,986,000 spent on the Airship Scheme. R100 had cost £337,000.

12 Atherstone, diary, October 2, 1929.

13 Atherstone, October 3, 1929.

14 "World's Largest Airship: R101 Ready for Trial Flights," *Scotsman*, October 3, 1929.

15 "Can R101 Make Good?"

16 Higham, *British Rigid Airship*, 297.

17 Cecil L'Estrange Malone, speaking in House of Commons debate, May 13, 1930, *Hansard*, c1666.

18 This number includes the twenty-two airships built by the Schütte-Lanz company.

19 Though Maitland was not, strictly speaking, a "technical" person, he had ten years of lighter-than-air experience behind him and a good deal of airship knowledge.

20 Swinfield, *Airship*, 159.

21 Johnston, *Airship Navigator*, 174–75.

22 Masefield, *To Ride the Storm*, 58.

23 Johnston, "Richmond of R101"; Higham, *British Rigid Airship*, 293; "V. C. Richmond, O.B.E."

24 Roxbee Cox, *Wrack Behind*, 188.

25 Swinfield, *Airship*, 303.

26 "R80: Launched on 19th July 1920, the R80 Was the First Truly Streamlined British Airship," Airship Heritage Trust online.

27 Davison, "R.101 Story."

28 Wallis letter to J. E. Morpurgo at Leeds University, January 11, 1971.

29 Morpurgo, *Barnes Wallis*, 173.

30 Peake, "Big Airship Programme." Among the R101 engineers working for Vincent Richmond were Harold Roxbee Cox, who would go on to become one of Great Britain's most prominent aeronautical engineers, devising among other things the kite balloon barrage, which brought down many German V-1 missiles in southern England; Hilda Lyon, who became a principal scientific officer at the Royal Aircraft Establishment in Farnborough; Alfred Pugsley, who became head of structural and mechanical engineering at the Royal Airship Establishment and

was later knighted and became president of the Institution of Structural Engineers; and Thomas Reginald Cave-Browne-Cave, who became head of the engineering school at University College, Southampton, and invented an innovative supersonic wind tunnel.

31 Davison, "R.101 Story," citing "Wallis Papers V57."

32 It should be noted that Scott and Colmore did visit Wallis occasionally in Howden, but these visits entailed no significant exchange of technical information. Neither Scott nor Colmore was in a position to offer such information. The men had known each other since before the start of the project. The Scotts and the Wallises knew each other well, and indeed Molly Wallis felt burdened by having to stock extra bottles of hard liquor when the Scotts visited.

33 Hoare, *Empire of the Air*, 222–23.

34 Shute, *Slide Rule*, 50.

35 Commander Joseph Kenworthy, Member of Parliament for Kingston upon Central Hull, in debate in the House of Commons, March 12, 1929, *Hansard*, c1030.

36 Chamberlain, *Airships—Cardington*, 115.

37 Shute, *Slide Rule*, 43.

38 Shute, 39.

39 Airship Heritage Trust online.

40 Morpurgo, *Barnes Wallis*, 154.

41 Originally only one shed had been in the Short Brothers' complex. In 1928 the large shed at RNAS Pulham was taken down and moved to Cardington. The original shed was lengthened by work that was finished in 1926.

42 Chamberlain, *Airships—Cardington*, 6.

43 "R33," Airship Heritage Trust online.

44 Chamberlain, *Airships—Cardington*, 6.

45 Higham, *British Rigid Airship*, 275.

46 Norman Peake, "Innovations in R100," *Dirigible*, 1999.

47 Hammack, *Fatal Flight*, 104.

48 Thomson, "Notes on the Manufacture."

49 In many descriptions of this process, the ceca are said to be from oxen. Oxen are a small percentage of steers (castrated bulls) that are used as work animals. Given the huge numbers of ceca needed, there is no way they all could have come from oxen. *Cattle* is a more accurate term to describe their source.

50 Walmsley, *R101*, 61.

51 Chollett, "Balloon Fabric Made," 258–62.

52 *Report of the R101 Inquiry*, 24; Air Ministry report on fabrics, AIR 5/905.

53 Masefield, *To Ride the Storm*, 107.

54 *Report of the R101 Inquiry*, 24.

55 Swinfield, *Airship*, 286–87, citing diary of Granville Watts.

56 Swinfield, 176, author interview with Stopes-Roe.

57 "R33: Civil Registration G-FAAG."

58 Thomson, *Air Facts and Problems*, 107.

59 "R33," Airship Heritage Trust online.

60 Thomson, *Air Facts and Problems*, 111. Thomson makes the assumption that R33, or any other large rigid airship, could have landed in such a gale. More likely her alternative would have been to "free-balloon" until the wind abated.

Chapter Nine: Trial by Error

1 "R101: Successful Launch."
2 Atherstone, diary, October 10, 1929.
3 Masefield, *To Ride the Storm*, 47; Thomson's conversation with his secretary Christopher Bullock from June 19, 1929, related to Sir Peter Masefield by Bullock on May 14, 1970.
4 Masefield, 47; AIR 2/349.
5 In Thomson's short 1927 book, *Air Facts and Problems*, he wrote in detail about the flight of the crippled R33 over the North Sea, among other air accidents.
6 This was not the first time that British airship authorities arranged "joyrides" for politicians and members of Parliament. In 1919 the trials of the British airship R32 were affected by such considerations. "All too frequently," wrote airship historian Robin Higham of R32, "this [trial] routine was stretched to the point of uselessness by the short duration of the flight owing to the presence of Members of Parliament aboard who had commitments elsewhere at a certain hour." Higham, *British Rigid Airship*, 214.
7 "R36," *Dirigible*; Atherstone, diary, October 15, 1929.
8 Davison, "R101 Story," 69.
9 Johnston, *Airship Navigator*, 139.
10 Charles Grey, "R.101," *Aeroplane*, October 23, 1929.
11 Sutherland, *Enchantress*, 188–89.
12 Marthe Bibesco, diary, July 8, 1929.
13 Bibesco, *Lord Thomson of Cardington*, 171.
14 Bibesco, 171.
15 Masefield, *To Ride the Storm*, 92.
16 "Notes for Press Use: Flight of HM Airship 100 to Canada; Notes on Officials and Officers," Airships online; Colmore biography, Bedford Archives online; Howlett, *Development of British Naval Aviation*, 101.
17 "R101," *Manchester Guardian*, October 19, 1929.
18 Minute from AMSR Higgins to Thomson, October 22, 1929, AIR 5/14.
19 Meager, *My Airship Flights*, 150.
20 Richmond, diary, cited in *Minutes of Proceedings*, 7:381.
21 Atherstone, diary, August 13, 1929.
22 Atherstone, November 6, 1929. Taking civilian passengers on test flights was not entirely unknown in Great Britain. On July 13, 1928, an Imperial Airways Vickers Vulcan airliner on a test flight from Croydon aerodrome crashed after takeoff, killing four joyriding airline employees. Imperial Airways decided to forbid the practice.
23 Atherstone, diary, November 8, 1929.

24 Atherstone, November 22, 1929.

25 Atherstone, November 23; there is no evidence that he was ordered to take the parachutes off the ship. He presumably believed he was following the more general order to prepare the ship for flight.

26 Royal Airship Works memorandum, AIR 20/159.

27 Letter from A. B. Jones to F. Rawlings at the Air Ministry, November 25, 1929, AIR 20/159.

28 Atherstone, diary, November 23, 1929.

29 "R101: Flight of Over 1,000 Miles."

30 *Report of the R101 Inquiry*, 40–41; Masefield, *To Ride the Storm*, 137.

31 Minute from Sky Hunt to First Officer Atherstone, November 11–12, 1929, AIR 5/906.

32 Air Ministry report on meeting with Professor Bairstow on R101's airworthiness, AIR 5/912.

33 Masefield, *To Ride the Storm*, 138.

34 *Too heavy* does not mean, as some writers have construed the term, that the airship could not take off, or that it could only fly using dynamic lift. *Too heavy* generally refers to the idea that the fixed weights of the ship are so heavy that proper amounts of fuel and/or ballast cannot be carried. Less fuel and less ballast mean, simply, less safety. This phenomenon was painfully apparent during R101's trials.

35 Roxbee Cox, *Wrack Behind*, 188.

36 Memorandum dated November 18, 1929, from Colmore and Richmond to AMSR John Higgins, AIR 2/349.

37 Letter from Vincent Richmond to Air Ministry, January 22, 1930, AIR 5/14.

38 Letter from Vincent Richmond.

39 Davison, "R101 Story."

40 R101 was not the first airship to be lengthened. The process had been done before, most notably with the German *Bodensee* and the British R36.

41 Minute from AMSR John Higgins to the secretary of state for air, November 21, 1929, AIR 2/349.

42 Thomson memo to AMSR Higgins, December 23, 1929, AIR 2/349.

43 Colmore memorandum to Reynolds, December 20, 1929, AIR 2/349; *Minutes of Proceedings*, 1:63, AIR 5/902.

44 Letter from Lord Thomson to Marthe Bibesco, August 20, 1930.

45 Atherstone, diary, January 29, 1930.

46 Shute, *Slide Rule*, 66.

47 Shute, 67.

48 Meager, *My Airship Flights*, 167.

49 "Notes from Conference at Air Ministry (Higgins, Bairstow, Colmore, Richmond, Chief Inspector Airships, S.9 [Louis Reynolds])," February 7, 1930, AIR 5/978; see also "Outer Cover of R100," *Dirigible* 50 (Spring 2007).

50 Masefield, *To Ride the Storm*, 195.

51 Minute from Higgins to Thomson, March 11, 1930, AIR 2/364.

52 Bairstow statement to Court of Inquiry, AIR 5/904.

53 "Notes from Conference"; AMSR pointed out that no records of the behavior of gasbags or outer covers existed.

Chapter Ten: France, and the Midnight Hour

1 The wire sent from the ship at midnight says that the passengers "sighted the French coast," which I take to mean that some or all of them were on the promenades sometime between 11:00 p.m. and 11:36 p.m.
2 Masefield, *To Ride the Storm*, 326.
3 Masefield, 390.
4 Wireless message from R101 to Cardington base, AIR 5/903.
5 Meager, *My Airship Flights*, 16.
6 Cave-Browne-Cave, "Rigid Airships."
7 Richmond, "Development of Rigid Airship."
8 Rose, *Empires of the Sky*, 153.
9 Masefield, *To Ride the Storm*, 200.
10 Shute, *Slide Rule*, 62–63; Shute had the wisdom of hindsight, but there is little doubt that he carried the knife, or that he intended to use it for such an emergency.
11 Haran, hydrogen balloon experiment.
12 Notes taken by Thomas R. Cave-Browne-Cave from interviews with R101 foreman engineer Harry Leech from August and September 1962 and March 1966. Cave-Browne-Cave wrote the notes up in a January 1967 report. United Kingdom Archives.
13 Ship captains did not always function as officers of the watch, but on this voyage Irwin was alternating three-hour shifts with Noel Atherstone and Maurice Steff.
14 Masefield made an analysis of R101's navigation and argues persuasively that R101 changed course over Poix. Masefield, *To Ride the Storm*, 394.

Chapter Eleven: The Perfectly Safe Experimental Prototype

1 Speech at House of Commons by Cecil L'Estrange Malone, Member of Parliament for Northampton, March 18, 1930, *Hansard*.
2 Sir Richard Wells, MP Bedford, in House of Commons, March 18, 1930, *Hansard*.
3 Lord Thomson, speech before House of Lords, June 3, 1930, *Hansard*.
4 Report of Vincent Richmond and Michael Rope of their April 26–27 trip aboard the *Graf Zeppelin* from Cardington to Friedrichshafen, dated May 7, 1930, AIR 5/912.
5 Report of Richmond and Rope.
6 Dick and Robinson, *Golden Age*, 39.
7 "Air Transport—Scheduled," 224.
8 Thomson speech to Fourth Imperial Press Conference in London, AIR 5/904.
9 Rose, *Empires of the Sky*, 329.
10 Dick and Robinson, *Golden Age*, 38; Swinfield, *Airship*, 234.
11 Dick and Robinson, *Golden Age*, 39.

12 Rose, *Empires of the Sky*, 312.

13 Dick and Robinson, *Golden Age*, 56.

14 Lord Thomson, speech before House of Lords, June 3, 1930, *Hansard*.

15 Richmond, "Development of Rigid Airship," 341ff.

16 Rope's note, cited by Masefield, Thomas R. Cave-Browne-Cave Papers, Imperial War Museum.

17 Atherstone, diary, July 2, 1930.

18 Richmond, diary, June 27, 1930.

19 *Minutes of Proceedings*, Booth testimony.

20 *Minutes of Proceedings*, Hugh Dowding testimony, November 6, 1930.

21 Meager, *My Airship Flights*, 190.

22 The first ship he worked on was the *Nulli Secundus*.

23 McWade note to Colmore, AIR 5/905.

24 Letter from Colmore to Outram, July 8, 1930, AIR 5/905; *Report of the R101 Inquiry*, 51.

25 *Report of the R101 Inquiry*, 51.

26 Outram minute to McWade, July 11, 1930, AIR 5/905.

27 Masefield, *To Ride the Storm*, 228.

28 *Report of the R101 Inquiry*, statement by Higgins, AIR 5/905.

29 Meager, *My Airship Flights*, 193.

30 Meager, 193.

31 "Secrets of the St. Lawrence."

32 Meager, *My Airship Flights*, 193.

33 Shute, *Slide Rule*, 82.

34 In a July 28, 1930, memo from AMSR Higgins, just before R100's departure, he wrote, "It would appear that the press generally are under the impression that Major Scott will command R100 on her Atlantic flight. This is not the case and I should like the position to be made clear before R100 starts." AIR 5/13.

35 Masefield, *To Ride the Storm*, 249.

36 Shute, *Slide Rule*, 81.

37 Shute, 81.

38 Atherstone, diary, September 2, 1930.

39 Giles Camplin, "On Second Thoughts," *Dirigible*, Summer 2022.

40 Colmore letter to Salmond, August 21, 1930, AIR 5/906.

41 Shute, *Slide Rule*, 67.

Chapter Twelve: The Violent, Unseen World

1 Chapple, *Great Grey Ghost*, interview with Joe Binks.

2 Lucien Lechat, statement, AIR 2/375.

3 Lechat; Masefield, *To Ride the Storm*, 396.

4 Davison, "R.101 Story."

5 Harry Leech, statement, Beauvais Hospital, October 5, 1930, AIR 5/906.

6 Leech, October 5, 1930.

Chapter Thirteen: Fools Rush In

1 Masefield, *To Ride the Storm*, 316, letter from Thomson to Mrs. T. G. Conrad of San Francisco, September 28, 1930.

2 Hart, "Lord Thomson."

3 Letter from Thomson to Marthe Bibesco, August 20, 1930.

4 Sutherland, *Enchantress*, 193.

5 Marthe Bibesco, diary, and her essay "Le Destin de Lord Thomson."

6 Masefield, *To Ride the Storm*, 316, letter from Thomson to Conrad.

7 Bibesco, diary; Sutherland, *Enchantress*, 194.

8 Just prior to R101's departure, Colmore told Thomas R. Cave-Browne-Cave, "If the ship does not succeed in getting the secretary of state to India in time for the Imperial Conference, no further money would be available for airship development and none would be asked for." Johnston, *Airship Navigator*, 145.

9 Masefield, *To Ride the Storm*, 316, letter from Thomson to Conrad.

10 Gratton, "Flight Testing the *Titanic*."

11 Shute, *Slide Rule*, 78–88.

12 Richmond, diary, September 24, 1930.

13 Masefield, *To Ride the Storm*, 302; worth noting is his comment on 305: "Had time permitted the right course would clearly have been to renew all those sections of the cover where the original, pre-doped fabric remained; some 33,000 square feet of it in all. But there was no prospect of doing that and maintaining the schedule that had been given to the Air Ministry."

14 Atherstone, diary, October 1, 1930.

15 Sir John Higgins was taking the job as chairman of Armstrong Whitworth Aircraft, one of Great Britain's largest aeronautical companies.

16 Air Ministry history of the Aeronautical Research Council, AIR 5/902.

17 Dowding minute saying that Bairstow and Pippard had approved the design as modified, subject to the director of aeronautical inspection's final approval. "I therefore recommend the issue of a 'Certificate of Airworthiness' as the Indian flight is expected to start on the evening of October 3. I would suggest the C of A be sent to the AIR inspector in Cardington, who should be instructed to hand it to the DAD [Director of Airship Development Colmore]." AIR5/904.

18 *Minutes of Proceedings*, Dowding testimony, 443–44.

19 *Minutes of Proceedings*, Dowding testimony, 445.

20 *Report of the R101 Inquiry*, Dowding testimony, 67.

21 Thomson, *Smaranda*, introduction.

22 Statement of Major Villiers to the Court of Inquiry, November 24, 1930, AIR 5/912.

23 *Death by Misadventure*, statement by Roger Gordon Thomson.

24 Masefield, *To Ride the Storm*, 324–25.

Chapter Fourteen: A Very Violent End

1 *Report of the R101 Inquiry*, 76.
2 The narrative here is drawn from survivor accounts, both to the Preliminary Investigation (hospital interviews) and later in interviews conducted before the Court of Inquiry. AIR 5/906 and 5/903.
3 *Report of the R101 Inquiry*, 78.
4 Chamberlain, *Airships—Cardington*, 160.
5 "Flame Temperatures Table."
6 Letter from Mr. Tyrrel at British Embassy in Paris to Arthur Henderson, MP, October 8, 1930, AIR 5/903.
7 Rabouille statement to Gendarmerie, AIR 5/903.
8 Letter from Tyrell to Henderson.
9 Report of R. H. Tottenham Smith, British vice-consul general in Paris, October 6, 1930.
10 Chamberlain, *Airships—Cardington*, 162.
11 Bibesco, *Lord Thomson of Cardington*, 183–84; in December 1930 Marthe visited Allonne and spoke with the worker.
12 List of personal items from crash, AIR 2/347.
13 Handwritten report of Bernard H. Pillsbury, HM Pathologist, Home Office, November 5, 1930, AIR 2/1247.
14 Report of Group Captain R. J. Bone, Major H. Jones, and F. S. D. Collins, October 6, 1930, AIR 5/903; memo from Mr. Pillsbury, pathologist to the Home Office, October 8, 1930, AIR 2/2147; Masefield, *To Ride the Storm*, 42, 186.
15 Bibesco, diary, and letter to Abbé Mugnier, in Masefield, *To Ride the Storm*, 185.
16 Sutherland, *Enchantress*, 195.
17 Sutherland, 196.
18 Chamberlain, *Airships—Cardington*, 162; historian Geoffrey Chamberlain witnessed this scene in front of the newspaper office as a boy.
19 "Silent, Endless Crowd," *Daily Express*.
20 "R101: Plans for Last Tributes."
21 Masefield, *To Ride the Storm*, 413.
22 "Great Grave," *Daily Express*.
23 "Bitter Tragedy," *Children's Newspaper*.
24 Holloway, "In Sacred Memoriam."
25 Telegram from the prime minister of Romania to Prime Minister Ramsay MacDonald, PRO 30/69/1522.
26 Johnston, *Airship Navigator*, 179.

Chapter Fifteen: Solving the Mystery: What Caused the Crash?

1 *Report of the R101 Inquiry*, 82.
2 Lawton, "R.101 Airship Disaster," 110. Engineers at the Goodyear-Zeppelin Corporation, an Ohio-based German-American joint venture, were appalled that

neither bags nor cover had ever been subject to extensive testing and had never been tested at all in bad weather.

3 *Report of the R101 Inquiry*, 87.

4 *Report of the R101 Inquiry*, 81; "At least 1,000 feet" was the inquiry's conclusion.

5 Williams and Collar, "Motion of RMA R.101." Collar was an aerodynamicist at the National Physical Laboratory.

6 Peter Masefield, February 15, 1987, manuscript relating to the Simpson study, Masefield Archive, Brooklands Museum. Note that Masefield and Ernest A. Johnston consulted on Simpson's project.

7 "The computer survey did not find any cause to disagree radically with the conclusion of the 1931 investigation," wrote airship historian Edwin Mowthorpe, who analyzed the computer inputs. "Indeed, Professor Simpson commented in his own paper that 'results from the Williams-Collar theory [NPL] are generally in very good agreement with those from the present model.'" Mowthorpe, "Technical Aspects of the R.101 Crash."

8 Johnston, *Airship Navigator*, 181–90, for Johnston's reconstruction of Simpson's crash scenario.

9 See chapter 11: The *Graf* had crashed near Pernambuco, Brazil. When she came to rest, the chimney of one of the local huts was sticking up into the belly of the ship; a fire was burning in the stove inside the hut. Still the airship did not catch fire.

10 Chamberlain, *Airships—Cardington*, 176–77.

11 Johnston, *Airship Navigator*, 167.

12 It is impossible to know if Irwin had assumed command or not. If the crew had been aware of a crisis developing after, say, 2:04 a.m. or 2:05 a.m., he may have been summoned from his berth before the first dive. In the computer-driven model later published by Masefield and Simpson, the increased drag and loss of airspeed at around 2:05 led to their assumption that "the OOW must have called the captain in accordance with standing instructions." Either way, Steff or Irwin, the OOW made what appears to be the correct call.

13 Johnston, *Airship Navigator*, 162.

14 *Report of the R101 Inquiry*, 78.

15 Johnston, *Airship Navigator*, 163; *Minutes of Proceedings*, vol. 3.

16 Lawton, "R.101 Airship Disaster," 106–7.

17 Author's correspondence with Bryan Lawton.

18 Lawton, "R.101 Airship Disaster," 119.

19 Lawton, 115.

20 Lawton, 118.

21 Lawton, 115.

22 A control cable rated for a strength of 27 cwt broke under testing at 22 cwt.

23 H. Bard, Beauvais resident, letter to "Commission of Enquiry," October 10, 1930.

24 *Report of the R101 Inquiry*, 84.

25 On September 25, 1930, little more than a week before R101's ill-fated flight, navigator Ernest Johnston was shopping for a new altimeter. He visited the offices

of a company called Eck and Brook, a British agent for scientific instruments. According to an October 10, 1930, letter from Justus Brook, a principal of Eck and Brook, to "The Commission to Investigate the R101 disaster" (AIR 2/365), "Squadron Leader Johnston . . . told us that he was not quite happy with the instruments which were at the moment on R101 and asked us to give him again prices and particulars of the instruments we quoted previously."

26 Letter from Dr. Eckener to Dr. Simpson, October 28, 1930.

Chapter Sixteen: Bloody End of a Bloody Era

1 *Report of the R101 Inquiry*, 95.
2 *Report of the R101 Inquiry*, 95.
3 *Report of the R101 Inquiry*, 95–96.
4 The full version of the hearings is available at the National Archives of the United Kingdom.
5 Chamberlain, *Airships—Cardington*, 192–94.
6 "R100: Registration G-FAAV."
7 Chamberlain, *Airships—Cardington*, 195.
8 "Dirigible Disasters," 6. The chief forecaster of the Weather Bureau said that a forecast earlier that day "was loaded with dynamite."
9 "Dirigible Disasters," 6.
10 "Dirigible Disasters," 7.
11 "Dirigible Disasters," 8; Dan Grossman, "Worst Airship Disaster in History: USS *Akron*—April 4, 1933," airship.net, April 4, 2013.
12 Rose, *Empires of the Sky*, 384.
13 Stopford, *Maritime Economics*.
14 Robinson, *LZ-129 "Hindenburg."*
15 Rose, *Empires of the Sky*, 421.
16 Rose, 421–22.
17 Dick and Robinson, *Golden Age*, 95.
18 Chamberlain, *Airships—Cardington*, 180.
19 Rose, *Empires of the Sky*, 476.
20 The flag has been in the church since September 28, 1931.
21 Thomson, *Smaranda*.
22 Thomson, introduction.
23 Roger Thomson, "Biographical Note on Brigadier General the Right Honourable the Lord Thomson of Cardington," November 1930, Brooklands Museum.
24 Bibesco, *La Vie d'une amitié*, 2:389.
25 Bibesco, 2:389.

BIBLIOGRAPHICAL NOTE

One of the first questions people in the airship community asked me when I started working on this book was "Do you agree with Nevil Shute?" If you are not familiar with the name, Nevil Shute was the pen name of Nevil Shute Norway, one of the most popular English authors of the middle twentieth century, author of such bestsellers as *On the Beach* (which I read when I was fourteen) and *A Town Like Alice*. He was also an Oxford-educated engineer who became the chief calculator under Barnes Wallis on the R100, the sister airship of R101. His first novel was published while he was working on that project. Though his work was mainly in Howden, he was intimately familiar with the R101 project and with the people at the Royal Airship Works.

In 1954 Shute published a memoir entitled *Slide Rule*, in which he devoted considerable space to R100 and R101. He was highly critical of the competence of R101's staff and of the engineering in the ship itself, as was his boss, Barnes Wallis. They were so intensely prejudiced against R101 that they were prone to making statements about her that were simply not true. Because of their stature in the world—Shute as a leading novelist, and Wallis as one of the best-known British mechanical and aeronautical engineers of the twentieth century—their comments received considerable play. Included in those comments was Shute's patently false statement that one of the problems of R101 was that the same designers had built the airship R38, which crashed in 1921. Among Wallis's canards was his nonsensical assertion that R101 was too heavy to fly and had to be kept aloft by using dynamic lift.

Because the biases of the two men ran so deep—partly out of the same ingrained jealousy that made other members of the R100 team dislike R101's builders—and led to such erroneous and unfair assessments of the R101 project, I have not relied upon the word of either of them in taking stock of either the quality of R101's engineers or the quality of her engineering. I have used quotes from Shute concerning other subjects, including the culture of Howden, the flight of R100 to Canada, and the airship community. He had quite a sharp eye for that sort of thing. And there is a factually accurate quote from Wallis about the lack of airship-building experience on the R101 staff. Otherwise I have just stayed away from them.

Another key player in the historiography of R101 was Sir Peter Masefield, who must be reckoned with in any attempt to tell the R101 story. In 1982, Masefield published *To Ride the Storm*, a full accounting of the R101 story that was the result of more than forty years of dogged research. Masefield had been an aviation journalist, copilot and gunner in World War II, a prominent aviation executive, and chairman of British European Airways in the 1950s. He was later variously in charge of all major airports in the United Kingdom and chairman of all London transport. He personally knew many of the key people in the British airship establishment. His book is the pioneering work in the field, full of facts that he was the first to uncover. He was first with so many pieces of the R101 story that it is impossible for me to even imagine writing a book without having his work as a reference. I—and everyone else who writes about R101—stand on his shoulders.

His book is not perfect. One of his biggest agendas, hammered at again and again over the book's 560 pages, is his defense of Lord Thomson (about whom he also wrote an unpublished biography, "Catch the Sunlight"). He promotes the blamelessness of such characters as Vincent Richmond and Michael Rope. He tends to be much harder, when assessing blame, on Reginald Colmore and Herbert Scott. But in writing about Scott he still withheld most of what he knew about

Scott's drinking. Part of his bias can be explained by his closeness with the airship community and with the heirs and descendants of the men who died. He shared a sense with many other people—including the authors of the government inquiry into R101's crash—that the R101 designers and crew should be spared the harsh light of public inquiry. Such attitudes hurt *To Ride the Storm*'s overall objectivity.

To research this book, I spent time in the collections of the National Archives of the United Kingdom in Kew, just west of London. When friends ask what I found there, I tell them, "King Arthur's pipe and slippers." Seriously, the archive has everything imaginable, going back to Roman times, and holds a large collection of wonderfully indexed original documents relating to R101. In footnotes and endnotes I have indicated the specific file designations from the archives with the prefix AIR. I visited the Royal Air Force Museum in Hendon, on the north side of London. Peter Davison was gracious enough to allow me to access the Peter Masefield Archive at Brooklands Museum, in Weybridge, which Peter (Davison) collected and curated. One of the most valuable sources for the political story of R101 was the UK Parliament's online *Hansard* official record of parliamentary debates.

I took the train north to Blackpool (actually Poulton-le-Fylde) to visit airship historian Nigel Caley's large personal collection, which includes some unpublished jewels relating to R101.

By a happy coincidence, the Harry Ransom Center at the University of Texas in Austin (where I live) holds a useful collection of Marthe Bibesco material.

Though the public documents on R101 are voluminous, the literature is not. Relatively few books have been published about her. Many of the books that include R101 coverage are not exclusively about her. Of the extant literature, the Masefield book is de rigueur. I would also recommend *Airship Navigator* by Ernest A. Johnston, *Airships—Cardington* by Geoffrey Chamberlain, *R101: A Pictorial History* by Nick le Neve Walmsley, *The British Rigid Airship: 1908–1931* by Robin Higham, and

Airship: Design, Development and Disaster by John Swinfield. For zeppelin history I found the following works useful: *Dr. Eckener's Dream Machine* by Douglas Botting, *The Golden Age of the Great Passenger Airships:* Graf Zeppelin & Hindenburg by Harold G. Dick and Douglas H. Robinson, *LZ 129* by Douglas H. Robinson, and *Empires of the Sky* by Alexander Rose. An excellent lengthy paper on R101, and one of the best things written about her, is "The R.101 Story: A Review Based on Primary Source Material and First-Hand Accounts" by Peter Davison in *The Journal of Aeronautical History* (2015).

One final observation: the "official" designation of the airship that is the subject of my book is R.101. Note the decimal point. As an element of style, I have omitted it. I find it a bit pedantic and unnecessary and will answer any challenges by offering up the airship herself along with her prominent, decimal-point-free designation painted in black on her side: *R101*.

BIBLIOGRAPHY

Books and Manuscripts

Abbott, Patrick. *Airship: The Story of R.34 and the First East–West Crossing of the Atlantic by Air*. Redditch, UK: Brewin Books, 1994.

Acworth, Marion Whiteford. *The Great Delusion: A Study of Aircraft in Peace and War*. London: Dial Press, 1927.

Allen, Fredrick Lewis. *Only Yesterday*. New York: Blue Ribbon Books, 1931.

Allen, Hugh. *The Story of the Airship (Non-Rigid): A Study of One of America's Lesser Known Defense Weapons*. Akron, OH: Lakeside Press, 1942.

Anderson, John. *Airship on a Shoestring: The Story of R.101*. London: Bright Pen, 2013.

———. *Parallel Motion: A Biography of Nevil Shute*. Kerhonkson, NY: Paper Tiger, 2011.

Atherstone, Noel Grabowsky. Unpublished diary. Airship Heritage Trust.

Bain, Dr. Addison. Hindenburg: *Exploring the Truth*. Cocoa, FL: Blue Note Publications, 2014.

Bibesco, Marthe. *Lord Thomson of Cardington: A Memoir and Some Letters*. London: Jonathan Cape, 1932.

———. *La vie d'une amitié: Ma correspondance avec l'abbé Mugnier, 1911–1944*. Paris: Plon, 1951.

Birdwood, Field-Marshal Lord. *Khaki and Gown: An Autobiography*. London: Ward, Locke, 1941.

Botting, Douglas. *Dr. Eckener's Dream Machine: The Great Zeppelin and the Dawn of Air Travel*. New York: Henry Holt, 2001.

Burney, Sir Dennistoun. *The World, the Air, the Future*. New York: Alfred A. Knopf, 1929.

Campbell, Edwin. *Zeppelins: The Past and the Future*. St Albans, UK: Campfield Press, 1918.

Camplin, Giles. "An Old Cover Story: A Theory to Explain the Crash of the Airship R101" (manuscript). Courtesy of the author.

Chamberlain, Geoffrey. *Airships—Cardington: A History of Cardington Airship Station and Its Role in World Airship Development*. Lavenham, Suffolk, UK: Terence Dalton, 1984.

Cornford, L. Cope. *The Paravane Adventure*. London: Hodder and Stoughton, 1919.

Dick, Harold G., and Douglas H. Robinson. *The Golden Age of the Great Passenger Airships: Graf Zeppelin & Hindenburg*. Washington, DC: Smithsonian Institution, 1985.

Eckener, Hugo. *Count Zeppelin: The Man and His Work*. London: Massie, 1938.

―――. *My Zeppelins*. Stratford, NH: Ayer, 1994.

Falls, Cyril. *War Books: A Critical Guide*. London: Peter Davies, 1926.

Fegan, Thomas. *The Baby Killers: German Air Raids on Britain in the First World War*. South Yorkshire, UK: Pen and Sword Military, 2002.

Ferguson, Niall. *Empire: The Rise and Demise of the British World Order and the Lessons for Global Power*. New York: Basic Books, 2002.

Friedrich, Otto. *Before the Deluge: A Portrait of Berlin in the 1920s*. New York: Harper and Row, 1972.

Fritzsche, A. *A Nation of Fliers: German Aviation and the Popular Imagination*. Cambridge, MA: Harvard University Press, 1992.

Fuller, John G. *The Airmen Who Would Not Die*. New York: Penguin, 1979.

Gilbert, James. *The World's Worst Aircraft, 1935–2006*. London: Hodder and Stoughton, 1980.

Gott, Richard. *Britain's Empire: Resistance, Repression and Revolt*. London: Verso, 2022.

Gurney, John. "The R101" (poem). Ransom Center, University of Texas.

Hammack, Bill. *Fatal Flight: The True Story of Britain's Last Great Airship*. New Zealand: Articulate Noise Books, 2017.

Hartcup, Guy. *Achievement of the Airship*. London: David and Charles, 1974.

Hedin, Robert. *The Zeppelin Reader: Stories and Poems from the Age of Airships*. Iowa City, IA: Harris Collection, 1998.

Higgins, John, et al. Memos concerning responsibilities of captain, 1930. AIR 5/13.

Higham, Robin. *The British Rigid Airship, 1908–1931*. London: G. T. Foulis, 1961.

Hoare, Samuel (Viscount Templewood). *Empire of the Air: The Advent of the Air Age, 1922–1929*. London: Collins, 1957.

Holanda, R. *A History of Aviation Safety: Featuring the U.S. Airline System*. Bloomington, IN: Authorhouse, 2009.

Holmes, Enid R. *Line Squall*. Privately published.

Howlett, Alexander. *The Development of British Naval Aviation, 1914–1916*. New York and London: Routledge, 2021.

Jamison, T. W. *Icarus over the Humber: The Last Flight of Airship R38*. London: University of Hull Press, 1994.

Johnston, Ernest A. *Airship Navigator: One Man's Part in the British Airship Tragedy, 1916–1930*. Stroud, UK: Skyline, Littleworth, 1994.

Kennedy, Greg, ed. *Britain's War at Sea: The War They Thought and the War They Fought*. London: Routledge, 2016.

Kirby, M. W. *The Decline of British Economic Power Since 1870*. London: George Allen and Unwin, 1981.

Lamond, Kathleen (Scott). *First Memory: Recollections of a Bygone Age*. Lulu Press, 2010 (published by her son).

Leasor, James. *The Millionth Chance: The Story of the R101*. London: self-published, 1957.

Lewitt, E. H. *The Rigid Airship: A Treatise on the Design and Performance*. London: Sir Isaac Pitman and Sons, 1925.

Macmillan, Norman. *Sir Sefton Brancker*. London: William Heinemann, 1935.

Maitland, Air-Commodore E. M. *The Log of H.M.A. R34: Journey to America and Back*. Introduction by Rudyard Kipling. London: Hodder and Stoughton, 1920.

Masefield, Peter G. "Catch the Sunlight" (unpublished manuscript, including handwritten sections). Sir Peter Masefield Archive, Brooklands Museum, Weybridge, UK.

———. *To Ride the Storm: The Story of the Airship R101*. London: William Kimber, 1982.

Meager, G. *My Airship Flights, 1915–1930*. London: William Kimber, 1970.

Miller, Nathan. *New World Coming: The 1920s and the Making of Modern America*. New York: Scribner, 2003.

Morpurgo, J. E. *Barnes Wallis: A Biography*. London: Longman, 1972.

Morris, James (Jan). *Farewell the Trumpets: An Imperial Retreat*. New York and London: Harcourt Brace Jovanovich, 1978.

Mowthorpe, Ces. *Battlebags: British Airships of the First World War*. Stroud, UK: Allan Stutton, 1995.

Paris, Michael. *Winged Warfare: The Literature and Theory of Aerial Warfare in Britain, 1859–1917*. Manchester, UK: Manchester University Press, 1992.

Richmond, Vincent Crane. Unpublished diary. Royal Air Force Museum.

Robinson, Douglas. *LZ-129 "Hindenburg."* New York: Arco, 1964.

———. *The Zeppelin in Combat*. Henley-on-Thames, UK: Foulis, 1971.

Robinson, Douglas, and Charles L. Keller. *Up Ship! A History of the US Navy's Rigid Airships, 1919–1935*. Annapolis, MD: Naval Institute Press, 1982.

Rose, Alexander. *Empires of the Sky: Zeppelins, Airplanes, and Two Men's Epic Duel to Rule the World*. New York: Random House, 2020.

Rosendahl, Charles E. *Up Ship!* New York: Dodd, Mead, 1931.

———. *What About the Airship? A Challenge to the US*. New York: Charles Scribner's Sons, 1938.

Roxbee Cox, Harold (Baron Kings Norton). *A Wrack Behind*. Cranfield, UK: Cranfield University Press, 1999.

Scott, G. H., and V. C. Richmond. *A Detailed Consideration of the Effect of Meteorological Conditions on Airships* (R38 Memorial Prize Paper). London: Royal Aeronautical Society, 1923.

Shute, Nevil. *Slide Rule*. 1954. Reprint, Thirsk, Yorkshire, UK: House of Stratus, 2000.

Simon, Viscount John. *Retrospect: The Memoirs of the Rt. Hon. Viscount Simon*. London: Hutchinson, 1952.

Smith, Julian. *Nevil Shute: A Biography*. Boston: Twayne, 1976.

Spanner, E. F. *This Airship Business*. London: Williams and Norgate, 1927.

———. *Tragedy of R101*. Self-published, 1931.

Stopes-Roe, Mary. *Mathematics with Love: The Courtship Correspondence of Barnes Wallis, Inventor of the Bouncing Bomb*. Camden, UK: Palgrave MacMillan, 2005.

Stopford, M. *Maritime Economics*. 3rd ed. London: Routledge, 2009.

Storey, Neil. *Zeppelin Blitz: The German Air Raids on Great Britain during the First World War*. London: History Press, 2015.

Sutherland, Christine. *Enchantress: Marthe Bibesco and Her World*. New York: Farrar, Straus and Giroux, 1996.

Swinfield, John. *Airship: Design, Development, and Disaster*. Annapolis, MD: Naval Institute Press, 2012.

Tharoor, Shashi. *Inglorious Empire: What the British Did to India*. London: C. Hurst, 2017.

Thomson, Christopher Birdwood. *Air Facts and Problems*. New York: George H. Doran, 1927.

———. *Old Europe's Suicide or the Building of a Pyramid of Errors: An Account of Certain Events in Europe during the Period 1912–1919*. New York: Thomas Seltzer, 1922.

———. *Smaranda: A Compilation in Three Parts*. London: Jonathan Cape, 1931.

Thurman, Judith. *Secrets of the Flesh: A Life of Colette*. New York: Ballantine Books, 1999.

Tombs, Robert. *The English and Their History*. New York: Vintage Books, 2016.

Toye, Richard. *Churchill's Empire: The World That Made Him and the World He Made*. 2010. Reprint, New York: St. Martin's Griffin, 2011.

Van Treuren, Richard. Hindenburg: *The Wrong Paint; Hydrogen: The Right Fuel*. Atlantas Productions, 2001.

Ventry, Arthur Frederick Daubeney Eveleigh-de Moleyns. *Airship Saga: The History of Airships Seen through the Eyes of the Men Who Designed, Built, and Flew Them*. London: Blandford Press, Sterling Publishing, 1982.

Walmsley, Nick le Neve. *R101: A Pictorial History*. Stroud, UK: History Press, 2010.

Wasson, Ellis. *Aristocracy and the Modern World*. New York: Palgrave/Macmillan, 2006.

Williams, Captain T. B. *Airship Pilot No. 28*. London: William Kimber, 1974.

Online and Printed Articles on R101

Bibesco, Marthe. "Le destin de Lord Thomson of Cardington." *La Revue universelle*, February 15, 1932.

Burney, Dennistoun. "Air Power." *Naval Review* 1 (1913): 118.

———. "Should We Develop Airships?" *Field* 155, no. 4022 (January 25, 1930): 111.

Callanan, Tim. "*Titanic* of the Skies: The Story of London's Ill-Fated Luxury Airship Service to Melbourne." ABC News.net Australia, December 29, 2018.

Cave-Browne-Cave, T. R. "Rigid Airships and Their Development." *Aeronautical Journal* 24 (1920): 143.

———. "Some Airship Personalities." *Aeronautical Journal* 70, no. 661 (1966): 52–53.

Chollett, Captain L. "Balloon Fabric Made of Goldbeater's Skins." *L'Aeronautique*, August 1922, 258–62.

Colmore biography. Bedford Archives online.

Crafts, Nicholas. "The Met Office Grows Up in War and Peace." *Royal Meteorological Society Specialist Group for the History of Meteorology and Physical Oceanography*, March 2009.

———. "Walking Wounded: The British Economy in the Aftermath of World War I." VoxEu, Vox Multimedia, August 27, 2014.

Crewe, M. E. "Meteorology and Aerial Navigation." *Royal Meteorological Society Specialist Group for the History of Meteorology and Physical Oceanography*, September 2002.

Davison, Peter. "The R.101 Story: A Review Based on Primary Source Material and First-Hand Accounts." *Journal of Aeronautical History*, paper no. 2015/02.

Dean, Sir Maurice. "The Loss of Airship R101." *Air Ministry Journal*, May 1966, 20.

Eckener, Hugo. "Commercial Possibilities of the Airship." *Journal of Air Law* 7 (1936): 211.

Gratton, G. B. "Flight-Testing the *Titanic*: Revisiting the Loss of His Majesty's Airship R.101." *Journal of Aeronautical History*, paper no. 2015/05.

Hall, C. P. "Two Conflicting Patents." *Dirigible* 84 (Summer 2018): 18.

Hart, Basil Liddell. "Lord Thomson." *Fortnightly Review* 134 (November 1, 1930).

Harvey, A. D. "Against London: A Zeppelin Officer's Account." *Air Power History*, Summer 2010.

Holloway, F. A. "In Sacred Memoriam: His Last Laurel." Public Records Office, UK, 30/69/1522.

Johnston, Ernest A. "Richmond of R101." *Dirigible*, October–December 1990.

Kings Norton, Lord (Harold Roxbee Cox). "A Wrack Behind." *Aeronautical Journal* 103, no. 1022 (April 1, 1999): 187–88.

Lawton, Bryan. "Control, Response, and Crash of HMA R.101." *Journal of Aeronautical History*, April 7, 2018.

———. "R.101 Airship Disaster and the Broken Elevator Cable." *International Journal for the History of Engineering and Technology* 87, no. 1 (2017): 96–124.

Masefield, Peter, and Alan Simpson. "The First Overseas Voyage and Flight Path of HMA R.101." International Convention of the Royal Aeronautical Society, the Airship Association, and the Airship Heritage Trust, July 5–7, 1996.

Meager, Tim. "A Theory to Explain the R101 Crash." *Dirigible* 76 (Autumn 2015).

Mieth, Otto. "Shot Down by the British: A Zeppelin Officer's Story." *Living Age*, April 17, 1926. Originally published in German in *Frankfurter Zeitung Illustrierte Blatt*, February 28, 1926.

Mitchell, Harley W. "Is the Dirigible Utterly Worthless?" *Popular Aviation* 11, no. 3 (September 1932).

Mowthorpe, Edwin. "Technical Aspects of the R.101 Crash." *Dirigible*, Summer 2006.

Peake, Norman. "The Big Airship Programme." *Dirigible*, Fall 1999.

———. "The Life and Death of Major Scott." *Dirigible* 11, no. 2 (Summer 2000).

Price, G. Ward. "How the *Deutschland* Was Wrecked." *London Magazine* 26, no. 16 (April 1, 1916). Reprinted in *Dirigible* 73 (Autumn 2014).

Richmond, V. C. "The Development of Rigid Airship Construction." *Engineering*, September 12, 1930.

———. "Organisation of a Colonial Airship Service." *Aeronautical Journal* 25, no. 131 (November 1921). (The date of this is surprising, so far in advance of Burney's campaign, apparently.)

———. "Some Modern Developments in Rigid Airship Construction." Paper read on March 30, 1928, to Sixty-Ninth Session of Institution of Naval Architects. AIR 5/903.

Salter, James. "The Curiously Underwhelming Reaction to the Wright Brothers' First Flight." *Financial Review*, August 19, 2015.

Scott, George Herbert. "Airship Piloting" and "The Present State of Airship Development" (two papers presented to the Royal Aeronautical Society). *Journal of the Royal Aeronautical Society*, December 1, 1921.

Southwell, R. V. "R.101." Article reprinted from *Nature*, December 14, 1929. RAF Museum.

Spanner, E. F. "The Tragedy of R.101." *Journal of the American Society for Naval Engineers*, August 1932.

Thomson, Jack C. "Notes on the Manufacture of Goldbeater's Skin." *Book and Paper Group Annual, American Institute for Conservation* 2 (1983).

Tonsing, Gertrude. "'Earth's Proud Empires Pass Away . . .': The Glorification and Critique of Power in Songs and Hymns of Imperial Britain." *HTS Theological Studies* (Pretoria, South Africa) 73, no. 3 (2017).

Upson, Ralph. "Directional Stability and Control of Airships." *Aviation and Aeronautical Engineering* 8 (April 1 and 15, 1920).

Williams, D. H., and A. R. Collar. "The Motion of HMA R.101 under Certain Assumed Conditions." Reports and Memoranda no. 1401, HMSO, May 1931.

Wintringham, T. H. "The Crime of R101." *Labour Monthly*, December 1930.

Articles from Airship Heritage Trust Online (airshipsonline.com)

"Historical British Airships, 1909–1930."

"R33."

"R34, the Record Breaker: Final Life."

"R36, Registration G-FAAF."

"R38/ZR-2: The First of the Admiralty A Class."

"R100: Registration G-FAAV."

Articles from Miscellaneous Publications

"Air Transport—Scheduled Air Transportation, Domestic Only, 1926–1945." *Historical Studies of the United States*, 224.

"Bitter Tragedy We Shall Forget." *Children's Newspaper*, November 1, 1930.

"Can R101 Make Good?" *Dundee Evening Telegraph*, October 16, 1929.

"Dr. Hugo Eckener: Zeppelin's Apostle." *Living Age* 350 (1936): 320. Translated from *Prager Tagblatt*.

"Du Plessis and *Dixmude*." *Dirigible* 14 (Summer 1993).

"Eckener Has Clue for R101 Inquiry: Commander of *Graf Zeppelin* Says Barometric Disturbance Upset His Altimeter." *New York Times*, October 13, 1930.

"Ex-Larchfield Pupil Died in Airship Disaster." Helensburgh Heritage Trust, April 2, 2010.

"Flame Temperatures Table for Different Fuels: Adiabatic Flame Temperatures for Common Gases in Air and Oxygen." ThoughtCo online.

"The Great Grave." *Daily Express*, October 11, 1930.

"Major G. H. Scott: A Great Airship Captain." *Times*, October 6, 1930.

"R36." *Dirigible* 11, no. 1 (Spring 2000).

"R101." *Flight* 21, no. 1085 (October 11, 1929).

"R101: Flight of Over 1,000 Miles." *Times*, October 19, 1929.

"The R101: Plans for Last Tributes." *Times*, October 9, 1930.

"The R101: Successful Launch." *Times*, October 14, 1929.

"Requiem for *Roma*." *Virginian-Pilot*, February 16, 1997.

"*Roma* Crashed in Virginia, 34 Dead: Hydrogen Fireball." *Virginian-Pilot*, June 29, 2010.

"Secrets of the St. Lawrence." Government of Canada Environment and Climate Change Canada website.

"Silent, Endless Crowd." *Daily Express*, October 11, 1930.

"The U.S. Navy's Curtiss NC-4: First across the Atlantic." history.net.

"V. C. Richmond, O.B.E." *Nature*, October 18, 1930.

Government Papers, Documents, Studies

"Dirigible Disasters: Report of the Joint Committee to Investigate Dirigible Disasters." United States Senate, 73rd Congress, 1st sess., April 13, 1933, 6.

Documents of the R.101 Disaster Fund at the office of the town clerk, Bedford.

Hansard: The Official Record of Parliamentary Debates online resource.

"Imperial Air Communications Special Subcommittee Report." Imperial Conference 1926. Hathitrust digital library.

Jones, R., and A. H. Bell. "Experiments on a Model of the Airship R.101 with Application to Determine the Steady Motion of the Airship." Reports and Memoranda no. 1400, Aeronautical Research Committee, May 1931.

———. Various papers on technical features of R101 in the Aeronautical Research Committee's Reports and Memoranda 1168, 1169, and 1400.

Lloyd, Geoffrey (Secretary to Samuel Hoare, Air Minister). "The Approach toward a System of Imperial Air Communications." Prepared for 1923 Imperial Economic Conference.

Minutes of Proceedings at Public Inquiry into the Loss of the Airship R.101. Institution of Civil Engineers, Great George Street, Westminster S.W., 1931.

"Programme for Government Research, Experiment and Development of Airships." Memorandum by the Secretary of State for Air, March 7, 1924, AD 24 (2). AIR 8/74/06990.

"Progress of Imperial Air Communications." Air Ministry, 1924 and 1930 versions.

"Report of the Airship Stressing Panel." Aeronautical Research Committee's Reports and Memoranda no. 800, August 1922, AIR 5/903.

"Report of the Airworthiness of Airships Panel." Aeronautical Research Committee's Reports and Memoranda no. 970, October 1924. AIR 5/903.

Report of the R101 Inquiry. Presented to Parliament by the Secretary of State for Air, 1931.

Rosendahl, C. E. "Reflections on the Airship Situation." United States Naval Institute Proceedings 53, no. 7 (1927): 745–58.

Teed, Major P. L. "The R101 Disaster." Paper prepared for the R101 Inquiry, AIR 5/919.

Video Sources

Airship R-80 and Roma. British Pathé, 1922. https://www.youtube.com/watch?v= SGx1lSXqbro.

Amy Johnson Tribute, featuring Lord Thomson. The Old Fliers Group, Jandakot Western Australian. https://www.youtube.com/watch?v=SroH_2ehwog.

Chapple, Len, producer. *The Great Grey Ghost*. Documentary by the Canadian Broadcasting Company, Vancouver, BC, 1966.

Davison, Peter, and Dr. Giles Camplin. "The R101 Airship Disaster: Revisited 89 Years On" (lecture). https://www.aerosociety.com/news/audio-rewind-the-r101 -airship-disaster-80-years-on-by-peter-davison-dr-giles-camplin/.

Death by Misadventure: HMA R101. Documentary on Granada Television, produced in Manchester, UK, 1967. Courtesy of Nigel Caley.

Documentary footage of USS *Akron*. https://www.youtube.com/watch?v=oZt6Y DumVM4.

The Flying Carriers: First Flight, video compilation.

Haran, Brady. Hydrogen balloon experiment, University of Nottingham. Film. periodic videos.com. https://www.youtube.com/watch?v=qOTgeeTB_kA.

History of Airships. https://www.youtube.com/watch?v=a6irdBtsaQ4.

Lighter-than-Air History: Rigid Airship Documentary. Periscope Film. https://www .youtube.com/watch?v=tjtGB1wC_hY.

The LZ4 Meets with Disaster. https://www.youtube.com/watch?v=hfaA4TrSPPA.

Norris, Dave, and Ron Mash, producers. *The US Navy Airship* Shenandoah. Tales of Southeastern Ohio. https://www.youtube.com/watch?v=jJsD1JTwcDc.

Pritchard, Wendy. "Jack Pritchard and the R38 Disaster." RAeS Video Webinar.

Survivors of Catastrophe Tell of Miraculous Escape. Paramount Sound News. https://www .gettyimages.com/detail/video/survivors-of-catastrophe-tell-of-miraculous-escape -man-in-news-footage/516313580.

The USS Akron. Principal Distributing Corp. https://www.youtube.com/watch?v= KtlmPe2e3eA.

USS Akron *Incident—1932*. Fox Movietone News. https://www.youtube.com/watch?v= cLFLAj-9-vU.

Video interviews from 1962 with R.101 survivors. http://www.eafa.org.uk/catalogue /109675.

The World's Biggest Airship Launched: The Trial Trip of the R.33. Pathé Gazette, 1919. https://www.youtube.com/watch?v=g1jsSG_58RM.

Zepp Arrives! Giant Airship Joins R100 at Air Base. British Pathé. https://www.youtube .com/watch?v=-dsKa15y-Ww. Footage of Scott and Eckener.

Zeppelin Attack! The Battle to Destroy L-33. Mark Felton Productions. https://www .youtube.com/watch?v=SS3zWo7UXxA.

ILLUSTRATION CREDITS

Insert

1 George Grantham Bain Collection, Library of Congress, LC-DIG-ggbain-37114
2 Mirrorpix/Reach Licensing
3 George Grantham Bain Collection, Library of Congress, LC-USZ61-1758
4 Romanian National Archives
5 Romanian National Archives
6 Public domain, via Wikimedia Commons
7 Airship Heritage Trust
8 George Grantham Bain Collection, Library of Congress, LC-DIG-ggbain-37952
9 Public domain
10 George Grantham Bain Collection, Library of Congress, LC-DIG-ggbain-02128
11 George Grantham Bain Collection, Library of Congress, master-pnp-ggbain -16000-16090u
12 Rol, CC BY-SA 4.0 https://creativecommons.org/licenses/by-sa/4.0, via Wikimedia Commons
13 Mirrorpix/Reach Licensing
14 Airship Heritage Trust
15 Public domain, via Wikimedia Commons
16 Public domain, via Wikimedia Commons
17 Airship Heritage Trust
18 Nigel Caley Collection
19 Mirrorpix/Reach Licensing
20 NH 89488, Naval History and Heritage Command, Washington, DC
21 NH 98997, Naval History and Heritage Command, Washington, DC
22 Jorge Kfuri (1893–1965), public domain, via Wikimedia Commons
23 Guy Warner Collection
24 Mary Evans Picture Library
25 Airship Heritage Trust
26 Mary Evans Picture Library
27 Mary Evans Picture Library
28 Mary Evans Picture Library

INDEX

ABOUT THE AUTHOR

S. C. Gwynne is the author of the *New York Times* bestsellers *Empire of the Summer Moon*, which was a finalist for the Pulitzer Prize and the National Book Critics Circle Award; *Rebel Yell*, which was also a finalist for the National Book Critics Circle Award and was shortlisted for the PEN Literary Award for biography; and *The Perfect Pass*. Gwynne is an award-winning journalist whose work has appeared extensively in *Time*, for which he worked as a bureau chief, national correspondent, and senior editor from 1988 to 2000, and in *Texas Monthly*, where he was executive editor. His work has also appeared in *Outside* magazine, the *New York Times*, the *Dallas Morning News*, the *Los Angeles Times*, the *Los Angeles Herald Examiner*, *Harper's*, and *California* magazine. He lives in Austin, Texas, with his wife, the artist Katie Maratta.

**R101 cruising over Hyde Park in London
on her maiden voyage, October 14, 1929:**
With her enormous bulk and habit of flying
low, she was a sensation wherever she went.
There was something implausible and
physical-law-defying about such a gigantic
object floating weightless in the sky.